The United Nations: Re

Also by Peter R. Baehr and Leon Gordenker

The United Nations at the End of the 1990s

De Vereinigde Naties: Ideaal en Werkelijkheid

Also by Peter R. Baehr

The Role of Human Rights in Foreign Policy (*with Monique Castermans-Holleman*)

Human Rights in the Foreign Policy of the Netherlands (*with Monique Castermans-Holleman and Fred Grünfeld*)

Human Rights: Universality in Practice

Innovation and Inspiration: Fifty Years of the Universal Declaration of Human Rights (*editor with Cees Flinterman and Mignon Senders*)

De Rechten van de Mens: Universaliteit in de Praktijk

Human Rights: Chinese and Dutch Perspectives (*editor with Fried van Hoof, Liu Nanlai and Tao Zhenghua*)

The Netherlands and the United Nations: Selected Issues (*editor with Monique Castermans-Holleman*)

Mensenrechten: Bestanddeel van het Buitenlands Beleid

Policy Analysis and Policy Innovation (*editor with Björn Wittrock*)

Also by Leon Gordenker

The UN Secretary-General and Secretariat

NGOs, the UN and Global Governance (*editor with T.G. Weiss*)

International Cooperation in Response to Aids (*with others*)

The Challenging Role of the UN Secretary-General (*editor with Benjamin Rivlin*)

Soldiers, Peacekeepers and Disasters (*editor with T.G. Weiss*)

Refugees in International Politics

The United Nations Secretary-General and the Maintenance of Peace

The United Nations: Reality and Ideal

Peter R. Baehr
and
Leon Gordenker
Fourth Edition

First Edition (The United Nations in the 1990s) 1992
Second Edition (The United Nations in the 1990s) 1994
Third Edition (The United Nations at the end of the 1990s) 1999
First published 2005 by
PALGRAVE MACMILLAN
Houndmills, Basingstoke, Hampshire RG21 6XS and
175 Fifth Avenue, New York, N. Y. 10010
Companies and representatives throughout the world

PALGRAVE MACMILLAN is the global academic imprint of the Palgrave Macmillan division of St. Martin's Press, LLC and of Palgrave Macmillan Ltd. Macmillan® is a registered trademark in the United States, United Kingdom and other countries. Palgrave is a registered trademark in the European Union and other countries.

ISBN-13: 978–1–4039–4904–2 hardback
ISBN-10: 1–4039–4904–2   hardback
ISBN-13: 978–1–4039–4905–9 paperback
ISBN-10: 1–4039–4905–0   paperback

This book is printed on paper suitable for recycling and made from fully managed and sustained forest sources.

A catalogue record for this book is available from the British Library.

Library of Congress Cataloging-in-Publication Data
Baehr, P. R. (Peter R.)
    The United Nations : reality and ideal / Peter R. Baehr and Leon Gordenker.–4th ed.
        p. cm.
    Rev. ed. of: The United Nation at the end of the 1990s. 3rd ed. New York : St. Martin's Press, 1999.
        Includes bibliographical references and index.
        ISBN 1–4039–4904–2 (cloth) – ISBN 1–4039–4905–0 (pbk.)
            1. United Nations. I. Gordenker, Leon, 1923– II. Baehr, P. R. (Peter R.). United Nations at the end of the 1990s. III. Title.

JZ4984.5.B34 2005   2005046333
341.23–dc22

10   9   8   7   6   5   4   3   2   1
14 13 12 11 10 09 08 07 06 05

Printed and bound in Great Britain by
Antony Rowe Ltd, Chippenham and Eastbourne

To the memory of
Belia Emilie Gordenker-Strootman
Felix Baehr

Contents

List of Tables

Preface to the Fourth Edition

Since the last edition at the end of the 20th century of this deliberately condensed account of the fortunes of the United Nations, its record has grown in complexity and breadth. The organization has taken part in legitimizing the use of force and even directing it and has also been excluded from the decisional circle that at times decreed armed intervention. It has preserved its position as one of the many devices of international cooperation on development and as a center for the difficult task of protecting human rights. It has become more central in coping with human and some political disasters. As forecast in earlier editions, it has never either vanished from participation nor receded into disuse.

In considering the United Nations, as well as all forms of international organization, each passing year seems to reemphasize the rapidly growing interconnection of societies, economies and security issues. What could once perhaps be brushed aside as too obscure for the international agenda, now is propelled into view by the speed and extent of electronic communication. One result for the authors of this book is a dilemma: if one excludes new detail of international life, the story is less rich than actuality; if one includes too much, the detail submerges the main lines. For instance, governments have begun the long process of complex structural reforms, proposed by the Secretary-General. These involve even the size and membership of the Security Council. What will emerge is now anything but certain.

It is our hope that what we have written not only helps to clarify the developments of UN structure and practice over decades but also encourages readers to mine on their own for additional knowledge the ever growing and easily accessible documentation as well as a formidable body of scholarly writing. Finally, we want to thank Niels Blokker, Nico Schrijver, Paul Peters en Tiemo Oostenbrink, who read and commented on parts of the manuscript, as well as Princeton University for various kindnesses and support.

Peter R. Baehr
Heemstede, Netherlands

Leon Gordenker
Princeton, NJ, USA
May 2005

Preface to the Third Edition

This book, which is the third edition of *The United Nations in the 1990s*, fulfills at least some of our expectations that were set out in its predecessor, five years ago. We noted then that the organization would likely remain an integral part of world politics, as it has, but that the policies of members could hardly be predicted.

The present edition builds on precisely the same expectations. So much has happened in the last five years, moreover, that a short volume such as this must be concise as to detail. Moreover, it probably gives less attention to activity outside the security agenda than would be our ideal preference. Yet that seems hardly avoidable, given the remarkable rapidity of development and change with regard to maintaining peace.

As in the previous editions, we hope to introduce the United Nations, its structure and its history in such a way as to stimulate informed judgment and further enquiry. We have no doubt at all that such enquiry is rewarding and that worthy critical conclusions on the United Nations require the kind of basic understanding we hope to stimulate.

We acknowledge with gratitude the assistance of Saskia Bal and Maaike Hogenkamp of the Netherlands Institute of Human Rights (SIM), who helped to revise the bibliography.

PETER R. BAEHR
Heemstede, Netherlands

LEON GORDENKER
Grijpskerke, Netherlands
April 1998

Preface to the Second Edition

As this revision of *The United Nations in the 1990s* is completed, it is obvious, if it were not before, that the organization now constitutes an integral part of international politics. Whether it will maintain that position – or decline or grow yet more – remains anyone's guess. As international politics probably will not freeze in place, it seems likely that the fortunes of the United Nations will, as before, reflect dynamic factors outside its control or purview.

Those varied and largely unpredictable activities of governments and other actors that we include in the term international politics have during the last three years deepened and broadened the agenda of the United Nations. This revised edition of *The United Nations in the 1990s* tries to sum up some of those additions and to show how they relate to earlier practice. As developments within the UN, especially with regard to peace and security, have so quickly and unexpectedly burst into the news, we cannot pretend to set out the last word on the organization. We have tried here, however, to sketch some of the most important changes since the last edition.

These changes include the far-reaching intervention of the organization in Iraq after its attack on Kuwait, the mounting of peace-keeping in Yugoslavia and Somalia and the apparent emergence of a new sense of international responsibility with regard to humanitarian disasters. But as with almost everything else in the experience of the United Nations, one decision or program soon leads to supplements, complements, withdrawals or other changes. We have revised the earlier edition in order to take into account changes wherever they could be observed. Some earlier errors were also corrected.

We wish to acknowledge the assistance with this revision of Ms Saskia Bal and Francine van Lenthe of the Netherlands Institute of Human Rights and Ambassador N. Biechman of the Netherlands Permanent Mission to the United Nations.

PETER R. BAEHR
Heemstede, Netherlands

LEON GORDENKER
Grijpskerke, Netherlands
February 1993

Preface

While the last lines of this book were written in mid-1991, the usefulness, the promise and the fragility of the United Nations seemed evident. The great crisis in the Middle East, caused by the seizure of Kuwait by Iraq in August 1990, at once pulled the world organization into the central decision-making vortex. The Security Council provided the legal basis for international coercion to force Iraq to withdraw from Kuwait. It demonstrated a broad consensus among governments in every part of the world that Iraq's invasion of Kuwait was unacceptable. In the background, some parts of the UN system dealt with the needs of people who fled from Iraq to the neighboring countries. Still other parts monitored the economic sanctions ordained by the Security Council and investigated Iraq's compliance with the complex terms of a cease-fire.

Decision-making in the Security Council was led by the United States government. The United Nations was used to define the aggression in the Persian Gulf but hardly to coordinate the military and political actions. Unlike the initial response to the attack on Korea in 1950, for the Persian Gulf in 1991 no unified military command was established. In both cases, the United States and its allies engaged the United Nations to establish legal and political reference points and to emphasize the breadth of international approval for their actions.

Both the quality of the public discussion of the Persian Gulf crisis and the role of the United Nations more generally relate to the origins of this book. The work reflects the beliefs of its authors that the United Nations is important enough in world politics to deserve an accurately informed public opinion of it. Our hope is that a clearly sketched introduction to the United Nations would help fill some of the recurrent gaps in understanding in public and classroom discussion. This book does not pretend to develop new knowledge, but it does attempt to set out the essential elements of forty-five years of experience with the UN system. It deliberately emphasizes historical development and legal institutional aspects, for some acquaintance with these is essential to informed judgment.

The framework of the book is formed by those principal topics which the United Nations Charter defines and which, baring cataclysmic change, can be expected to preoccupy the UN system into the

21st century. It attempts to avoid illusions about the role of the United Nations in international politics and about the benefits or costs it may have in terms of the foreign policies of its members. Finally, it is necessarily selective in the face of an enormous amount of UN activity.

Our transnational collaboration bridges the Atlantic Ocean. This, we hope, helps to discourage nationalistic partisanship and to encourage a cosmopolitan point of view. While we avoid policy recommendations, we do offer occasional judgments as to whether the United Nations has developed according to plans and expectations for it. The book concentrates on the UN system while attempting to remain sensitive to the world political context that conditions it. At the same time, we neither explain nor assay the world scene at every juncture, nor do we offer a general theory to cover everything that has or could happen to the United Nations.

Although we attempt objectivity, we bring to this work convictions about the value of international cooperation. Cooperation among governments, we hold – as did the founders of the United Nations – is essential to a peaceful world. That may be an unattainable goal. A great deal of cooperation nevertheless remains an unmistakable daily practice, a stable foundation, for the way governments relate to each other much of the time. Not all international cooperation works out to the benefit of all or is necessarily productive of a peaceful world in the long term. But the concept that international relations need to be organized and that institutions are useful in encouraging and supervising cooperation seems unassailable, especially after the end of the Cold War and the astonishingly quick reorganization of East and Central Europe.

Our collaboration began while we were fellows in the early 1970s at the Netherlands Institute of Advanced Study in the Humanities and Social Sciences (NIAS) at Wassenaar. A forerunner of this book was then developing. With another fellow at NIAS, P.J.G. Kapteyn, then Professor of International Law at Utrecht University, Baehr was drafting parts of what became *De Verenigde Naties: ideaal en werkelijkheid*, published in 1976 by Het Spectrum. Gordenker read the original manuscript and offered his comments. From the ensuing discussion came the first English-language cousin of this book, *The United Nations: Reality and Ideal*, published in 1984 by Praeger. A revised Dutch version with the earlier title was published in 1985 by Boom.

Our confidence that this book may prove useful was bolstered by the willing help that we received from scholars, international civil servants, diplomats and national civil servants. They, as well as students in universities in the many countries where we have lectured, all deserve our thanks, although not all of them can be named here. Among those who can are Professor Theo van Boven of the Rijksuniversiteit in Limburg, who kindly read the chapter on human rights; Dr Johan Kaufmann, whose own writings have enlightened students of international organization and his fellow diplomats; and Mr Gerben Ringnalda, a veteran official of the Netherlands Ministry of Foreign Affairs, who commented on the chapter on international cooperation and development. Gordenker owes specific thanks to the Rockefeller Foundation and the Ford Foundation for support for his research and to the Center of International Studies at Princeton University for its many services over the years, including those that made possible his continuing contact with the Netherlands and its scholarly community; and to the Graduate Institute of International Studies at Geneva for its many kindnesses while he taught there.

It is hardly necessary to say that we accept personal responsibility for the interpretations and errors of this book.

Leon Gordenker
Princeton, NJ
Peter R. Baehr
Heemstede, Netherlands

List of Abbreviations

ACC	Administrative Committee on Coordination
CEB	Chief Executives Board
ECLA	Economic Commission for Latin America
ECOSOC	Economic and Social Council
EPTA	Expanded Program of Technical Assistance
FAO	Food and Agricultural Organization
G-77	Group of 77 (developing nations)
GATT	General Agreement on Tariffs and Trade
IAEA	International Atomic Energy Agency
ICAO	International Civil Aviation Organization
ICJ	International Court of Justice
IDA	International Development Association
IFAD	International Fund for Agricultural Development
IFC	International Finance Corporation
IFOR	Implementation Force (in Yugoslavia)
ILO	International Labor Organization
IMF	International Monetary Fund
IMO	International Maritime Organization
IBRD	International Bank of Reconstruction and Development (later the World Bank)
ITU	International Telecommunication Union
MINURSO	United Nations Mission for the Referendum in Western Sahara
NATO	North Atlantic Treaty Organization
NGO	Non-governmental Organization
NIEO	New International Economic Order
OAS	Organization of American States
OAU	Organization for African Unity
ONUC	Opération des Nations Unies au Congo
ONUSAL	United Nations Observer Mission for El Salvador
OPCW	Organization for the Prohibition of Chemical Warfare
OPEC	Organization of Petroleum Exporting Countries
OSCE	Organization for Security and Cooperation in Europe
PLO	Palestine Liberation Organization
SWAPO	South West African People's Organization
UNBRO	United Nations Border Relief Organization

UNCDF	United Nations Capital Development Fund
UDI	Unilateral Declaration of Independence (of Rhodesia)
UNCTAD	United Nations Conference on Trade and Development
UNDOF	United Nations Disengagement Observer Force
UNDP	United Nations Development Program
UNDRO	United Nations Disaster Relief Office
UNEF	United Nations Emergency Force
UNEP	United Nations Environmental Program
UNESCO	United Nations Educational, Scientific and Cultural Organization
UNFICYP	United Nations Force in Cyprus
UNFPA	United Nations Population Fund
UNHCR	United Nations High Commissioner for Refugees
UNICEF	United Nations Children's Fund
UNIDO	United Nations Industrial Development Organization
UNIFIL	United Nations Interim Force in Lebanon
UNIIMOG	United Nations Iran-Iraq Military Observer Group
UNIKOM	United Nations Iraq-Kuwait Observation Mission
UNMIH	United Nations Mission in Haiti
UNMOVIC	United Nations Monitoring, Verification and Inspection Mission
UNOSOM	United Nations Operation in Somalia
UNPROFOR	United Nations Protection Force (in Yugoslavia)
UNRRA	United Nations Relief and Rehabilitation Administration
UNRWA	United Nations Relief and Works Agency (for Palestine Refugees)
UNSCOM	United Nations Special Commission
UNTAC	United Nations Transitional Authority for Cambodia
UNTAG	United Nations Transition Assistance Group (in Namibia)
UNTEA	United Nations Temporary Executive Authority (over West Irian)
UNTSO	United Nations Truce Supervision Organization
UNU	United Nations University
UNV	United Nations Volunteers
UPU	Universal Postal Union
WFP	World Food Program
WHO	World Health Organization
WIPO	World Intellectual Property Organization
WMD	Weapons of Mass Destruction
WMO	World Meteorological Organization
WTO	World Trade Organization
WTO-OMT	World Tourism Organization

1
Introduction

Representatives of 50 countries met on 25 April 1945 in San Francisco to write a document that, it was hoped, would guide the world to an era of peace and well-being. As the United Nations Conference on International Organization opened, the reek of war was fresh but hope for the future surged among the people of the nearly victorious Allied states. The Conference debated and eventually approved the Charter of the United Nations and thus the creation of a new world organization.

However novel the statesmen at San Francisco may have wanted their handiwork to appear, familiar difficulties and specific historical baggage accompanied them. During the next six decades, these difficulties remained while new ones arose. Yet the San Francisco Charter has endured almost as it was drafted, while the organization based on it resisted, bent, rebounded, and adjusted to the turbulent political currents that are characteristic of international relations. This book deals mainly with the fate of the organization created at San Francisco. But the United Nations, if it is to be clearly understood, must be set against the background of international politics and the history of international organization.

Independent states

Although the San Francisco Conference claimed to speak in the name of 'We, the peoples of the United Nations,' its participants acted on behalf of governments. In turn, those governments represented states – those legal and political abstractions for social structures within which people are governed. In some states, the people or their elected representatives can change the government or even the national constitution. Within others, woe befalls those who even breathe a criticism of governmental

1

policy. In treating with each other, most governments pretend that they rule in their states without the slightest responsibility to others unless they specifically undertake it. Each state is said to be sovereign and independent. The UN Charter faithfully reflects this assertion.

If each state is sovereign and independent, then the new world organization could not be a government. Nor did the San Francisco Conference leave any doubt on this point. Yet the new United Nations was mandated to produce and supervise some order in the world, to foster welfare and very specifically to maintain peace and security. How to do so raises a central issue in international politics: how to govern the ungovernable states? Despite earlier attempts to cope with this issue and despite nearly 60 years of practice by the United Nations, it remains largely unresolved.

Interdependent societies

The concept of sovereignty describes no actual behavior, especially during our time when societies daily become more closely linked. Interdependence among societies, manifested by such visible activity as commerce or transportation, reaches back to the beginning of human history. But during the last century, it was extended to the whole globe. Never before has communication among individuals and organizations within distinct societies taken place so quickly and so penetratingly.

Examples of the depth of interdependence abound. The oil boycott in 1973, ordered as weapon against Israel by governments of Arab oil-producing lands, almost strangled automobile traffic in Western Europe and North America. An increase in interest rates, ordered by the government of the United Kingdom, raises the price of the British pound to foreigners, reducing their purchases of British goods. That slows the whole economy of the United Kingdom. In turn, workers in factories abroad who make goods that importers in the United Kingdom bought lose business. A SARS epidemic in China affects transatlantic air traffic. The support by the Sudanese government of Arab militia causes a flood of African refugees into neighboring Chad, where they congregate in refugee camps mainly financed by funds from North America, Western Europe and Japan. Sabotage attacks on oil pipelines in Iraq and disturbances in Nigeria lead to higher fuel prices all over the world. An epidemic of AIDS costs millions of lives. The possibility of global warming resulting from high consumption of fossil fuels leads the governments of low-lying islands and beaches to fear flooding.

In a world so interconnected that these and other transnational phenomena appear, metamorphose and turn up again, international responses and governance seem imperative. Global interdependence involves all with all but not equally and not always with desired effects. Yet no one government in a world of states can by itself wipe out evil or benefit all equally. It would seem that only cooperative behavior – or else a world government and the end of the national states – can lead to regulation and order in a situation of interdependence. But how insure cooperation or even acceptance that some human activity leads to a threat to all?

Without ever using the not-yet-fashionable terms, 'interdependence', or 'globalization', the San Francisco Conference hoped to create an institution to cope with its effects. It did so by trying to channel and encourage cooperative behavior by governments through standing institutions. These would seek out common interests and recommend common policies which governments could then carry out. The permanent institutions could assume a perspective which extended beyond the horizons of any one government.

International law

The UN Charter consists of rules for an organization of states and for some limits of action on the part of their governments. These rules are cast in the form of legal obligations, binding on states and accepted as such by their governments. The UN Charter itself is described by jurists as a multilateral convention, a binding treaty that makes new law. Moreover, the new organization received the task of progressively developing international law. The UN Charter thus unmistakably has the nature of public law, which serves to organize polities; in form, it resembles such documents as the United States Constitution. Yet this global compact was intended to apply in a world of nominally independent sovereign states whose very existence suggests the absence of general rules.

Thus the UN Charter poses the issue of whether law really can be applied to states and raises again one of the hoary issues of international relations. In fact, governments had for some 300 years recognized the existence of legal obligations, most of which were explicitly undertaken in the form of treaties. Others were attributed to custom recognized by all governments. No one questioned the ability of governments to take on legal obligations, even if their desirability could cause debate. But the execution of these obligations remained in hands of governments.

On the whole, the body of international law is usually applied without challenge. Thousands of treaties and negotiations and judicial settlements of disputes give evidence of the application of international law. Just as with domestic law, however, violations take place. In the national jurisdictions, examples would include breaches of contract, damage to others by negligence, embezzlements, murders or narcotic smuggling and sale. Generally, they are quickly dealt with in a court without fundamentally disturbing the society or implying a challenge to the validity of law. Domestic courts routinely apply international law. At the international level of states, a violation may not end in a trial and a judicial decision. A breach of law could result in a tense crisis, deprivation of important advantages to one or more countries and even a devastating war.

The San Francisco Conference tried to adjust to the issue of applying and extending international law by seeking a consensus among governments. Presumably, if they agreed to the rules of the Charter, then they could be depended on to cooperate in settling disputes and promoting cooperation. But the governments represented in San Francisco in no sense sought to legislate a coercive process as a national parliament might do. Only in one instance did they approve such a mechanism for the new organization. This, as will be explained in detail in Chapter 4 below, could be used only in case of a blatant *violation* of the peace and thus of the rules of the Charter. Aside from that, international law was to be applied among and within states and developed on the basis of a freely-reached consensus of governments.

Reforming world politics

Recurring, progressively more devastating war among states had long before San Francisco led to the notion that the manner in which international relations was conducted needed reform. A long list of normative thinkers, including Immanuel Kant, Jean-Jacques Rousseau, the Quaker leader William Penn, the American President Woodrow Wilson, and hundreds of others had turned their minds to redesigning international politics. However little or much their notions penetrated the thinking of the mass of people and their governors, no one could remain unaffected by the destruction that modern military technology had made possible. The deaths of a 800,000 young men in the Battle of the Somme of World War I and of whole cities in one blow in the nuclear bombings of Hiroshima and Nagasaki raised an issue that could not be ignored. In the wake of World War II, during which damage to civilians had far exceeded military casualties, the question of whether the nature of international politics was at fault figured high on an unacknowledged agenda at San Francisco.

The query as to whether and how much the international political system could be reformed linked to the difficulty of controlling a collection of sovereigns. It was out of the question somehow to abolish sovereignty and to form a world government. None of the victorious governments, headed by such redoubtable figures as Churchill, Roosevelt, and Stalin, would entertain such a notion for an instant. Yet all three of these seasoned political leaders specifically endorsed a new approach to organizing world politics. So did the mass of people wherever they could express themselves. In the United States in 1945, for instance, some 90 percent of a representative sample of the population polled in attitude surveys favored joining the United Nations. Fifty years later, incidentally, more than 70 percent of those polled favored continuing that membership.

To some extent, the tension between the rejection of old style international politics and retention of the idea of the sovereign, national state was resolved by giving extraordinary roles to the greatest of them. Thus, the United States, the Soviet Union, the United Kingdom, France and China were expected to exercise special responsibilities for maintaining peace. The first three of this quintet had taken the lead in developing the ideas for a new international organization and had written the drafts placed before the San Francisco Conference. Together the 'Big Five' would form a directorate for governance with narrowly defined emergency powers; Roosevelt thought of them as the policemen of the world. They would further be expected to use their prestige in the service of peace.

These ideas, resting on experience with power politics, became a keystone of the new UN Charter. But the finished document went much deeper in a reformist direction wherever the emphasis was not on short-term settlement of specific disputes. The reforms, it was thought, would help promote international peace and security. Partly they involved institutional devices and partly novel subject matter for international cooperation.

As any 'peace-loving' state could become a member of the new organization, the ultimate aim was universal membership. The initial test of peace-loving ironically was whether a state had declared war on Germany and Japan. The members would have votes in the various deliberative organs. They would make decisions, which usually took the form of recommendations, on the basis of debates that usually were open to any witness who entered the room. Majority voting patterns, sometimes qualified, were to replace the old diplomatic formula of consensus or nothing. At the same time, the 'Big Five' would have a weighted vote in matters of peace and security. Both the universality of membership and the provisions for voting might be called novel.

For the first time, an international organization was charged with promoting the international protection of human rights. This mandate could not avoid touching sensitive political nerves in many countries. Yet in the world of 1945, when the murderous behavior of the Nazi regime in Germany had become common knowledge, protection of human rights answered a need felt by many people and leaders. But it was also an idea with revolutionary content, as will be explained in Chapter 5.

The Charter implies a theory that the conditions in which wars are bred have to do with economic deprivation and shortcomings in society, including violations of human rights. Consequently international cooperation was to seek to create conditions in which peace would flourish. Such cooperation could cope with economic and social problems that ignored national frontiers. Thus, the new United Nations would have to find a way to deal with sweeping issues of interdependence in a world of sovereigns.

In the colonial world, still very extensive in 1945, both economic and social problems and issues of human rights, such as the right to participate in government, visibly merged. The new organization included an instruction to improve the conditions of colonial peoples, to bring some of them to self-government or independence and to open all colonies to some measure of international scrutiny. Were this not done, the Charter implicitly assumes, it might become impossible to keep the peace.

The reformist goals set out by the Charter would obviously involve more than a few quick decisions. They implied eliminating social evils and changing the scope and depth of international cooperation beyond all precedent. Thus, they can be understood as reflecting a strong current of dissatisfaction with a past that comprised so much strife and suffering.

Conferences and decisions

Despite the lofty new aims of the San Francisco Conference, it proceeded in a time-honored manner. The delegates to it represented governments and therefore were bound to follow instructions from their capitals. They negotiated with their colleagues to gain for themselves as much as they could without losing the promise of collaboration. This followed diplomatic practice and also the decision-making mode of confederations, such as the original Swiss state, the first version of the United States of America, and the Dutch Republic of the 17th century.

The diplomatic model of instructed delegates reigned in the League of Nations as well as in two sorts of early forerunners of the United Nations. As for the League of Nations, which had many tasks that resembled those of the new organization, it was decided even before the San Francisco meeting to start afresh. That would allow the governments to distance themselves from an organization that had a reputation as a failure.

The other forerunners included the international conferences to organize the peace at the end of European wars and a varied collection of functional organizations. The peace conferences did not constitute permanent organizations. The functional agencies had a continuing existence in order to regulate specific, specialized relationships among governments, such as navigation on the Rhine River, and to administer and supervise agreements among governments.

The first of the great postwar conferences was the Congress of Westphalia (1648), which marked the end of the Thirty Year's War and the emergence of the modern concept of the sovereign state as a basis for international relations. In a 'world' that was limited to Europe, almost every state, however minor, was represented. Other examples were the Congress of Utrecht (1713) and the crucial Congress of Vienna (1815) which reorganized Europe after the Napoleonic Wars. The governments represented in Vienna accorded conclusive legitimacy to the modern sovereign state and worked out many lasting rules for international conferences. Among the most important of these was the notion of equality among sovereigns; it meant that no state could claim special privileges in rank or in making decisions. This rule of equality underlies the one-nation, one-vote principle used in the League of Nations and the United Nations. The Congress of Vienna encouraged the formation of the first of the international functional organizations.

Functional cooperation in the 19th century

A pioneer functional organization involved the Rhine River, which flowed through and touched on the claims of several states affected by the Napoleonic wars. Negotiations stemming from Congress of Vienna resulted in the establishment of the Central Commission for Navigation on the Rhine in 1832. All the riparian states except Switzerland joined it. It successfully organized cooperative governmental action to maintain the river channels and supervise traffic. Its success led to the creation of a similar commission for the Danube in 1856. It had delegated power to collect tolls and dredge the river channels.

By the second half of the 19th century, technological advances offered benefits that no government could obtain alone. Like using the Rhine, this was true of postal and telegraphic traffic, weather reporting and transport generally. In order to promote international cooperation on such matters, standing institutions were required. With a permanent secretariat and a regular schedule of meetings, instead of occasional conferences, institutions could develop and oversee international standards. The secretariats could carefully prepare studies and expert advice for the periodic meetings of governmental delegates. This pattern of meetings, preparations and a permanent bureau offered a model and experience for later, more ambitious organizations.

The new mode of organizing international relations was employed for no less than 33 international public unions, as this form of international institution was then called, between 1865 and 1914. Some of the most important of the new agencies were the International Telegraphic Union (1868), the early version of the contemporary International Telecommunication Union (ITU); the International Bureau for Weights and Measures (1875); the Universal Postal Union (UPU) (1878); and the International Institute of Agriculture (1905). Founding governments narrowly defined the tasks undertaken by the international public unions. Unlike the peace conferences, the delegates to the meetings of the unions were usually experts and technical personnel. They were nevertheless subject to instructions from their governments. While the secretariats assured continuity, governments provided for supervision by manning small executive committees elected by larger general conferences.

Parallel to the intergovernmental agencies, private individuals also formed agencies that extended across national frontiers. The organizations strove to coordinate work carried out at the national level. As early as 1864 in his native Switzerland, Henri Dunant formed the Red Cross movement. In 1868, the Interparliamentary Union was established. The International Olympic Committee began meeting in 1894 and in 1899 the International Bureau for Prevention of Traffic in Women and Children began to operate. These private agencies are merely examples of some of the 182 international non-governmental organizations that existed between 1865 and 1914. They frequently stimulated the growth of intergovernmental agencies. Their personnel sometimes joined delegations or staffs of the official bodies.

The Concert of Europe

A series of international conferences through the 19th and early 20th century followed the lead given by the Congress of Vienna. Bringing together the European sovereigns or their spokesmen, these gatherings served to some degree to regulate political relationships and make adjustments after relatively small armed conflicts. This practice of conferring constituted the Concert of Europe which helped to prevent a general European war for a century.

The Congress of Vienna had produced a rudimentary political organization of Europe in the so-called Grand Alliance. This was an agreement among England, Prussia, Austria-Hungary, Russia, and later France to ensure that the decisions of the Congress were carried out. It aimed at maintaining the political *status quo*. England, however, set as its primary goal limiting the influence of the defeated France, while the other powers showed more interest in suppressing political and social change. In 1822, England withdrew from the alliance in protest against its conservative intervention in Spain. Nevertheless, all of the governments in the Grand Alliance continued the policy of conferring about political issues in Europe. They dealt with such questions as Greek independence from the Ottoman Empire (1827), the separation of Belgium from the Netherlands (1831), peace after the Crimean War, developments in the faltering Ottoman Empire, and the tension between the Austro-Hungarian and Russian empires. The last major gathering of the Concert, the London Conference of 1912–3, again involved the Balkan area and foreshadowed the antagonisms that set off World War I.

Even if the governments that hewed to the Concert process had their own ends in mind, they laid down principles that were important for the later development of international organization. They met periodically. They used the end of international conflicts, especially the Napoleonic War, as a means for reorganizing their relationships. They avoided punishing the defeated, especially France, in such a way as to exclude its future cooperation. They relied on the leadership of great powers. They sought to avoid war by conferring in advance of using military power. They limited the scope of military activity. But they did not adopt the features of the public international unions: formal permanent institutions, fixed rule of procedure, formal agendas, and periodical meetings. Nor did they establish a permanent secretariat.

The Hague Peace Conferences

The experience with conferring, periodic meetings, international law and technical preparations, as well as pursuit of national foreign policy goals, all underlay an unusual initiative by the Russian emperor. He sought to protect his land from its own weakness by using the customary organizational techniques to promote disarmament. This resulted in the summoning of the Hague Peace Conferences of 1899 and 1907.

The first of these conferences developed rules for making the conduct of war more humane. They still have some application. Furthermore, rules were discussed to bring about pacific settlement of international disputes. From that beginning, the second conference created the Permanent Court of Arbitration, which in fact was a list of eminent jurists available to form international tribunals whose decisions would have binding effect, plus a permanent international secretariat. Governments had *specifically* to agree in advance to submit their disputes to such arbitration. This, too, still exists.

A noticeable increase in interest in the Hague Peace Conference rapidly developed. The first meeting in 1899 included representatives of 26 governments. The second in 1907 enjoyed participation of 44 governments, including some from Latin America for the first time. Although World War I nullified the plan for continuing meetings, a definite trend towards universal participation in international law-making and creation of means to settle disputes had become clear.

The League of Nations

Far and away the most important embodiment of the experience with international cooperation during the 19th century was the League of Nations. It was equally the direct forerunner of the United Nations, whose Charter borrowed heavily from the League Covenant. It served as a testing laboratory for the ideas of its time.

The central idea underlying the League was formulated by President Woodrow Wilson of the United States in the last of the famous 14 points that set out the war aims of his government:

A general association must be formed under specific covenants for the purpose of affording mutual guarantees of political independence and territorial integrity to great and small states alike.

While that statement proposed no fundamental change of the system of sovereign states, it projected a new legal contract among governments, the creation of a permanent institution of universal member-ship and a system of guarantees intended to maintain international peace and security.

Wilson's 14th point initiated planning efforts in Great Britain and France, as well as the United States, and a vast public discussion. Fed into negotiations at the Versailles Peace Conference of 1919, this activ-ity resulted in agreement on the Covenant of the League of Nations. As a formal part of the treaty intended legally to end the First World War, the Covenant predictably was aimed at preventing the recurrence of another such disaster.

A novel political commitment – collective security – provided the foundation of the peace-keeping system in the Covenant. It relied on the notion that governments would honor their legal obligations and on their repeated declarations after wars that they did not want another – at least at once. Collective security thus assumes a common interest in peace. It also assumes a rudimentary community of states. If any one government orders an attack on another, then all of the rest view this anti-social action as an attack on them. They have the legal obligation to resist by individual and joint means. Thus, the notion of self-defense, long accepted as a sovereign right, is broadened to all in the community. Neutrality is excluded. As the community includes all states, including those with great military power, an agreement on collective security would effectively deter armed aggression.

The assumption of a community of states draws on the 19th century experience with developing international law and with the functioning of the Concert of Europe. The League institutionalized the *ad hoc* conferences of the Concert. Now they would meet according to a regular calendar. For specialized purposes, including maintenance of peace, smaller bodies would meet periodically. A headquarters was established at Geneva, where a permanent secretariat, headed by the Secretary-General, was appointed.

The commitments needed to make collective security effective were set out in the League Covenant. Conflicts among members were to be solved without war. The organs of the League were available to help find such solutions. Some would be legally binding. This approach to peace through negotiation or legal judgment incorporated the diplo-matic experience of the previous century. Only after all other means were tried was the use of force permissible. Only if the commitments were disregarded, the penalties implied by collective security would be involved automatically and legally.

The two main representative organs of the League, the Assembly and the Council, shared the responsibility for the political handling of dis-putes as well as other matters within the competence of the organization.

All members were represented in the Assembly, which met annually, and the great powers were always members of the smaller Council which met more frequently and could be summoned on short notice. The Council usually took up disputes which might threaten peace although some came before the Assembly. The voting arrangements clearly reflected the customary practices of international conferences which could not force sovereigns to submit to the will of the majority. Therefore voting in the League was by unanimity. That meant that each member state had the veto. Formally, the League thus faced narrow limits in the face of resistance by a government.

Nevertheless, the carefully elaborated procedures for settling disputes had the backing of two centuries of diplomatic experience. The League system institutionalized the practices that had often served well. Members were expected to try to settle disputes themselves. If they could not, the Council was open for political handling, including mediation and investigation. If the parties consented, the Council could arbitrate a dispute. Or alternatively, they could submit it for a binding decision to the new Permanent Court of International Justice in The Hague.

If the Council could not settle a dispute after a serious effort, it then had the duty of reporting on the facts and making recommendations for resolving it. After that report or arbitral or judicial proceedings, the members undertook not to resort to war during a three-month cooling off period. If they did, all members were to treat it as a breach of the Covenant, invoking automatic sanctions.

The procedure by which the principle of collective security would be brought into play derived from the conception of a balance of power among the European powers. This device meant that no single power could dominate the area and that the rest of the governments would rather fight to restore the balance than to let that happen. Thus, expansion would be deterred and independence of states preserved. But the League system envisaged regulating disputes through a standing institution.

That institution would have duties much beyond merely serving as a framework for automatic reaction. If any government broke the rules, the Council could organize the sanctions and even supply armed forces to check the transgressor. In order to act against aggression, members of the League declared themselves ready to offer mutual financial support. They also would permit armed forces to pass through their territory to act against the aggressor.

If the League created a new form of guiding political relationships, it also established a novel judicial organ in the Permanent Court of

International Justice. This was more than the directory of experts of the Permanent Court of Arbitration. The new body consisted of a bench of 15 independent judges, appointed by the Council and the Assembly of the League acting jointly. That guaranteed the prestige of this new body, the first of its kind. It could draw upon the substantial body of international rules already respected most of the time by most governments.

The first decade of the League's short life included institutional construction, including the first international civil service, and several promising attempts at dispute settlement. The latter included hostilities between Bulgaria and Greece and the judicial settlement of quarrels between Sweden and Finland over the Aaland Islands. During the 1930s, however, the lack of community, the limited membership of the League and the unwillingness to renounce war or to treat its use as an attack on all sapped its capacities.

The assumption of universal membership had almost immediately proved unwarranted. The government of the United States, the originator of so much that went into the Covenant, was the first to abandon it. President Wilson failed to get the consent of the Senate for ratification of the Treaty of Versailles; his successor campaigned on and applied a policy of hostility to the League. The new Soviet Union, isolated as it consolidated the revolution that replaced the Russian empire, joined only in 1934. That left only France and Great Britain as the great powers and, as Japan was the only non-European member of general importance, emphasized the European character of the League. Japan quit after having been condemned for swallowing Manchuria in 1931. Italy, soon to have a Fascist government, became an uncomfortable member and withdrew in 1937, after breaking the Covenant by conquering Ethiopia (then called Abyssinia). Germany joined in 1926, but its new Nazi government abandoned membership in 1933.

An unmistakable sign of retreat from the Versailles order came with Japan's disregard of demands by the League to end its expansion into China. Soon thereafter Mussolini's Italy secretly began preparing to attack Ethiopia. The League responded to aggression in 1935 with economic sanctions, excluding oil and military steps, but that did not prevent the conquest of a weak African country. After that, the League no longer had much political significance. Although Italy, Germany and the Soviet Union all intervened in the Spanish Civil War, the League barely reacted. Hitler's successful pressure for the cession of Czechoslovakia in 1938 was handled outside of the League.

Finland got little help from the expulsion from the League of the Soviet attacker. The League did not take up the German attack on Poland in 1939, which began the Second World War. The formal dissolution of the organization took place in 1946 in Geneva.

Had they been faithfully used, the admittedly imperfect means at the disposal of the League for settling disputes could perhaps have made important differences in international politics. At least they would have complicated matters for an aggressor as they did for Italy when sanctions were applied at the end of 1935. Yet chroniclers of the League have left little doubt that because the major powers – only England and France throughout its life – declined to use its devices, what was left of the collective security system was doomed. In fact, the absence of the United States and most of the time, the Soviet Union, Germany and Japan, gave evidence of even more lack of agreement than did the hesitance of Britain and France. The lack of commitment was only compounded by the unanimity rule for voting. Even so, when the conflicts involved small states and limited aims, useful effects came from the League. But whether any institution depending on cooperation could have resisted deliberate aggression from such sources as Japan, Italy, Germany and the Soviet Union can be doubted.

World War II and the UN

Long before victory in World War II was on the horizon, the idea took root among the leaders of the allied powers that the postwar world would require a general international organization. It would help to maintain the reestablished peace and much more. As Woodrow Wilson made the creation of the League of Nations an aim of the war, so too did Franklin Roosevelt and Winston Churchill.

Four months before the United States joined the battle, the British Prime Minister and the American President discussed war aims in August 1941 aboard an American cruiser off the Canadian shore. The result was the Atlantic Charter, the first open statement of principles about the postwar world. Supporting FDR's Four Freedoms – of expression and religion, from want and fear – which he had set forth earlier as policy aims, Churchill and Roosevelt favored restoration of independence to those states that had lost it to German aggression. They rejected territorial gains for their own countries. They mentioned that 'pending the establishment of a wider and more permanent system of general security', governments that threatened aggression should be disarmed. Although Churchill preferred a clear statement that an effective international organization was desirable, Roosevelt was held back by the fear of a negative reaction from the United States Senate. Nevertheless, the message was clear. The Soviet Union, the British Dominions and the Western European governments in exile approved the Atlantic Charter a month later.

In the succeeding months, winning the war preoccupied the leaders, but a series of conferences and intense planning, especially in the United States and the United Kingdom, gave shape to a postwar world organization. On January 1, 1942, less than a month after the Japanese attack that brought the United States into the war, 26 governments signed the 'Declaration of the United Nations', which set out principles for a 'wider and more permanent system of general security.' In it, the originators of the Atlantic Charter were joined by China, Poland, Czechoslovakia, Yugoslavia and several Latin American states. They viewed the Atlantic Charter as a common program for the allied states and pledged mutual support in the war effort and rejected any separate peace or armistice.

At that stage, even the term, 'United Nations', was tentative. The memoirs of Cordell Hull, then U.S. Secretary of State, relate that Roosevelt suggested the title, 'Declaration by United Nations', to Churchill who lay in his bathtub. 'The distinguished bather', Hull recalled, 'agreed and thus the term "United Nations" came into being.'

The planning for a postwar organization quickly evolved in 1943 from bathtub to professional diplomacy. Planning began in earnest in the foreign ministries of several governments and above all in Washington. The foreign ministers of the three leading allied powers, the United Kingdom, the United States, and the Soviet Union, convened in Moscow to draft the 'Declaration of Moscow' and later got a Chinese signature. It sought a general international organization as soon as possible. Aimed at maintaining international peace and security, it would be based on the sovereign equality of member states.

A further, brief glimpse of the progress towards an international organization came with the Teheran Conference of 1943, attended by Churchill, Roosevelt, and Stalin. This was followed by the Dumbarton Oaks Conference in a mansion in Washington from August to October 1944. This was the most concerted, detailed international effort so far. The discussion was based on drafts set out by the American State Department.

At Dumbarton Oaks, representatives of China, the Soviet Union, the United Kingdom, and the United States formulated the governing principles of the United Nations. Among them was the name, 'United Nations', to proclaim the intention of continuing peacetime cooperation on the basis of the common purposes of the war. All the sovereign members would be represented in the General Assembly which would have a broad agenda. The Security Council members (originally 11, later 15) would have the specialized task of keeping the peace. This distinction compromised the Soviet preference for separate organizations for peace and for economic and social cooperation. Other differences, such as the Soviet demand for 16 votes for the component republics of the USSR and the British opposition to any treatment of colonial territories, could not be settled. The remaining points at issue at Dumbarton Oaks were passed to the Yalta Conference of February 1945, where Churchill, Roosevelt, and Stalin found formulae for them.

The disagreement over membership and the Soviet demand for 16 votes yielded when Roosevelt proposed giving a vote to each of the then 48 United States. Yet the Ukrainian and Byelorussian Soviet Socialist Republic, never before identified as sovereign states, did get votes. Stalin argued that this advantage was offset by Washington's influence in Latin America. The list of 'sponsoring powers' of the United Nations would be expanded from the Big Three of Yalta to include China and France, both to have permanent places on the Security Council. Invitees to the founding conference at San Francisco would include all states whose governments had declared war on the Axis powers before March 1, 1945, and that had signed the Declaration of the United Nations of January 1, 1942.

Related to membership was the question of voting, a principal agenda item at Yalta. Except on procedural matters, the five Great Powers had to agree unanimously in the Security Council in order that a resolution be adopted. That meant that any of them had a veto. Procedural resolutions and those to which the Great Powers agreed required a seven-member majority in the 11-member Council. The earlier Soviet opposition to the Anglo-American proposal that a party to a dispute should not vote on it in the Council was overcome by treating pacific settlement differently from enforcement action. In the former, a party to a dispute could not vote but could in the latter.

As for colonies, Churchill was assured at Yalta that no part of the empire would be put under UN control without British consent. Great Britain, or any country, could put a colony under the supervision of a trusteeship system that would extend only to territories voluntarily put into it; to former mandates of the League of Nations (that had been seized from Germany and Turkey after the First World War) which had not gained independence; and additional territories that might be taken from Germany and Japan. Administration of other colonial territories would remain as before.

Within an hour of taking office after Roosevelt's sudden death on April 12, 1945, President Harry Truman announced that the founding conference for the United Nations would be held as planned. Accordingly, the United Nations Conference on International Organization opened on April 25, 1945, in San Francisco.

The San Francisco Conference

In what was probably the most public diplomatic conference to that time, 260 representatives of 50 states attended the conference that met in the San Francisco Opera House. More than 2,500 press and radio correspondents churned out the news. More than 40 citizens' organizations, encouraged by the United States, sent representatives. The intergovernmental agencies that had survived the war dispatched their spokesmen. All were served by a staff of more than 1,000, organized by the Department of State.

As with earlier diplomatic conferences, each governmental delegation had an equal vote. But as in the past, everyone understood that without the concurrence of the Great Powers no real results could be booked. The debates took place in a plenary session, four main committees, and 12 subcommittees, all of them aiming at finding ways to resolve issues.

Issues there still were, despite the long preparation at Dumbarton Oaks and the subsequent agreements at the Yalta. At the same time, the San Francisco Conference had solid, careful drafts on which to base its deliberations.

In addition to the never quite vanished differences among the Great Powers, two cleavages that sometimes involved overlapping groupings of states appeared at San Francisco. One of these was between small and large states; the other between colonial and non-colonial states. The small powers gained persuasiveness when the major powers drew apart. The non-colonial powers usually sought to make the colonial powers, some of which were small states, more accountable for their policies. Generally the smaller states tried to strengthen the powers of the General Assembly, in which they had the advantage of numbers and equality, against the more exclusive Security Council with its veto for the Permanent Five. Strong interest in economic and social cooperation through the United Nations also was characteristic of the smaller powers.

Nowhere did the divergent tendencies among the great and small surface more visibly than in committee sessions that dealt with the

Security Council. The smaller states resisted the provision for Great Power unanimity in the Council. The Permanent Five responded that no Council would ever be established without the veto. The small powers won provisions to ensure that the best contributors to peace from their ranks, as well as an 'equitable' geographical representation, would be elected to the Council.

As for the colonial issue, two categories of territories were defined for different treatment. The new drafts distinguished territories placed under UN supervision or trusteeship from the rest of the colonial world. All colonies except those placed under trusteeship were to be known as non-self-governing territories. For them, the administering states had duties of advancing the people but not granting them independence; self-government was retained as a goal. Administering states would be obliged to report to the General Assembly.

The trusteeship system was less controversial, because it was familiar from the League of Nations mandates system and because it extended only to old mandates or new ones identified voluntarily. Even so, the U.S. navy insisted that a special category of strategic trust territories be created for the Pacific islands that the United States extracted from Japanese control. These supposedly had strategic value; their supervision was therefore made a duty of the Security Council, not the Trusteeship Council and the General Assembly. The general aim of the Trusteeship System, unlike that of the other colonies, was independence.

No procedure for withdrawal from the new organization entered its constitution, but obviously any government that wished would do so. This most transparent of conferences formally named the new organization the United Nations, despite misgivings of French-speaking delegates who noted that the acronym 'NU' in their tongue meant naked.

The vote of approval for the completed Charter of the United Nations came on June 25, 1945. Representatives of 50 states formally signed it on the next day. After the Permanent Five and a majority of the signatories ratified it, it came into force on October 24, 1945, the first United Nations Day. The new General Assembly, joined by a 51st member, met for the first time on January 10, 1946, in London.

2
Charter and Structure of the United Nations

The structure and some of the most important procedures of the United Nations are set forth in its Charter (For full text, see Appendix, p. 159). This constitutional document, approved by the San Francisco Conference, has remained formally unchanged, except for the enlargement of the Security Council and the Economic and Social Council. It provides the legal, institutional framework for the organization. Examining its main features helps in estimating the UN's success in reaching its main goal: the maintenance of international peace and security. Moreover, knowledge of the constitutional structure is essential for useful discussion of possible reforms.

The aims of the organization are introduced in soaring and yet sober language, as was doubtless appropriate at the end of a terrible war. The preamble, which has no strict legal application, contains a well-known, inspirational example:

> WE, THE PEOPLES OF THE UNITED NATIONS DETERMINED to save succeeding generations from the scourge of war, which twice in our lifetime has brought untold sorrow to mankind...

It is followed by two articles which describe the concrete purposes of the institution and the means provided to meet its lofty ends.

Among its broad range of activities, the central purpose is the maintenance of peace and security, the first aim set out in Article 1 of the Charter. A series of related purposes follow. These include friendly relations among nations, achieving cooperation to solve international problems of an economic, social, cultural or humanitarian character, and harmonization of the action of members so as to attain these ends. The implied assumption of the aims holds that broad cooperation would prevent war.

Two of the most elaborate chapters of the Charter contain the provisions for activities intended to maintain peace. Yet 'peace' is nowhere explicitly defined. It may be taken to mean only an absence of international violence and the protection of the territorial *status quo* from forceful alteration. Chapter VI of the Charter deals with the peaceful settlement of disputes which if continued might lead to a breakdown of the peace. Chapter VII authorizes coercive '...action with respect to threats to the peace, breaches of the peace, and acts of aggression.'

Arrangements for international economic and social cooperation intended to underpin a peaceful international order make up Chapters IX and X of the Charter. They include a wide-ranging declaration of principles that extend the scope of international organization beyond precedents. That prominent feature of international politics in 1945, the colonial empires, is treated in Chapters XI and XII. Chapter XI consists of a 'declaration regarding non-self-governing territories' in which members that administer territories that have not yet attained a full measure of self-government, accept a set of regulating principles. To the people of such territories, the Charter promises self-government but not necessarily independence.

A Trusteeship System that includes closer UN supervision of a special set of non-self-governing territories is set out in Chapter XII. These lands were to be brought at least to self-government and perhaps independence. Included in the system were at least the territories taken from the vanquished in the two world wars. Thus, it succeeded the League of Nations mandates system. All but one of the territories, South West Africa (now called Namibia), that the League supervised, were made Trust Territories. Other colonies could have been placed under the system, but none ever were.

Close relatives

Whatever the wishes of the wartime planners who framed the UN Charter, it closely resembles the Covenant of the League of Nations. The drafting committees that worked on the Charter, sought to start with a clean slate in order to scotch fears that the new organization merely revived a failure. They developed significantly different features for the United Nations but nevertheless were bound by basic facts of international politics.

As with the League, only sovereign states could join the UN. In both cases, the purpose was to prevent a breakdown of international stability as defined after a war. Both organizations established permanent formal organs to reach decisions consonant with the organizational purposes. Both created an assembly with broad concerns in which all members were represented and a limited-membership council that met more often than the assembly. Both established permanent secretariats, headed by a secretary-general. Both organized an international court legally to settle disputes. Both sought to coordinate the operations of related organizations that dealt with functional issues, such as social welfare or health.

Yet the new organization departed significantly from the old pattern along lines intended to strengthen political power and broaden and deepen the scope of international cooperation. Perhaps the boldest change sought to provide the Security Council with military power to deter or halt aggression. It was to have at its disposal armed forces regulated by special agreements with governments and ready for action when the Council decided to use them. This new approach, far more substantial than the provisions for coercion under the League, never resulted, however, in the creation of the envisaged force.

The Security Council itself represented a new degree of specialization for the established organs. It had specific responsibility for maintaining the peace, unlike the League Council that had general supervisory duties over the entire agenda. Furthermore, the UN General Assembly was barred from dealing with disputes under consideration in the Security Council. The principle of specialization extended to other forms of cooperation through the creation of an Economic and Social Council and Trusteeship Council.

In the case of the Trusteeship Council, the specialized subject matter was matched with a broader scope of supervision and was intended to have a higher level of governmental representation than the analogous organ in the League. Moreover, going well beyond the limits imposed on the League, the General Assembly was given some, but limited, tasks with regard to colonial territories not brought under the Trusteeship System.

The UN Secretary-General, like his predecessor in the League, would serve the entire organization. But in the new organization, he has the independent power under Article 99 of the Charter to bring any matter before the Security Council that in his opinion threatened or breached the peace. Such explicit political authority goes far beyond the earlier model.

While the League used the time-honored diplomatic technique of making decisions on the basis of an unanimous vote, the UN replaces it with qualified majorities. For important matters in the General

Assembly, a two-third majority is required, while committees, which frame resolutions, make their decisions on the basis of a majority present and voting. Voting in the Security Council is somewhat more complex as all matters of substance require the concurrence of the five permanent members. Procedural decisions may be taken by a majority of all members, whether permanent or not. Thus, at least nine votes in the present 15-member Council (seven in the original 11-member Council) must be cast in favor of any successful resolution.

The design approved at San Francisco only partly predicted the actual operation of the UN, which turned out not very different in many respects from its predecessor. Over most of the history of the UN, fundamental disagreements among the permanent members of the Security Council, especially the United States and the Soviet Union, prevented quick, coercive intervention in international conflicts. The organization could not coordinate related international institutions with a strong hand any more than the League Council could in its time. Nor did the UN dependably serve even as well as the League at its best as an economic and social 'think-tank.' As for managing change in the colonial world, it did not smoothly and slowly proceed towards independence with the UN making the crucial decisions. But the organization certainly did reflect, preside over, influence and support the process.

The decline of empires related to the universal membership of the United Nations. The League membership never included any recently independent former colonial territory. At no time were all of the great powers represented. From the beginning, all great powers were UN members, even if a long quarrel preceded changing the representation of China from the government in Taipei to that in Beijing. As each colonial holding became independent, the successor government promptly joined the UN. The membership is well-nigh universal.

The six main organs of the UN – the General Assembly, the Security Council, the Economic and Social Council, the Trusteeship Council, the Secretariat, and the International Court of Justice – bear immediate responsibility for the policies and much of the activity of the organization. These organs will be examined in the following sections.

The General Assembly

Each UN member is entitled to a seat in the General Assembly and to cast one vote. The usual annual session takes place between September and mid-December. Special or emergency sessions may be summoned at other times.

As the most representative of the UN organs, the General Assembly takes up an agenda that covers almost every international issue brought by the members or emerging from the work of the Secretariat and associated organizations. With so much to do and so many members, it follows a rather formal procedural pattern. This always includes a lengthy general debate that in fact is neither a debate nor discussion, but rather a series of speeches by senior governmental representatives who set out national positions. As they include foreign ministers and even heads of governments, and sometimes personalities such as the Pope or the head of the Palestine Authority, new proposals may emerge in this unique setting.

The detailed discussion of reports on earlier work and new proposals takes place in the six permanent committees of the General Assembly. The committees are: the First (disarmament and international security); the Second (economic and financial); Third (social, humanitarian and cultural); Fourth (special political and decolonization); Fifth (administrative and budgetary); and the Sixth (legal). When the committees end their debate and agree on recommendations, these go to the plenary session of the General Assembly, where usually debate is cursory. The plenary session may, however, take up a question without prior committee consideration.

The scope of General Assembly concern is almost as broad as an inventory of international issues and as wide as the Charter itself. It may take up under Article 10 of the Charter any matter within the scope of the Charter or related to the powers and functions of another organ. Although this allows discussion of matters of peace and security, the Charter nevertheless sets apart specific disputes on which action, including conciliation and coercion, may be necessary. These are reserved under Article 11 (2) of the Charter to the Security Council. Logical though this may be in terms of specialized organs taking up their appointed tasks, the General Assembly tends to discuss whatever its members wish at any given time.

The hollowing-out of the Security Council's reserved territory even has the support of an informal amendment of the UN Charter. This is the 'Uniting for Peace' resolution (UN General Assembly Res 377 (V)), adopted by the General Assembly in 1950, during the Korean war, at the behest of the United States (see discussion, Chapter 4). It provides that if the Security Council fails to carry out its responsibility as the result of a veto by a permanent member, the General Assembly may deal with a situation threatening or involving a breach of the peace. This procedural shift occurs if a majority of the Council decides to hand over the matter to an emergency special session of the General Assembly. The larger organ may only recommend measures to deal with the situation, but these may include coercion, even including the use of armed force. Even such voluntary steps conceivably could have a substantial impact on a violator of the peace.

Although the then cohesive Soviet group denounced the Uniting for Peace procedure as illegal, they nevertheless acquiesced in its use as early as the Suez crisis of 1956 and again during the Congo conflict in 1960. Since then, the resolution opened the way to call the General Assembly into session to deal with the continuing conflicts around Israel and with South Africa's long occupation of Namibia (earlier known as Southwest Africa), the only remaining League of Nations mandated territory that gained independence only in 1990. As the United States can no longer count on a majority of votes for its proposals in the General Assembly, it now regards the Uniting for Peace procedure with reserve.

The agenda of the annual General Assembly session now includes more than 150 items. These reflect the troubles of the world and hopes of coping with them. A large number of items, such as the conflicts in the Middle East, economic development, protection of the world environment and promotion of human rights, recur repeatedly. Each session ends with a thick file of resolutions, some of them almost impenetrably complex. These are adopted by a variety of procedures that include majority votes, consensus, acclamation, and adoption without a vote. Among them each year is the budget of the organization, which is prepared by the Secretary-General and closely scrutinized. Unlike almost all of the other resolutions, the budget represents a formal legal obligation placed on the members.

The Security Council

The crucial point about both membership and voting in the Security Council is the special position of the five permanent members who were taken to be the Great Powers by the UN founders. Their presence and membership has remained constant, although the Council membership was increased in 1965 from 11 to 15 in the hope of improving representation by offering more places to be filled by election for two-year terms. In 1991, after the political disintegration of the Soviet Union, its Council seat was taken over by the Russian Federation, which was admitted to UN membership. Selection of non-permanent members by the General

Assembly follows a geographical formula: three African, two Asian, one Eastern European, two Latin American and two from Western Europe and other states. As for voting, only on procedural matters may a majority of nine take decisions; on other matters, the majority must include all of the permanent members (see Chapter 3 for more detailed discussion of voting). Over the years, many proposals have been circulating to expand the permanent membership and thus the representative character of the Council. Obvious candidates were Germany, Japan and beyond them possibly states from other regions and levels of economic development; among those mentioned were India from Asia, Nigeria from Africa and Brazil from Latin America. All of these proposals were greeted by the present members of the Council with obvious reserve and no decision had been reached by mid-2005.

Unlike the General Assembly, the Security Council is designed always to be ready to meet on a problem of peace and security. It has both conciliatory and coercive powers, which are to be exercised only after the parties to a dispute have tried to find their own solution. The Charter lists means for settlement of disputes: negotiation; enquiry; mediation; conciliation; arbitration; judgment by a court; proceeding through regional agencies; and other means parties may choose. The Council may take the initiative in a dispute that, if continued, would threaten the peace, or may wait for it to be brought to it. It can recommend means of settlement or offer conciliatory services or a plan for settlement. Under Chapter VI of the Charter, it cannot employ coercion. It is legally limited to persuasion.

The legal limits on Council action expand if a direct threat or breach of the peace occurs. In such a case, it has the right to take stronger action under Chapter VII of the Charter. First, it must decide whether the matter before it does threaten the peace (Article 39). If so, it may recommend provisional measures, such as a cease-fire or further negotiation. Or it may call at once on member governments to apply diplomatic and economic sanctions (Articles 40 and 41). If the Council does so, it places a legal obligation to act on the members. Furthermore, the Council has the legal capacity to use armed forces placed at its disposal by members (Articles 42 and 43). In deciding on enforcement action under Chapter VII, a member who is a party to dispute may vote, but under Chapter VI a disputant must abstain.

The Economic and Social Council

Although the United Nations structure separates the organs dealing with maintenance of peace from those of economic and social cooperation, the Economic and Social Council (ECOSOC) deals with some obviously political issues, such as the creation and supervision of a system to protect human rights that may be closely related to international conflict. Moreover, the mere existence of this specialized organ does not ensure that governments will be represented by persons with special knowledge of the subject matter.

Election to ECOSOC, as with other organs with limited tasks, was supposed to foster representation of a broad segment of organizational membership. It began with 18 members, but formal amendment of the Charter raised membership first in 1965, to 27 and in 1973, to 54. The five Permanent Members of the Security Council invariably are elected, as befits high prestige and economic capacity, while other members are chosen proportionally for three-year terms from the main geographical groups.

Fostering the general welfare in the belief that this will create conditions for peace constitutes the main task of ECOSOC. It depends primarily on member governments to carry out recommendations, which it may make directly or, more usually, via the General Assembly; therefore it has no operating tasks. Its main work includes making and initiating studies and reports with respect to international economic, social, cultural, educational, health and related matters.

ECOSOC has negotiated agreements for coordination and cooperation with the specialized agencies associated with the UN and receives regular reports from them. Agency representatives also participate in ECOSOC meetings. These relationships are intended to coordinate the work of the specialized agencies. The Council also may initiate the formation of new international organizations, as it did with such members of the UN family as the World Health Organization (WHO), the World Meteorological Organization and the World Intellectual Property Organization (WIPO). The Council prepares draft conventions (law-making multilateral treaties) on matters within its competence and submits them to the General Assembly for reference to governments. It summons special international conferences on matters within its wide jurisdiction.

The Trusteeship Council

Its task now a mere shadow of what it once was, the Trusteeship Council has a complex composition intended to insure impartiality in administering the trust territories. It always includes the permanent members of the Security Council and then balanced the members that administered colonies with others that did not. It reports annually to the General

Assembly, except in the case of so-called strategic trust territories for the welfare for which the Security Council is responsible. The supervisory methods of the Trusteeship Council have included examination of annual reports from the territories and the dispatch of visiting missions to them. It can also accept petitions from groups and individuals.

Some of the important trust territories that once were supervised by the Council were a legacy from the League mandate system. Examples are Tanganyika, administered by the United Kingdom; Ruanda-Urundi, administered by Belgium; and Togo and Cameroon, administered by France. All of these territories and others, except for a part of the Trust Territory of the Pacific, administered by the United States as a strategic territory, have exercised self-determination to the satisfaction of the Council and have become independent. With no work, the Council no longer meets.

The International Court of Justice

In most respects a carbon copy of the Permanent Court of International Justice which was founded with, but functioned outside of, the structure of, the League of Nations, the new International Court of Justice (ICJ) is a main UN organ. All UN members must be parties to the ICJ statute. The court is composed of 15 independent justices, serving nine-year terms. They are elected by an absolute majority of both the General Assembly and the Security Council.

Non-members of the United Nations may become party to the Statute upon recommendation of the Security Council and on conditions determined in each case by the General Assembly. The Holy See has availed itself of this possibility.

The jurisdiction of the court covers all questions that states refer to it and its decision are binding in a dispute. States can refer cases in two ways. The first is by way of a prior agreement. An existing treaty between the parties may provide for reference. Or a special agreement, setting out the dispute and providing for reference, may be reached between the parties. The second way of referring cases to the court involves advance agreement on compulsory jurisdiction, as specified in Article 36 of the Statute of the court. A signatory to the optional clause declares that, in relation to any other state accepting the same obligation, the ICJ has jurisdiction over a case that either of them submits concerning:

  a) the interpretation of a treaty;
  b) any question of international law;

c) the existence of any fact which, if established, would constitute a breach of an international obligation;

d) the nature or extent of the reparation to be made for the breach of an international obligation.

In 2004, compulsory jurisdiction had been accepted by 65 states, but their declarations often contain reservations excluding certain kinds of disputes or disputes with certain states. Thus, for many years, the United States accepted compulsory jurisdiction, except in cases falling under the jurisdiction of US courts. President Ronald Reagan withdrew even from this commitment in 1986, after Nicaragua won a judgment against the United States for mining its harbors and aiding the 'contra' rebels.

Apart from adversary proceedings, the ICJ may give an advisory opinion, requested by another UN organ or by a specialized agency, on any legal question. One such advisory opinion, for example, concerned the question of whether expenses of UN peace-keeping activities were to be considered 'expenses of the Organization' under Article 17 of the Charter and thus to be apportioned by the General Assembly as a charge on the members. (The answer was 'yes.') Since 1946, the Court has issued 25 advisory opinions on such topics as admission to UN membership, reparation for injuries suffered by persons serving the UN, and the territorial status of South-West Africa (now Namibia) and Western Sahara. The most recent advisory opinions concern a request by WHO on the use of nuclear weapons in armed conflicts; and requests by the General Assembly on the legality of threatening to use nuclear weapons and the construction of a defence wall by Israel on Palestinian territory.

The Court has had little effect on peace and security. In the almost 60 years of existence of the ICJ, the average yearly number of decisions has been less than two. None of these concerned solution of an international conflict involving serious violence. In the absence of accepted international legislation, many inter-state disputes do not so much concern the nature of the legal situation as the question as to whether the law should be developed or changed. That is beyond the competence of the ICJ.

More frequent use of the Court – desirable though that may be from the perspective of the development of the rule of law – cannot be expected. Most governments tend to consider the recognition of the compulsory jurisdiction of the Court as infringing on their sovereignty. Many of them doubt the non-partisan character of the Court.

Governments in recently independent states view it as too dominated by western legal thinking and too concerned with great power interests. The Communist world in particular used to doubt the impartiality of such international organs.

The Secretariat

The Secretary-General of the United Nations is the chief administrative officer of the organization and directs the permanent staff, the Secretariat. The appointment of the Secretary-General begins with a recommendation of a candidate by the Security Council to the General Assembly, where the formal election takes place (Art. 97). The usual term of office is five years and reappointment is possible.

The Secretariat is organized in departments which have functions related to the other principal organs, such as political affairs and security affairs, economic and social affairs, coordination of humanitarian action and legal counsel while other departments deal mainly with internal management and services. In early 1998, for the first time a Deputy Secretary-General was appointed to fill in for the Secretary-General when he requires it.

The Secretariat is omnipresent in the functioning of the organization (Art. 98). Its officers keep the records, interpret, translate documents in the several working languages and collect statistics and prepare numerous reports and papers. The latter serve as the basis for most of the discussions in the deliberative organs. The Secretary-General usually personally attends sessions of the General Assembly, the Security Council, and the ECOSOC. In other meetings, he is usually represented by designated officers.

The Charter provides that the Secretariat should be an international civil service (Art. 100). The Secretary-General appoints the Secretariat under regulations adopted by the General Assembly. The paramount consideration is stated as 'the necessity of securing the highest standards of efficiency, competence and integrity.' But this provision is modulated by an instruction to pay due regard to recruiting the staff 'on as wide a geographical basis as possible.' (Art. 101).

The standards and international character of the UN staff, as with the first international civil service in the League, have continually come under pressure. The wide geographical basis keeps the nationals of any one government from dominating the staff, but the General Assembly has often urged the Secretary-General to improve the distribution, which is tantamount to giving priority to country of origin, rather than qualifications. Furthermore, from the beginning, governments have intruded in the appointment process. This tends to weaken the effect of the oaths of office taken by international servants as well as a Charter provision (Art. 100) that they may accept no instructions from national governments, their own or other, as well as the undertaking by governments to respect the international character of the staff.

Who gets the second-level jobs, just below the rank of Secretary-General, was the subject of an informal agreement among the great powers during the earliest days of the UN. Below this so-called 'political level', many governments promote the candidacy of their own nationals. For instance, governments in Eastern Europe and the Soviet Union, until 1989, used to submit lists of their nationals whom they considered qualified. Until 1986, the United States communicated to the Secretary-General the results of security checks – that is, information as to whether they may be Communists – on its nationals who are under consideration for appointment. Other governments concentrate their efforts on particular openings, putting forward candidates who sometimes, not entirely by accident, are the representatives at headquarters. As a practical matter, the Secretary-General could hardly go much beyond these 'suggestions', or for that matter, conduct impartial searches and examinations for the best among thousands of possible candidates. Geographical distribution, agreements among the great powers, campaigning for nationals and limiting those who would be allowed to accept appointments all tend to dilute the international character of the Secretariat.

Beyond organizing and directing the staff, the Secretary-General takes on a special, frequently difficult, political role that reaches farther than any assigned to any other international official. It derives primarily from Article 99 of the Charter, giving him the right to bring any matter that in his opinion may threaten peace and security to the attention of the Security Council. Thus, his personal judgment and readiness to take initiatives is crucial. In addition, he can state his views in his annual report and use opportunities given by his presence, or that of senior staff members, in hundreds of intergovernmental meetings. Governments may, of course, ignore his initiatives. Consequently, his influence depends on persuasiveness and good political analysis.

The use of Article 99 has been rare and restrained. Dag Hammarskjöld, the Swede who was the second Secretary-General, expressly invoked it to convene the Security Council in 1960 to deal with a crisis in the Congo.

His predecessor, Trygve Lie, a Norwegian national, claimed that he acted in the Korea case in 1950 under Article 99. So did Kurt Waldheim, the Austrian fourth Secretary-General, who put the seizure of the United States embassy in Iran by radical student groups before the Council. But in the latter two incidents, the legal basis of the call by the Secretary-General was less explicit than in the Congo case.

Apart from the dramatic use of Article 99 to summon the Council, it offers the Secretary-General a basis for an important behind-the-scenes diplomatic role. This activity does not necessarily become visible or even the subject of discussion in the Security Council. 'Quiet diplomacy' was the way Hammarskjöld described it. It received its first test in 1954, when he flew to China in his 'personal capacity' to negotiate freedom for US military airmen who had been captured during the Korean war.

The political role of the Secretary-General achieves full development when he is given instructions by a global deliberative body, such as the Security Council or the General Assembly. Typically, he has a substantial share in designing such instructions. This was the case during the Suez crisis of 1956, when Hammarskjöld improvised the first UN peace-keeping force. Similarly he was in the public eye in the Congo. Other incidents include the actions of U Thant, the Burmese third Secretary-General, in 1964 in Cyprus and Waldheim in 1975 in the Middle East and later in Lebanon. Javier Pérez de Cuéllar, the fifth Secretary-General, a Peruvian, acted in the so-called Gulf war between Iraq and Iran, helped negotiate the Soviet retreat from Afghanistan in 1988, and South Africa's withdrawal from Namibia in 1990. Boutros Boutros-Ghali, the former deputy foreign minister of Egypt, who succeeded Pérez de Cuéllar in 1992, bluntly accused the rich, northern countries of neglecting the UN operation in Somalia in favor of what was once Yugoslavia. Kofi Annan, the national of Ghana who is Secretary-General as the 21st century begins, has promoted in UN action in numerous conflicts, such as the implosions of government in Liberia and Sierra Leone, and in dealing in various ways with the results of the two wars in Iraq.

Most of these cases involved the formation and direction of some sort of a presence in the field and negotiations with the conflicting parties under rather broad authority from a UN organ. Usually, such incidents open political opportunities for the Secretary-General to seek a lasting settlement of the dispute.

The exercise of discretion easily involves the Secretary-General in controversy. After all, the states involved in a quarrel are almost always

UN members and have divergent ideas about what servants of the organization should do. Both government officials and public figures nevertheless praised Hammarskjöld for his energetic, effective creation of peace-keeping forces in the Sinai Peninsula and in the Congo. Both he and U Thant retained political support when they directed the use of force by UN troops in Katanga province of the Congo. Annan was able to criticize the American build-up to the second Iraq war in 2003 without a sharp public controversy with the United States.

Yet U Thant was stridently accused of giving up too quickly to Egyptian pressure to withdraw the UN Emergency Force (UNEF) from Sinai in 1967, at the beginning of the Arab-Israeli war of 1967. Both Trygve Lie, for his role in the Korean war, and Hammarskjöld for his generally restrained policy in the Congo were berated by the Soviet Union, which boycotted them. Chairman Khrushchev moved from demanding Hammarskjöld's resignation to an onslaught on the office itself. The Soviet notion was that the unitary Secretary-General should disappear in favor of a three-member organ (a 'troika', or carriage drawn by three horses) that would represent Western, Communist and non-aligned states.

Hammarskjöld had early on both occasions assumed considerable leeway and argued in meticulous reports that both the Charter and the instructions he received would be the basis for the activities of the Secretary-General. His response to Khrushchev was made in a still-famous speech on September 3, 1960, before the General Assembly. The UN, he declared, primarily served the smaller states, not the Soviet Union or any Great Power. As long as the smaller states wished, he would remain in office, serving their interests. Hammarskjöld, not the Soviet Union and its allies, prevailed in the Assembly, but that did little to diminish the tension before the Secretary-General was killed in an aircraft accident in 1961 in Zambia. After that, the 'troika' remained in the barn and the Soviet Union eventually supported the election of U Thant. He soothed relations with the Soviet Union but irritated official Washington with his sharp criticism of the Vietnam War.

How an incumbent Secretary-General interprets his function obviously conditions his political role, but in the end the major powers have the strongest voice in determining how wide the limits of the office may be. Lie and Hammarskjöld sought to expand the office, their successors less directly so. Waldheim dealt with the great powers with much caution, even while inserting himself into every possible international negotiation. Any Secretary-General must be tactful and use diplomatic skill in dealing with all member country representatives and estimate carefully how far to go in taking initiatives. Lie and

Hammarskjöld sometimes went beyond the limits set by one or another of the Great Powers and paid dearly. Thant and Waldheim were more circumspect and less influential. During his second term, Pérez de Cuéllar showed a rising ability to make use of his opportunities to play an active role in the management of international conflicts and by 1990 was entrusted with increasing conciliation and peace-keeping assignments. Boutros-Ghali openly favored political activism and close management of a growing number of field missions. This brought him into conflict with the United States which vetoed the reappointment that he wanted. Kofi Annan sought with diplomatic finesse to accommodate to the wishes of the United States. He was able to restore some of the lost cooperation with Washington and developed considerable persuasiveness on security matters aside from the extra-UN expedition in Iraq mounted by the United States in 2003.

Cluster of UN agencies

Grouped around the United Nations itself are some 20 intergovernmental agencies (see Table 2.1, below). Each of these concentrates on particular economic, social or cultural programs. The most independent of these bodies, formally known as 'specialized agencies', were foreseen in the UN Charter. They have memberships that overlap the United Nations but are not identical, sometimes including non-members of UN. Their establishment rests on constitutional documents that like the UN Charter have the status of treaties among their members. Their relationship to ECOSOC is governed by the special agreements mentioned earlier. (Art. 63). Other agencies owe their existence to specific resolutions of the UN General Assembly and in principle could be dissolved by it.

Coordinating the work of these agencies is left primarily to ECOSOC (Art. 64), which is hardly endowed with more power than making recommendations and negotiating. Each agency tends to develop its own constituency in national governments and among technical specialists. Some of them date back to the middle of the 19th century and have steady financial support. Some have closely defined purposes, such as the supervision of certain copyright regulations; others represent special interests, such as the rapid economic and industrial development for the Third World. Yet others deal with notions as broad as the fostering of human intellectual progress generally or the protection of health everywhere. Although each of them is in touch with experts in their fields, that does not mean that firm agreement exists on how to approach particular issues. The lending agencies successfully claim special exemption from UN examination of their specific deals. As a consequence of these factors, the UN-associated agencies can sometimes compete or act as independent fiefdoms.

The system of UN agencies is as geographically decentralized as it is functionally differentiated. Six agencies are located in Geneva: the World Trade Organization (WTO); the International Labor Organization (ILO); the International Telecommunication Union (ITU); the World Health Organization (WHO); the World Intellectual Property Organization (WIPO); and the World Meteorological Organization (WMO). Two agencies are headquartered in Washington, D.C.: the World Bank (formally the International Bank for Reconstruction and Development) and its daughters and the International Monetary Fund (IMF); two in Vienna, the International Atomic Energy Agency (IAEA) and the UN Industrial Development Organization (UNIDO). Paris is host to the UN Educational, Scientific and Cultural Organization (UNESCO) and Rome to the UN Food and Agriculture Organization (FAO), the World Food Program (WFP) and the International Fund for Agricultural Development (IFAD). Other agencies are located in Montreal (the International Civil Aviation Organization – ICAO); Berne (the Universal Postal Union – UPU); London (the International Maritime Organization – IMO); Nairobi (the UN Environment Program – UNEP); Madrid (Wolrd Tourism Organization – WTO-OMT); and The Hague (Organization for the Prohibition of Chemical Warfare – OPCW). Some of the organizations that are formally part of the UN itself, have headquarters in Geneva, including the UN Conference on Trade and Development (UNCTAD) and the High Commissioner for Refugees (UNHCR). The UN Children's Fund (UNICEF), the UN Development Program (UNDP) and the UN Population Fund (UNFPA) are located in New York. The UN University operates from Tokyo and UN University for Peace from San José, Costa Rica.

For the perhaps hopeless task of coordinating this organizational tangle and interrelated activity, the UN has an intergovernmental mechanism in ECOSOC and a bureaucratic device in the Chief Executives Board (CEB) (formerly the Administrative Committee on Coordination (ACC).) ECOSOC invites the heads of specialized agencies with which formal agreements are in effect to give oral reports. In addition, it reviews written documentation. The agencies have the right to initiate a discussion in ECOSOC and sometimes do in order to promote their programs.

ECOSOC has available to it studies by the UN Secretariat and its own Committee on Program Coordination, based on a program budgeting analysis covering the whole system, except for the World Bank and the IMF. Nevertheless, the specialized agencies make their own budgetary decisions, which may or may not reflect the priorities and guidelines set out by ECOSOC, usually after negotiations with the institutions concerned.

Those organizations responsible to the General Assembly, such as UNHCR or UNCTAD, submit their reports through ECOSOC. The review there may be very light indeed as the documentation will again be taken up in the committees of the General Assembly.

The other coordinating device, the CEB, brings together the executive directors of the specialized agencies as well as the chief officers of IAEA, GATT, UNCTAD, UNHCR and other similar agencies. Governments are not represented in this structure, which resembles a 'summit' of feudal lords who supervise the several territories of functional international cooperation under the presidency of the UN Secretary-General. He also heads the staff that serves CEB. Aside from exchanging the information that each agency offers, its result depends on the effectiveness of the Secretary-General's leadership, the independence of the executive heads of the agencies, and the demands of their constituencies.

Organizational tension

The simultaneously elaborate and vague coordinating machinery for the UN economic and social activities illustrates a general tension that runs through all international institutions. Governmental representatives repeatedly praise centralization of some sort, along with a tight program for the general welfare. They seek efficiency, simplicity, defined priorities and directness. Yet the same governments strongly support the programs of functional agencies, even when they diverge from the guidance offered by ECOSOC; they presume that technical cooperation inherently produces desirable benefits. At the same time, some of the same governments inject ideological issues into technical programs, while others simply stay out of or leave organizations whose programs contain objectionable aspects. For instance, the United States, the United Kingdom and Singapore at one point withdrew from UNESCO, but have since returned. The Arab governments have pressed for the expulsion or limitation of Israeli participation at every opportunity; and the Soviet Union never took part in the World Bank or the IMF, but by 2004 nearly all of the former Soviet Republics had joined both organizations. Consequently, the weak impetus towards centralization leaves parts of intergovernmental cooperation largely unaffected.

The governmental oversight of the agencies formally emanates from assemblies that resemble the UN deliberative organs. As a rule, each member state has one vote. Usually, a general conference or congress meets every year or every other year. Between these meetings, an elected executive committee or council supervises the program and the work of the executive head. Like the UN Secretary-General, the agency executive directors head permanent international secretariats. These sometimes carry out large-scale programs to assist governments and even individual persons. Only government officials represent states, except in the case of the ILO, which was deliberately built on a tri-partite base. Each member delegation in the International Labor Conference, the analogue of the UN General Assembly, consists of two governmental delegates and one each for employers and workers. For the ILO Governing Body, the executive council, members are elected from any of the three constituencies.

The IMF and the World Bank do not follow the one-state, one-vote pattern of the other agencies. They determine voting strength on the basis of capital investment in the agencies. The weighted voting principle extends to the standing executive bodies, which make principal decisions on loans. There, each large contributor sends a member, but the smaller contributors are grouped together for common representation by a joint delegate. Although these arrangements clearly apply the principle that who pays the piper calls the tune, only rarely do issues come to a vote in the two financial agencies. Most decisions are taken by consensus.

The usual organizational structure in the agencies is centralized along the lines of the United Nations. A permanent secretariat is housed in a central headquarters; its expert personnel controls information which gives the secretariat a powerful voice in policy decisions. WHO, however, created a unique decentralized structure. Six regional organizations, each with a regional committee of governmental representatives from the area, take responsibility for executing much of the WHO program, which is broadly outlined through the central organization in Geneva. Other agencies maintain regional offices with much less responsibility for programs. Taken as a whole, the UN system shows some degree of decentralization in the wide geographic distribution of the headquarters of the component agencies. That distribution also reflects the competition of governments for the international prestige and financial benefits of hosting the headquarters of an intergovernmental agency. So far, however, no agency has been invited to establish its headquarters in Eastern Europe.

Table 2.1 lists the specialized agencies, the years in which they were set up, the number of members, the headquarters location, and the main purposes. Some important organizations that are, strictly speaking, not formal specialized agencies are also included because of their similar functions. These are IAEA, WTO, the UN University, UNEP and UNHCR.

Table 2.1 The United Nations System

Organization	Founded	Membership	Headquarters	Purpose & Operation
International Labor Organization (ILO)	1919	177	Geneva	To develop international minimum standards of labor and to draft international conventions on subjects such as human rights, freedom of association, wages, hours of work, etc..
Food and Agricultural Organization (FAO)	1945	188	Rome	To raise levels of nutrition and standards of living; to improve production and distribution of all food and agricultural products; and to improve the conditions of rural populations.
International Fund for Agricultural Development (IFAD)	1977	163	Rome	To mobilize additional resources for agricultural development in developing states by providing finances for projects and programs to introduce, expand or improve food production systems.
United Nations Education, Scientific and Cultural Organization (UNESCO)	1946	190	Paris	To promote collaboration among nations through education, science, culture, and communication in order to further universal respect for justice, for the rule of law and for human rights and fundamental freedoms.
World Health Organization (WHO)	1948	192	Geneva	The attainment by all peoples of the highest possible level of health; to stimulate the fight against epidemics and other infectious diseases; to disseminate information on the effect on human health of environmental pollutants; to set global standards for antibiotics, vaccines, etc.

Table 2.1 The United Nations System – *continued*

Organization	Founded	Membership	Headquarters	Purpose & Operation
World Bank; International Bank for Reconstruction and Development (IBRD)	1946	184	Washington D.C.	To assist in the reconstruction and development of territories of members by facilitating the investment of capital for productive purposes; to promote private foreign investment and to supplement it by providing loans for productive purposes.
International Development Association (IDA)	1960	164	Washington D.C.	To promote economic development and increase productivity, thus raising standards of living by providing its membership with finances to meet important development requirements on flexible terms
International Finance Corporation (IFC)	1956	176	Washington D.C.	To provide risk capital for productive private enterprise in association with private investors and management, to encourage the development of local capital markets and to stimulate the international flow of private capital.
International Monetary Fund (IMF)	1945	184	Washington D.C.	To promote international monetary cooperation and the expansion of international trade; to promote exchange stability; to maintain orderly exchange arrangements and to avoid competitive exchange depreciations; to assist in the establishment of a multilateral system of payments with respect to the currency transactions between members and to the elimination of foreign exchange restrictions that hamper world trade.
International Civil Aviation Organization (ICAO)	1947	188	Montreal	To facilitate the safety, regularity, and efficiency of civil air transport and to study the problems of international standards and regulation for civil aviation.

Table 2.1 The United Nations System – *continued*

Organization	Founded	Membership	Headquarters	Purpose & Operation
Universal Postal Union (UPU)	1878	190	Berne	To form a single postal territory of countries for reciprocal exchange of letter-post items; to secure the organization and improvement of postal services; and to take part in postal technical assistance.
International Telecommunication Union (ITU)	1865	189	Geneva	To maintain and extend international cooperation for the improvement and rational use of telecommunication facilities in order to increase their usefulness and to make them generally available to the public; and to harmonize the actions of nations in the attainment of these common ends.
World Meteorological Organization (WMO)	1951	187	Geneva	To facilitate international cooperation in the establishment of networks of stations and centers to provide meteorological services and observations; to promote the establishment and maintenance of systems for the rapid exchange of meteorological and related information; and to promote standardization of meteorological observation and to ensure the uniform publication of information and statistics.
International Maritime Organization (IMO)	1958	164	London	To facilitate cooperation and exchange of information among governments on technical matters affecting shipping and, with special responsibility for the safety of life at sea, to assure that the highest possible standards of maritime safety and efficient navigation are achieved.

Table 2.1 The United Nations System – *continued*

Organization	Founded	Membership	Headquarters	Purpose & Operation
World Intellectual Property Organization (WIPO)	1970	180	Geneva	To promote the protection of intellectual property throughout the world through cooperation among states and, where appropriate, with other international organizations; and to administer the various 'unions'.
World Tourism Organization (WTO-OMT)	1974	141	Madrid	To promote the development of responsible, sustainable and universally accessible tourism.
United Nations Industrial development Organization (UNIDO)	1965	171	Vienna	To promote and accelerate the industrialization of developing countries and to coordinate the industrial development activities of the UN system.
International Atomic Energy Agency (IAEA)	1957	137	Vienna	To seek and accelerate and enlarge the contribution of atomic energy to peace, health and prosperity throughout the world and to ensure that assistance provided by it is not used to further any military purpose.
World Trade Organization (WTO – successor to General Agreement on Tariffs and Trade (GATT)	1948	147	Geneva	To provide international control over trade restrictions and thus to help expand world trade and contribute to higher living standards.
United Nations University (UNU)	1975	N/A	Tokyo	To help solve pressing global problems of human survival, development and welfare through internationally coordinated science and scholarship.

Table 2.1 The United Nations System – *continued*

Organization	Founded	Membership	Headquarters	Purpose & Operation
United Nations Environment Program (UNEP)	1972	N/A	Nairobi	To promote international cooperation in the field of the environment and to recommend policies to this end; to keep under review the world environmental situation in order to ensure that emerging environmental problems of wide international significance receive appropriate and adequate consideration by governments.
Office of the United Nations High Commissioner for Refugees (UNHCR)	1951	N/A	Geneva	To provide refugees with international protection and to seek permanent solutions for the problems of refugees. To promote the adoption of international minimum standards for the treatment of refugees and the effective implementation of these standards.
Organization for the Prohibition of Chemical Weapons (OPCW)	1997	164	The Hague	To implement the provisions of the Chemical Weapons Convention in order to achieve the OPCW's vision of a world both free of chemical weapons and in which cooperation in chemistry for peaceful purposes is fostered.
United Nations Children's Fund (UNICEF)	1946	N/A	New York	To protect and promote the rights and welfare of children and mothers in 161 countries. Works with UN agencies, state and NGO partners on projects to help children and mothers.
United Nations Population Fund (UNFPA)	1969	N/A	New York	To aid governments and NGOs in formulating programs of family planning and protection from disease, including HIV/AIDS, and violence against women.

3
Membership and Decision-making

In the almost 60 years of its existence, membership of the United Nations has more than tripled. In 1945, at its founding, the organization had 51 members. By 2004, membership had grown to 191 and is now almost universal. Since the 1960s, African and Asian states have occupied a dominant numerical position, as Table 3.1 shows.

Table 3.1   Geographical distribution of UN membership

	1945	2004
Western Europe	8 (16%)	25 (13%)
Eastern Europe	6 (12%)	22 (12%)
Americas	22 (43%)	35 (18%)
Africa	4 (8%)	52 (27%)
Asia	9 (17%)	43 (23%)
Australia and Pacific	2 (4%)	14 (7%)

Formal requirements for membership, listed in the Charter, require that the applicant state be 'peace-loving', accept the obligations contained in the Charter and, in the judgment of the organization, have the ability and willingness to carry out these obligations [Article 4]. Applicants for membership are admitted by the General Assembly, after having obtained the recommendation of the Security Council.

During the first 10 years, the process of application was anything but automatic. Repeatedly, coalitions led by the United States or vetoes cast by the Soviet Union prevented the admission of states. Between 1946 and 1955, only five states obtained membership: Pakistan and Yemen (1947), Burma (now called Myanmar, 1948), Israel (1948) and Indonesia (1950). In 1955, the United States and the Soviet Union agreed in a package deal to end their competitive blocking tactics. This led to the admission of 16 new members. Subsequent requests – mainly by former colonies – have caused little difficulty. The largest influx took place in 1960 when 17 new members entered. The German Democratic Republic merged with the Federal Republic of Germany and the two Yemens also became one state. The former Soviet republics, in addition to Belarus and Ukraine, which were original members, all became UN members. The 191st member, as of 2004, was Timor Leste (East Timor), admitted in 2002.

Chinese representation

The Chinese revolution, which brought the Communist Party to power in Beijing in 1949, caused a long, bitter controversy about which government had the right to represent China in the United Nations. The Nationalist government of Chiang Kai-shek, which had fled to the island of Taiwan, held the seat at the time of the communist take-over. Between 1949 and 1971, the government in Beijing vainly sought the eviction of the Nationalists from the United Nations. During those two decades, a majority in the General Assembly, led by the United States, rejected the claim of Mao Ze-dong's government that it represented China.

The United States succeeded in keeping the matter of Chinese representation off the agenda of the General Assembly until 1961. The United States secured the adoption of a procedural resolution calling the issue an 'important matter' that requires a two-thirds vote. Then on October 15, 1971, after Henry Kissinger, then U.S. national security adviser, had secretly flown to Beijing to arrange a visit for President Nixon, the General Assembly voted by 76 in favor, 35 against, and 17 abstentions to seat the representatives of the People's Republic of China. Since then, the Nationalist government which still rules Taiwan, has been excluded from the United Nations.

Divided states

Three divided states, the results of the Second World War or receding colonialism, caused controversy in the United Nations. After unification, all have joined the organization.

In the case of Germany, the Federal Republic (West Germany), awaiting reunification, opposed for a long time the admission of both parts of the country to the United Nations. Detente between East and West during the early 1970s set the conditions for the eventual admission of West Germany and the German Democratic Republic in 1973. After reunification in October 1990, the two seats became one.

The defeat of the Western-backed South Vietnamese government in 1975 by communist North Vietnam produced the forceful reunification of Vietnam and, in 1977, the state was admitted to the United Nations.

Korea had been the object of an effort by the United Nations between 1947 and 1950 to achieve peaceful unification. The North Korean attack on South Korea resulted in military action under United Nations auspices to restore the peace (see Chapter 4). The eventual armistice in 1954 brought the peninsula no closer to unification: it remains divided between a Western-oriented government in the South and a communist government in the North. Both governments applied for membership in mid-1991 and were unconditionally accepted.

Ministates

Although some general criteria for membership appear in Article 4 of the UN Charter, it contains no specification as to the minimum size for membership. A consequence is the problem of mini- or microstates. Indeed, two of the founding members of the organization – Iceland with 160,000 inhabitants and Luxembourg with 300,000 – would now be considered ministates. At the time, these exceptionally small members caused little concern. This equanimity turned into perplexity when very small colonies gained independence and began entering the United Nations as one of their first formal acts of government. A dozen members of the United Nations have fewer than 150,000 inhabitants. The smallest is the island of Nauru (12,000 inhabitants) in the Pacific Ocean.

In the General Assembly, ministates each have one vote, equal to that of the larger and more powerful states. As this equality does not reflect power and influence, the larger states become irritated by some activities of the smaller fry. Furthermore, the small and microstates pay only tiny parts of the organizational budget. Yet, through their voting strength, the tiny states can help majorities in the General Assembly to adopt sometimes expensive programs for which the organization as a whole must pay.

Practical ways around the difficulties caused by ministates have, so far, never been found. No one can agree on an answer to the question of what objective criteria should be used to decide the minimum effective size. Should it be one million inhabitants, as once was proposed? Or half a million? Even if it were possible to find agreement on criteria, how should the smaller states be represented?

A new type of associate membership for the ministates was once suggested by diplomats from larger countries. An associate member would be permitted to benefit from UN activity and be allowed to speak in the General Assembly on matters relevant to it, but it would have no right to vote. The newly independent ministates have kept their distance from this proposal. They suspected, rightly, that several of them that now enjoy status as full members of the UN would lose their rights. As more and more ministates joined as full members, it became less likely, under the present Charter provisions, that their rights would be curtailed.

Weighted voting

Apart from the issues posed by microstates, proposals to create a system of weighted voting in the General Assembly have been made, primarily by scholars and political leaders but rarely by governments. According to such criteria as size of population, gross national product, military power, or a combination of these factors, some states would cast more votes than others. The International Monetary Fund and the World Bank provide living examples. In these organizations, the number of votes per member state varies according to its capital contribution. In the United Nations, the criteria proposed for weighted votes immediately produce controversy. Small and poor states strongly oppose the whole idea, for it would mean loss of their formal status of equality. Because their co-operation is needed in order to alter the UN Charter, there is little prospect for change.

At the same time, domination of UN work by the small states poses the danger that the General Assembly may lose authority in coping with international issues. An Assembly led by such states as Saint Vincent and the Grenadines or Sao Tome would hardly reflect the facts of world politics.

From the point of view of newly independent states, no matter how small, UN membership has great symbolic and practical meaning. Raising the flag of a new state on the long row of poles on United Nations Plaza in New York signals self-respect and esteem in the wider world. A new delegation takes a seat in the main assembly hall with a vote equaling that of established and powerful states. The newcomers thus enhance feelings of national consciousness that have vital importance to them. This strengthening of national self-assurance paradoxically occurs in an organization founded to foster international solidarity.

The practical importance of membership derives partly from the network of permanent missions located in New York and Geneva. The new states can use their representation to the United Nations as a super-embassy. Contacts can be made there with ambassadors of every government in the world. A government can both obtain and supply information there. Many international agreements in the fields of trade and development, often of primary importance to new states, grow out of contacts first made in New York or Geneva. In both places, they can also consult the headquarters or representatives of other UN agencies.

Decision-making processes

International organizations customarily rely on defined voting procedures in decision-making organs. Proposals are put to the members of bodies such as the General Assembly or the Security Council in the form of draft resolutions. These are adopted or rejected. Such votes may require, depending on the organ and its rules of procedure, either an ordinary or a qualified majority of some sort.

As most public bodies in democratic states now reach decisions in this manner, it may seem almost natural that international organizations should employ the same procedure. Nevertheless, the practice of democratic voting procedures in international organizations is of relatively recent origin and doubts about its usefulness have never dissipated.

The big 19th century international conferences that served as models for contemporary organizations, usually arrived at decisions by consensus. This practice followed from the idea of absolute national sovereignty. No state could be committed to anything without its express consent. Thus any decision required approval by all participants. In practice, in other words, a rule of unanimity prevailed. In principle, this rule applied in the League of Nations, where each member state in fact held a right of veto.

Since then, members of international organizations have increasingly accepted decision-making by majority vote. This applies both to legally binding as well as to non-obligatory resolutions. In the case of non-binding resolutions, the choice of majority voting may not matter very much. Voting arrangements become much more important, however, when an organization deals with matters that governments consider pertinent to their national interests. Such issues frequently engage the United Nations. Consequently, the way in which decisions are reached in the Security Council and the General Assembly, where far-reaching debates on matters of peace and security take place, has unavoidable importance.

Not surprisingly, the United Nations heads the list of international organizations in which voting problems have attracted public attention and criticism. As the Charter allots serious powers to maintain the peace to the Security Council, majority rule in that body is restricted. As elsewhere in the United Nations, the principle of equality of member states applies. Yet, relative power continues to condition international relations, especially when resorting to force looms as a possibility. At the founding of the United Nations, the big powers successfully claimed the right to a veto in the Security Council as a means of protecting their power positions, over the opposition of the smaller states. Furthermore, even if the permanent members favor a resolution, a qualified majority of nine out of 15 votes in the Council is required for adoption of a proposal.

In this respect, the relatively small Security Council contrasts sharply with the much larger General Assembly, where a simple majority may take most decisions. The exception comes when the Assembly votes on 'important matters', which require a two-thirds majority.

Should this process of decision-making be called 'democratic'? Hardly. First of all, the system fails to satisfy on the basis of size of population. From a democratic point of view, it is obviously wrong that such countries as China, India, the Russian Federation, and the United States, each with many millions of inhabitants, have a vote equal to that of the Seychelles, with all of 80,000 people. But even if the United Nations were able to persuade all its members to adopt a weighted voting system that would better represent the elements of power and population, a great deal of difference would still remain in the degree to which governments truly represent their people. Few of the people or their elected representatives of the states gathered in New York are consulted while government delegates make up their minds. Most member governments cannot be considered even remotely democratic in the manner of the countries of Western Europe and North America. Even if the frequent argument is accepted that Western political concepts should not be applied to non-Western societies, this uncertainty remains

From the standpoint of democratic theory or of power politics, the present voting system may stand as the least objectionable. As long as the world is divided along existing political lines, there is no reason to expect that the system will be changed. The question will then remain as to how the voices of 'We, the peoples of the United Nations ...' to whom the Charter refers in its preamble, can make themselves heard and accurately understood.

Fundamental changes

The expansion of membership during the 1950s and 1960s wrought fundamental changes in the United Nations. The most important of these occurred in political affairs. During the first years of its existence, the organization responded to the United States and its allies: for practical purposes, it was a Western organization. At present, it is in many respects dominated by African and Asian states. The new alignment can be seen most vividly in the General Assembly. There, the Afro-Asian group, whenever it reaches internal agreement, can secure the adoption of any resolution. In the Security Council too, where a decision requires nine votes, the relative importance of the African and Asian states has increased. They furnish five of the 10 non-permanent members.

The voting strength of the African and Asian governments strongly affects the decision process in the General Assembly. In order to secure adoption of their proposals, sponsors of resolutions must assemble many more votes than in the early years. Approval of even slightly controversial resolutions demands extensive lobbying. The smallest and most obscure members enter the process, for their votes count for as much as any other government's. Many more than one delegation has too few people to cover all meetings in progress. In those circumstances, friendly delegations that do have enough manpower take on the task of alerting their friends among the small delegations. Delegates of small states sometimes rush into a room just before a crucial vote takes place, cast their ballot, and move on to the next meeting.

Voting groups

Traditional diplomacy is carried on outside the range of the public eye. The UN decision-making process includes public debates in the deliberative organs. This style of negotiation is called 'conference diplomacy' or 'parliamentary diplomacy.'

Nevertheless, confidential meetings usually precede important decisions, which are subsequently confirmed in public. This has been strikingly true of the Security Council, where private conversations among the representatives of the Permanent Members now lay the basis for any important decisions. Some knowledgeable observers consider confidential consultations more important than the actual resolutions or formulae that formally record decisions. This is all the more true in the General Assembly, because of the limited legal obligation involved in most of its decisions. Pre-voting consultations offer a chance for governments to set out their positions and to learn of others so that possibilities of reaching a compromise may emerge without the sometimes embarrassing glare of publicity. The give and take of the ensuing negotiations itself becomes an important factor in regulating the behavior of governments.

Many of these negotiations take place in group meetings. Such groups, or caucuses are not mentioned in the Charter and have no official status. Yet, they are of crucial importance in the decision-making process. The main geographical groups are the African, the Asian, the East European, the Latin American, and the West European and others. In addition, groups form around particular subject matter. When economic issues are at stake, the African, Asian and Latin American representatives meet as the 'Group of 77' ('G-77', a term taken over from the designation of the developing countries in UNCTAD (see Chapter 6). On political issues affecting the non-Western world, such as colonialism, they usually meet as the Non-Aligned Movement, signifying their formal detachment from the defence alliances sponsored by the superpowers. The 25 members of the European Union have meetings of their own.

Further analysis discloses a complexity that in itself argues against the notion that these groups somehow have iron-bound definitions. The African and Asian groups sometimes meet together. Their Arab members may meet as a separate group. The Islamic Conference, which exists outside of the United Nations, sponsors meetings of the Muslim countries on issues in General Assembly of interest to them. Although purely geographical criteria would dictate membership in the Asian group for Israel, it has been for obvious political reasons, excluded as was the unreformed South Africa from the African group. For many years, the Latin American group excluded Fidel Castro's Cuba. Greece and Turkey belong to the West European group, while Turkey also attends the meetings of the Asian group on an informal basis. Cyprus has belonged to the Asian group but, as a member of the Council of Europe and now the European Union, would join with the West European and others. That word, 'others', refers to Australia, Canada and New Zealand. With the latter group, the United States is an observer and in fact joins it for the purpose of proposing candidates.

Regional groups that operate at the ambassadorial level, consisting of the permanent representatives of member states, can be distinguished from those at committee level, where the delegates on any one of the main committees meet together. At the ambassadorial level, representatives of the member states that make up the five geographical groups – African, Asian, East European, Latin American, and West European and others – meet approximately once a month. Their purpose relates to elections held in the General Assembly to fill the non-permanent seats in the Security Council, all of the seats in the Economic and Social Council, and those in some other bodies. The seats in the two important councils are allotted among the five groups according to a system set out in 1968 (General Assembly resolution 1991 [XVIII]). That resolution provides that, in the Security Council, three non-permanent seats are reserved for the African, two for the Asian states, one for the East Europeans, two for the Latin Americans, and two for West Europe and others. The 54 seats in the Economic and Social Council are similarly distributed.

The ambassadorial groups also decide on the distribution of the offices of vice-presidents of the General Assembly and chairmen and rapporteurs of the six main committees. Together with the permanent members of the Security Council, these officers of the General Assembly make up the important General Committee. A different geographical group each year provides the president of the General Assembly. Whoever receives the nomination of the group that has the office that year, automatically wins the acceptance of the other member states. In effect, the geographical groups, rather than the membership as a whole, elect the president on a rotating basis.

At the committee level, unlike the arrangement for ensuring geographical distribution, a large number of groups operate. These are convened whenever the members believe it politically opportune. For example, if a resolution must be drafted or if a resolution already before the Assembly requires some adjustment in order to gain approval, groups may meet. The membership of such groups varies considerably, depending on the issue and the timing. For example, Japan joins the Asian group on questions of self-determination in the Fourth Committee, but meets with the Western group on economic issues in the Second Committee. Such consultations have a rather informal organization and much flexibility of membership and procedure.

The group of West European and other states, comprising some of the richest and most influential UN members, has never developed its consultations to the point of reaching a common point of view or group position. Nevertheless, subgroups of West Europeans have increasingly sought to present a single position. Thus, the members of the European Union or the Nordic countries often speak with one voice. In the West European and others' group as a whole, however, consultations normally are nothing more than an exchange of views on candidates.

Some governments try to build up support for their views across geographical groups. Building such a common point of view may produce a majority in the General Assembly. The informal procedures of group gatherings lend themselves to easy relationships. Delegates speak languages that, for reasons of national prestige, they never would use in formal public sessions. Even French delegates have been heard to speak English! Such meetings take place in private and outsiders find it difficult to know whether, where, and when they take place, let alone to attend them. The results are treated as confidential.

Groups and voting positions

Even though the geographical groups at the ambassadorial level have no mandate to take important decisions, whatever consensus they do reach may still fail to hold. The ambassadors may declare during informal sessions that they intend to vote in a particular way. When the time comes, they may act differently, not necessarily because of bad faith or duplicity. In fact, good diplomacy requires honesty and keeping commitments. Yet, external circumstances, such as pressure from outside or from domestic public opinion, can sometimes change commitments. Under such circumstances, either consensus will not be achieved in the first place or it may evaporate. The result may well be a change in position, either at the committee level or at the plenary meeting that has to decide on committee recommendations.

In the meetings of the consultative groups of delegates at the committee level, however, some decisions have a fair chance of being carried out. That is often true for decisions pertaining to tactics. These include such matters as whether and when to introduce a draft resolution, or whether to ask for a paragraph-by-paragraph or roll-call vote. A related tactical consideration is the question of whether to try to get the General Assembly to define a particular issue as 'important,' requiring a two-thirds majority for adoption. Such deals can be undertaken by delegations on their own initiative, without detailed instructions from home governments.

Multilateral consultations in regional groupings indirectly contribute to making decisions at a higher, governmental level, according to some diplomats who are familiar with the process. During the consultations, numerous issues that do not have a direct bearing on the agenda of the General Assembly, come to the surface. Delegates can probe each other's views for better information or understanding. Such conversations are reported to the respective governments for consideration while they are preparing for more formal deliberations. Thus, the talks relating directly to the work of the General Assembly may have broad effects on the positions of governments.

The political significance of resolutions

The very process of proposing and deciding on resolutions engages the attention of governments. One or more members of the UN organ in question may take the initiative for submission of a draft resolution. Drafts may originate within the UN Secretariat or in a specialized agency. Even so, a representative of a member state in most cases must formally introduce the draft resolution. Resolutions always aim at having the UN organ speak out on a specific issue. A resolution may welcome, condemn, or applaud any situation or development. Usually, a resolution makes recommendations to governments or directs the Secretariat to undertake specified activities.

Resolutions of the General Assembly are only rarely legally binding: they are normally recommendations to one or more actors in world politics, but not legal obligations of the sort that courts can enforce. Furthermore, if the parties to whom recommendations are directed, ignore them, the General Assembly has no legal capacity to correct undesired behavior. It can, however, give direct, binding instructions to the UN Secretariat and it can underline its wishes by budgetary decisions.

If resolutions of the General Assembly have so little obligatory effect, why do the delegates of more than 190 governments spend at least three months each year polishing, promoting, and maneuvering resolutions? The answer is that the legal significance of resolutions represents a minor part of their meaning. Rather, recommendations may have substantial political significance. If that is so, how can an observer uncover the intentions embodied in a resolution?

Most resolutions include preambles in which the drafters explain the considerations that they believe should lead to an expression of opinion by the General Assembly. In many instances, their intention is actively to seek publicity on a given issue. The operative part of the resolution, which follows the preamble, contains a precise statement of the action desired. This can ensure additional attention to the issue. In some cases, by instructing the Secretary-General to write a report on the issue for consideration at the next session, a resolution guarantees additional publicity. Another technique for achieving the same result establishes an *ad hoc* committee to deal with the item, either at once or while the General Assembly is in recess. Such continued attention and consideration can sometimes lead to the establishment of entirely new international bodies. This was the case with UNCTAD and UNEP.

Another aim pursued by the sponsors of a resolution may be the expression of sentiments about a particular situation. Such resolutions concern, for example, the maintenance of international peace or displacement and deaths in an ethnic conflict. They have little more positive result in themselves than the recording of a widespread belief. Yet governments may find it useful as a response to pressure in their domestic settings. It permits leaders to claim legitimacy for their foreign policies and to demonstrate to followers that national goals have sympathetic support elsewhere.

Resolutions also may be introduced in the hope of creating norms of behavior in international relations. Such resolutions may eventually provide for the creation of multilateral conventions that have the force of law on governments that ratify them, and can be enforced in domestic courts. Sometimes, a resolution seeks the elaboration of general principles, mentioned in the Charter, such as the prohibition of violence, or the promotion of economic development. Two well-known examples of this process are the Universal Declaration of Human Rights (see Chapter 5) and the resolution declaring the seabed the common heritage of mankind. As for the seabed, resolutions of the General Assembly led eventually to the drafting of a comprehensive Convention on the Law of the Sea. It not only codifies existing international law, but also broadens its scope and sharpens its definitions.

Even when resolutions adopted in the General Assembly do not directly stimulate lawmaking, they nevertheless command a certain moral authority. This moral force grows when a resolution receives support from a large majority, is backed by representatives of several regional groups, or is favored by states that are considered 'influential.' The latter include such countries as India, Egypt, Brazil, and in some cases Canada, Pakistan, Argentina and Australia, which have special prestige as leaders or symbols of widely favored positions. During the 1960s, some international lawyers and other observers even argued that the moral authority of a resolution, if carried by a large majority, could be understood as demonstrating the existence of legally binding rules. Now, however, the predictability of votes on General Assembly resolutions as the result of regional caucusing has diminished their former moral force, especially in the Western states. Nevertheless, most governments will still try to avoid a direct confrontation with, or condemnation by, the General Assembly.

The actual formulation of resolutions varies a good deal. If the expression of a widely held sentiment is the aim, strong language may be used – the more so if the parties concerned are unlikely to heed the recommendation. South Africa used to provide a case in point. Resolutions condemning *apartheid* contained increasingly bitter language, but the South African government, for many years, simply refused to conform. When, however, some chance remains that compliance will result, more careful language may be chosen.

One way or another, however, resolutions proposed in the General Assembly force governments to take public positions on matters that they may sometimes prefer to handle privately. Even endlessly reiterated resolutions force governments to take positions anew. In doing so, governments sometimes must take into account strong or changing opinions at home. Furthermore, governmental politics may well change substantially over time: the votes reflect such change.

When the General Assembly deals with a proposed resolution, governments have three choices: they can vote in favor, oppose or abstain. (A fourth possibility sometimes practised is to refrain from participation in the vote, while present or not. It is akin to abstention.) Each of these choices can have diplomatic consequences. For example, the Arab governments and Israel closely watch the votes on resolutions dealing with the situation in the Middle East for signs of change. Finally, governments understand that on occasion UN members find ways outside of the organization to gain the ends sought by resolutions. Yet, unless the more powerful and influential governments are prepared to carry out the resolutions of the General Assembly, the verbiage of the resolutions may have no more effect than harmless blowing off steam.

Slow decision-making

The way in which the General Assembly proceeds on resolutions and other matters causes delegates to complain about slow and cumbersome decision-making. Almost anyone who observes the process from a spectator's seat would agree. Speeches stretch from minutes into hours, the same points are repeated with differing emphasis by a series of delegates from different countries, the arguments wander from the point and they often include quite extraneous comment. What is more, during the first weeks of the Assembly, many hours are consumed by the so-called general debate, which has little to do with a real debate. The suggestions made in the general debate, to no one's surprise, seem to favor the interests of the speaker. The prepared texts inexorably find their way into the record, even if they get little attention in the General Assembly and have little to do with the points made by the previous speaker. This speech making has grown in length with the list of members of the organization.

In addition, paper descends on the desks of delegations in daily avalanches. Reports, minutes, proposals, draft proposals, amendments, texts of remarks, answers to assertions made earlier – all of these eventually come out in as many as six languages: English, French, Spanish, Russian, Chinese as well as Arabic. The situation is only compounded, when the General Assembly, unable to decide on a clutch of problems, sets up new committees, names subcommittees, creates commissions and appoints experts to try to find agreeable ways out of impasses. Complaints about this unwieldy process only stimulate the General Assembly to create yet another committee to design improvements in its working habits. Little has resulted from these efforts. Ambassadors of sovereign states do not accept limitations on their words, for that would imply denigration of the rights of a government. Consequently, they will not accept such obvious proposals as increasing the power of the presiding officers to call speakers back into line when they drift from the subject or make discourteous remarks. Furthermore, the speakers often look over the heads of the delegates, back to their own countries, when they speak; when they address home audiences from this global platform, they accept no abridgement of their remarks.

Yet, slow procedures offer advantages that cannot be laughed away. While one delegate carries on interminably, repeating what has been said thrice before, other representatives busy themselves with consultations on the texts of draft resolutions, work up amendments, and recruit co-sponsors. In the lobbies important decisions can be prepared while the scheduled meetings drone along. The time can be used to maintain contact with home governments. Without instructions, some delegates have no authority to proceed, so the discussion would falter in any case. Delegates also tend politely to overlook stalling tactics, knowing that they may themselves soon need time to maneuver or seek instructions. An outside observer could easily conclude from the assiduous use of the delays by delegates that they really find the slow existing procedures quite satisfactory.

Finances

Whatever the pace of decision-making, the member governments must adopt a budget and provide for finances if there is to be an international institution at all. The General Assembly considers and approves the budget of the organization, as provided in Article 17 of the Charter. The Secretary-General submits a proposed budget to the General Assembly to cover two years of operations. This proposal undergoes running examination during its formation by experts appointed by the General Assembly to the Advisory Committee on Administrative and Budgetary Affairs.

For the 2004–05 biennium, the budget to which member governments are obliged to contribute totaled some $2.9 billion. It had hovered around that figure for a decade. Important headings in budget include overall policy-making direction and coordination ($499 million), common support services ($441 million), staff assessment ($350 million), regional cooperation for development ($337 million), international cooperation for development ($273 million), political affairs ($150 million), public information ($145 million), and human rights and humanitarian affairs ($133 million).

In addition to the regular budget, based on obligatory contributions, several UN programs depend on voluntary financing. Examples of these programs include the UNDP, the UN Relief and Works Agency for Palestine Refugees (UNRWA), UNHCR, and UNICEF. The larger peace-keeping ventures also were budgeted separately.

Apart from the activities supported by voluntary contributions, the budget is covered by assessment of the member states. The assessment depends in an approximate way on ability to pay. Every three years, the Assembly decides how to allocate the assessments among the members. The minimum contribution was .04 percent before 1973 but has been decreased first to .02 percent and then to .001 percent. No state pays more than 22 percent. A large number of members pays only the minimum, and together this makes up a small fraction of the total. The sub-Saharan African countries, including South Africa, the largest single geographical group, pay less than 0.6 percent of the budget, while the stronger and more developed states each pay a substantial fraction. The following states are responsible for the largest contributions:

United States	22.0%
Japan	19.5%
Germany	9.8%
France	6.5%
United Kingdom	5.5%
Italy	5.1%

The precise budgetary shares are determined during negotiations in the Assembly's Committee on Contributions, according to criteria including national income, income per capita, foreign exchange available, and similar factors. The developing nations have insisted that these criteria must reflect their special financial disabilities.

Some budgetary provisions have led individual states to refuse to pay their assessments. The most important instance of this refusal grew out of the peace-keeping operations in the Middle East during 1956 and 1957, when the UN Emergency Force (UNEF) served there, and in the Congo from 1960 to 1964, when an expensive peace-keeping operation took place. The Soviet Union and France claimed that expenses for these operations were not 'expenses of the organization' that had to be apportioned among the members, according to Article 17 of the Charter. This led to a 'financial crisis' with critical political implications. The crisis actually centered on the application of the provision of the UN Charter in Article 19 that a government in arrears of paying its contributions for two years shall have no vote in the General Assembly. The Soviet Union and its allies took the position that the peace-keeping expenses should be paid by the 'aggressors', whom they identified as Great Britain, France and Israel in the Suez incident and Belgium in the Congo. Along with France, the Soviet Union also raised substantial legal objections. The Soviet Union pointed out that the relevant budgetary decisions rested, not on the Security Council acting as provided in the Charter, but on a resolution of the General Assembly. The legal argument was sharpened when the International Court of Justice, responding to a request by the General Assembly, issued an advisory opinion in 1962 to the effect that the expenses indeed were those referred to in Article 17 and thus subject to obligatory apportionment. The refusing states maintained their attitude until, in 1964, the issue reached a climax. The Soviet Union and some other members then owed more than two years' worth of contributions. The United States appeared determined to force the issue and to secure the suspension of the Soviet Union and its allies from voting in the General Assembly. Had the General Assembly gone through with this proceeding, the Soviet group almost certainly would have withdrawn from the organization. No votes were taken during that Assembly. Once the General Assembly was over, the United States reappraised its position. Tacitly acknowledging the failure of its attempt to force the Soviet Union and France to contribute, the United States decided that their continuing membership after all would be more important than a pyrrhic victory. France proved willing to pay at least part of its debt, but the Soviet Union continued to refuse to contribute money for the now terminated peace-keeping ventures until the Gorbachev-led policy changes. China has adopted a similar stance, refusing to pay for actions that it considers hostile or in violation of the provisions of the Charter, by which it means the response of the United Nations in Korea. Later peace-keeping operations have been financed through voluntary contributions. The United States announced after the crisis that it would also decide for itself when it was obliged to pay. This stance had little significance until the Reagan presidency, when the United States used it actively as a threat and put it into effect in minor instances.

U.S. debt to UN

Combined with a broad public distaste for financing foreign ventures, opposition to UN expenditures gradually permeated the American Congress. By early 1988, the failure by Congress to honor requests from the President for appropriations for UN contributions built up the American debt to the United Nations to more than $1 billion. Leading senators, who were in position to block financing for the UN debt demanded reforms of the UN system and reduction of personnel. Even after some adaptation by Secretary-General Boutros-Ghali and a much more sweeping reconstruction by his successor, Kofi Annan, of those parts of structure within his capacity, the reluctance to contribute to the UN budget continued. It also involved demands, endorsed by the foreign affairs policy makers, for a reduction in the percentage of the budget paid by the United States to 20 percent from its present

25 percent. This would require agreement by the General Assembly which declined to act on the matter until the backlog debt was paid up. The consequence of the reluctance by the American Congress to spend taxpayers' money, even the relatively small amounts involved in the UN budget, was a gradually increasing threat of bankruptcy for the organization. As alleged mismanagement of the United Nations entered the domestic political lexicon, the organization limped through a decade of increasingly stringent finances because of the very size of the missing American contribution, the largest of any member, and the irregularity of its payments. It signaled, moreover, an increasing willingness on the part of the Congress to use its appropriation power so as deeply to intervene in the UN policy process and the management of the Secretariat. Yet that organ has international status and a legal duty not to accept instructions from a member government, all of which have accepted the obligation not to issue such orders. (UN Charter, Article 100).

The American position on financing began to show signs of bending in the late 1990s, when Secretary-General Annan made special efforts to develop contacts with leaders in Washington. The strongest critic, then the chairman of the Senate foreign relations committee, Strom Thurmond, even appeared in the Security Council to recite his criticisms of the UN budget. But soon some arrears began to be paid. A sharp turn took place at once after the terrorist attack on New York and Washington on 11 September 2001. A payment that wiped out much of the arrears was authorized at once by Congress with support from the White House. The US level is now 22 percent.

The financial crisis deserves to be judged dispassionately, not merely on the basis of legal and moral obligations. The question should be raised as to whether it was sensible to assume that the General Assembly could force a great power to pay for an exercise that it opposed from the very beginning as legally and politically impermissible. Under a law adopted in 1979, for example, the U.S. Congress has forbidden its government to contribute to UN funds that in any way support the Palestine Liberation Organization. Major powers will not contribute financially to activities to which they are politically opposed.

Quite apart from the Article 19 crisis, a steady stream of criticism is directed at the level of expenses of the United Nations. In the past, this variety of criticism has been expressed both by the United States and the Soviet Union. Superfluous administrative activities are cited. In the General Assembly, delegates insist on the need to reduce expenditures, but then vote for countless requests for studies and reports to be prepared by the Secretariat, support new study committees, and summon new conferences in many distant corners of the earth. While it is easy to raise questions about how useful much of this activity really is, to demonstrate specific waste is equally difficult. The Secretariat is required by the General Assembly to make a report on all new expenses, to set out the cost-effectiveness of old activities, to produce a program budget, and to allow the watchdog Advisory Committee on Administrative and Budgetary Questions to give its advice. While it is not strictly germane, the perspective of judgments is improved by recalling that the total costs of the UN system fall below the costs of running even a modest military establishment.

Another criticism related to costs of the UN system calls attention to the many receptions and dinners given by the permanent mission to the United Nations in New York. The great majority of these fall exclusively within national accounts, not the UN budget, and resemble the functions that take place continually in national capitals. They are indispensable to diplomatic work. In New York, the number of these gatherings perhaps exceeds those held in any national capital; it is not unusual for a senior diplomat to appear at as many as three receptions in one evening. These occasions make it possible for diplomats to talk informally about matters that will be raised more officially later. They also use such occasions to speak with journalists and to send gestures of amity or disdain to others. This is the way some diplomatic business is normally conducted anywhere. Complaining in public and meeting later at parties is likely to remain a permanent feature at UN headquarters.

4
The Maintenance of Peace and Security

Two principal direct approaches to the maintenance of international peace and security, the fundamental purpose of the United Nations, are set out in the UN Charter.

The first is the pacific settlement of disputes, outlined in Chapter VI. The second comprises coercive measures against any state that threatens or breaks the peace. This is defined in Chapter VII. Specific issues of peace and security may in principle be handled by the General Assembly only when they are not before the Security Council or when the latter asks for the assistance of the larger body (Art. 12). The UN Charter traditionally foresees disturbances to the peace as involving conflicts between states, but recently practice has allowed UN action in some violent disturbances within states.

Of the two main approaches to conflicts, pacific settlement and its associated devices have been used far more often and with far fewer cascading difficulties than enforcement. They also receive far less publicity than more coercive approaches. This result differs little from what diplomatic experience and the League of Nations have taught, for the use of coercion demands elusive coordination of policy and action and can spur on a more serious crisis, great costs, upsetting effects on large populations and even more violence.

The initial responsibility for the peaceful resolution of differences rests on the parties to a dispute. They are forbidden from using armed force (Art. 2(4)) but rather must try to find a pacific solution without endangering international peace and security (Art. 2(3)). Beyond that, the UN Charter lists several specific means of settlement (Art. 33).

The list begins with <u>negotiations</u> to find a solution. An <u>enquiry</u> to develop better understanding of the positions in a tense international relationship could be set in motion. In this case, the Security Council could ask the Secretary-General to carry out this task or else establish its own commission or agent. The Council could offer <u>good offices</u> or direct the Secretary-General to do so. Formally, this merely provides a location with a suitable atmosphere for negotiation. The Secretary-General could also be instructed to send out <u>observers</u>, if the parties agreed, and would always report back on his activity. <u>Mediation</u> and <u>conciliation</u> also are listed in the Charter. These procedures, technically somewhat different, require the services of a third party that can make suggestions about the solutions to a dispute without obliging the disputants to accept them. The president of the Security Council, or the Secretary-General, or a group of persons or national representatives acceptable to the disputing governments could serve as third parties.

Third parties also figure in <u>arbitration</u>, but here an arbitrator or a commission is specially appointed to deliver a decision which the disputants agree in advance to accept as binding. Differences about the interpretation or application of international law can be appropriately settled by arbitration or by <u>judicial decision,</u> for example by the International Court of Justice, on the basis of questions defined by the parties or in accordance with a procedure agreed in advance (see Chapter 2). Finally, the Security Council is authorized to select other pacific measures which may be useful.

Pacific settlement of disputes

If fighting has actually broken out, the Security Council usually calls on the parties to stop practices that contradict obligations assumed under the Charter and to cease-fire. Such an appeal may succeed, not perhaps so much because it emanates from the Security Council but rather either because the goals of a party were achieved or else that further violence appears futile. If an appeal results in a cease-fire, the Council may dispatch international observers to ensure observance of its terms. This requires consent from disputants.

In all of the means for pacific settlement provided in Chapter VI of the Charter, the cooperation of the parties is unmistakably required. Generally, the disputants may prove amenable to accepting the intervention of the Security Council in the hope that their own aims will gain support. Whatever the tactics of the parties to a dispute, the underlying principle of pacific settlement assumes that force or war must be excluded as a means of conflict resolution. Rather, peaceful settlement techniques must prevail. Another principle underlying the Charter provisions holds that regional conflicts may lead to a danger to wider international peace and security. Although the Charter encourages the use of regional arrangements for pacific settlement, the Security Council is in principle authorized to intervene in regional conflicts. (Art. 52 (3,4)).

UN proceedings have succeeded in preventing a number of conflicts from spreading or have dulled the sharpest edges of others. The unresolved conflict over Kashmir between India and Pakistan provides an example of a UN presence in order to dampen new flare-ups. The Security Council convinced both parties as long ago as 1949 to accept the presence of a small observation group which can furnish reliable information about new outbreaks of violence. Such reports help in reasserting international concern about any disturbance. The Kashmir conflict also exemplifies the fact that the United Nations seldom has been able to put in place permanent solutions to end disputes. Rather it often brings the parties to arrest a conflict on the spot, after fighting, or else restores the pre-conflict situation. In that way the conflict is not resolved but simply checked for the time being. Such results do not settle the question of the merits of the case and in many respects remain unsatisfactory. Nevertheless, the most important assumption of the UN Charter insists gentler behavior is always preferable to the use of force.

The long-lasting Arab-Israeli conflict provides a striking example of both the successes and the limitations of UN performance. Time after time, in outright warfare during 1948, 1949, 1956, 1967 and lastly in 1973, as well as during Arab uprisings in Israeli-occupied territory, UN action achieved little more than a cease-fire and the temporary restoration of at least some of the pre-conflict situation. None of this eliminated the causes of the wars. Neither for that matter has good offices or intense bilateral mediation by the United States government, the Oslo agreement of 1993 among the parties or the widely-endorsed 'road-map for peace' process of the early 21st century.

Following the failure of the 1947 plan by the General Assembly to partition Palestine into two states, in the series of military engagements around Israel, the United Nations provided important services to encourage the maintenance of cease-fires and armistices. Above all, it furnished an important specific element in the form of 'peace-keeping forces' that were deployed between warring parties. (A peace-keeping force does not normally employ force.) (See discussion below.) Furthermore, the UN Relief and Works Agency (UNRWA) operates a large-scale program in the Middle East to assist hundreds of thousands of Palestinians, who include persons who fled from what is now Israel during the 1948 conflict or descended from them.

Although it would be overdrawn to claim that these activities ensure permanent peace in the Eastern Mediterranean, on occasion the UN has helped to moderate or contain the armed conflicts there. For many years it was the only impartial third-party available for this purpose. Its series of mediators – Folke Bernadotte, who was assassinated; Ralph Bunche, the American who won the Nobel Peace Prize for his work; and Gunnar Jarring, a Swedish ambassador, and several others – could hardly be blamed for the lack of progress in this complex situation. They could not persuade the disputants to agree on a permanent solution and abandon military means. Without the commitment of disputing parties, essential in any conciliatory proceedings, the third party must eventually fall short of full success.

Coercive measures

Aware of the limits to pacific settlement as well as of the failure of 'automatic sanctions' during the League of Nations, the authors of the UN Charter gave the Security Council in Chapter VII of the Charter coercive powers to counter aggression and threats to the peace. The Security Council can go beyond recommendations and to make binding decisions to prevent or force an end to aggression after it has declared that a threat to or breach of the peace exists (Art. 39). Such a finding implies that subsequent Council decisions have the quality of a legal obligation.

Before using a full array of coercion, the Council may decide on provisional measures that legally do not alter the claims or positions of the parties (Art. 40). Or it may go directly to stronger methods. These include non-military approaches; listed in the Charter are a partial or complete end to economic relations, breaking off of rail, sea, air, postal, telegraphic, radio and other communications, and cessation of diplomatic relations. Underlying these sanctions is the proposition that the attacker would suffer such unacceptable consequences that he would restore the situation before hostilities – that indeed he would be deterred from going on.

In practice, in the near term these sanctions usually appear to fall short of the desired effect. Either the party against whom they are invoked is so strong economically that the punishment can be shrugged off, or as is more often the case, the potentialities of the Charter are not fully invoked or the members do not honor the decisions of the Security Council. Or in some cases, one of the parties simply prefers enduring the costs to changing its course.

After the experience of the League of Nations and World War II, the UN planners knew that economic and diplomatic sanctions might not deter aggression. They therefore provided the Security Council with the authority not only to use but to prepare in advance for military pressure against flagrant violators of the Charter (Art. 43). According to the Charter, all UN members must make armed forces available to the Security Council on its request and in line with special agreements to be drawn up. These would include rights of passage and other assistance. Such agreements do not exist. (See discussion, below.)

Obviously, this system would not operate against the permanent members of the Security Council. They could be coerced only with great difficulty and the possibility of a general war. Furthermore, for them the unanimity rule provides the possibility of forestalling any decision. Nevertheless, they formed a keystone of the system, both in respect to expectations about their behavior and the services they would provide for the Council. The expectations grew out of the benefits of wartime cooperation and President Roosevelt's notions that international peace could be guaranteed by the 'four policemen', the leading victorious allies.

Precisely because this opportunistic friendship broke down in the Cold War, the other deterrent aspect of the UN system never came into being. This was to be a standing armed force, directed by the military commanders of the permanent members, which could act at the beck and call of the Security Council (Art. 45, 47). The Council was to be assisted by a Military Staff Committee, made up of the Chiefs of Staff of the permanent members. It would work out the details of the standing forces, to which any UN member could contribute but which clearly would rely mainly on the permanent members. The Committee reflected the split between the Soviet Union and the other permanent members. In July 1948, it reported to the Security Council that it could make no further progress unless the Council itself came to an agreement on specified issues. Such agreement has never been reached, although the General Assembly also has long had its own committee to study the issues. The Military Staff Committee formally still exists but has never made any progress.

Neither of the main antagonists in the Cold War then or afterward wanted to hand over decisional powers to the United Nations where the response to a political issue would be unpredictable. In the early years, the Soviet Union showed the greatest reluctance to accept broad authority for the Security Council. It was in a minority position both there and the General Assembly. While it could protect itself with the veto in the Security Council, this brought costs in terms of negative propaganda from its opponents. By 1970, the United States increasingly adopted political positions that left it isolated and it too used the veto. Only after Mikhail Gorbachev took over leadership of the Soviet Union did its position change to favor much more use of the United Nations in issues of peace and security. Russia, the Soviet successor, has followed a similar but less far-reaching line. China, the only remaining Communist government with a permanent Council seat, rarely has taken a leading position but generally favors a lower level of UN activity over a higher one.

In a sense, the designers of the UN Charter opted for a prudent approach to international peace. They showed a clear skepticism about the notion that they could simply set out binding rules for the maintenance of peace and expect them always faithfully to be followed. The Charter contains provisions that cover the contingency that Chapters VI and VII might not work. Accordingly, Article 51 of the Charter provides for a 'natural right' of individual and collective self-defense for all members until the Security Council has taken the necessary steps to maintain international peace. The inclusion of 'collective self-defense' opens the way for military alliances.

The collective self-defense provision offered some legal justification for the creation of the two principal alliances that grew out of the Cold War. These were the North Atlantic Treaty Organization (NATO) and the opposed and now defunct Warsaw Treaty Organization. The treaties on which they were based both referred to Article 51. The existence of the two organizations could be taken as evidence that collective security in the UN system had failed. It is clear that the governments involved in the Cold War had more confidence in their alliances than in the United Nations.

The fact that most new states in Asia and Africa took up explicitly 'non-aligned' positions demonstrated more distrust of the alliances than lack of confidence in the UN arrangements. At the same time, most of the new states had little reason to fear attacks on their territories. With the relaxation of the Cold War during the late 1980s, NATO began to look for tasks that had less military content and by the early 2000s had extended its membership into the former Soviet zone, while the Warsaw Treaty Organization simply crumbled. NATO forces took on the policing of Bosnia-Herzegovina in the mid-1990s and in 1999 used its bombers to interrupt what was seen as Serbian attempts at ethnic cleansing in Kosovo. These expeditions obviated the possible

Soviet or Chinese vetoes in the Security Council. Explicit UN blessing, however, led to stationing of NATO armed units to help with security in Afghanistan.

In addition to the mode of collective defense, the UN system offers its members the possibility of joining regional security arrangements. In Chapter VIII of the Charter, members are urged to use regional organizations to settle differences that come within their purview. This is supposed to take place in preference to engaging the Security Council. Examples of these regional arrangements are the Organization of American States (OAS), the Arab League and the more recently established African Union, which succeeded the Organization for African Unity (OAU). For the most part, these organizations have proved useful only in limited local issues, such as boundary disputes. They have only very rarely produced solutions to important disputes which involved serious threats to international peace and security.

Practical use of Charter concepts

Increasingly in the 1990s, the conceptual separation of pacific settlement and enforcement was pushed aside in UN organs in favor of a mixture of the two approaches to conflict and even, as noted, novel cooperation with military alliances. The hallmarks of UN engagement became improvisation and innovation. This provoked controversy between those governments that in debates over policies hewed to strict interpretation of the sovereignty of members and those that favored explicit international solidarity. This debate, which goes to the very heart of international organization, came to the fore, for instance, in the beginning of the 1990s with UN reactions to the strife in Somalia, Rwanda and the former Yugoslavia.

Israel and neighbors

Stretching or adjusting the approach to maintaining peace in the UN Charter began with the innovative precedent of peace-keeping. It emerged in the UN response to the joint attack by France, Israel and the United Kingdom following Egypt's nationalization of the Suez Canal in 1956. The first of such forces, the UN Emergency Force (UNEF) was hastily designed by Secretary-General Hammarskjöld under instructions from the General Assembly after the Security Council was deadlocked by French and British vetoes. This took place at a crisis point in the Cold War as Soviet forces put down an uprising in Hungary.

Despite its background in a shower of crises, UNEF embodied principles that were points of reference in all later combinations of peaceful settlement and military presence. These include the acceptance by the disputing parties of the UN force; its use of force only in self defense; impartiality in the existing political status which the UN undertakes not to change; and exclusion from the force of troops from interested parties. All peace-keeping forces fall under the direction of the Secretary-General and his appointed UN commander, who leads national units which retain their own command structure. UNEF and other peace-keeping entities formed during the Cold War also excluded troops from permanent members of the Security Council, thus augmenting their neutral stance. Soldiers from the peace-keeping forces patrol between armistice lines, collate factual accounts of alleged violations and mediate in minor disputes. They are not equipped to carry out military operations against enemies.

With a maximum of 6,000 soldiers, UNEF stayed in position until the outbreak of a new war between Israel and the Arab states in 1967, before which the peace-keepers were ejected by Egypt. After the 1973 war with Egypt, Israel allowed a new UNEF II for the first time on its soil, so that both sides of the border were under UN surveillance. But under pressure from the Soviet Union, UNEF was disbanded in 1979. Meanwhile, a smaller force, the UN Disengagement Observer Force (UNDOF), stationed on the Golan Heights between Syria and Israel, was still in place in 2005.

A bigger peace-keeping operation was dispatched by the Security Council after Israeli forces occupied part of the south Lebanon in 1978. There, the UN Interim Force in Lebanon (UNIFIL) succeeded for the next four years in maintaining reasonable tranquility. Then the Israeli military cut through UNIFIL lines on their way to Beirut. Since then, UNIFIL has hardly been able to function, although the Security Council continues to renew its mandate, perhaps in the hope that it can someday be more useful.

Cyprus

Another long-running peace operation separates Greek and Turkish claimants to authority on Cyprus. For this operation, the UN Force in Cyprus (UNFICYP) was stationed in 1964 after it was alleged that Turkey would attack the island. This fear grew out of unresolved tension between Turkey and Greece and their support for contending ethnic groups that threatened civil war on the island. Turkey finally invaded the northern part of the island in 1974. Before and since,

UNFYCIP, which initially included British troops, watches over a tense armistice from which despite repeated UN negotiations and mediation, no settlement of the rival claims has emerged. Moreover, in 2004, the Greek-speaking part of Cyprus, on its way to join the European Union, in a popular vote rejected a plan for unity proposed by Secretary-General Annan that had been accepted by the Turkish voters in the north.

Congo

While UNEF principles were applied by Hammarskjöld and the Security Council in response to an army revolt and an invasion by Belgium of its recently independent former Congo colony, the operation developed in ways that suggested enforcement action. When Belgium withdrew, four years of turbulence, during which UN experts in great part governed, followed. Hammarskjöld personally attempted to negotiate between a shaky central government and a rebellious group in rich Katanga province. On his way, he died in an aircraft accident. Amid contending Cold War pressures, the UN force, called ONUC after its French initials, eventually was built up to 20,000 men and included an air wing. This formidable grouping eventually ended a secession of the rich Katanga province in an operation that ostensibly restored freedom of movement to the UN force. Secretary-General U Thant, who had succeeded Hammarskjöld, ended the mission in 1964, by which time opinion in many third world governments had turned against the entire notion of peace-keeping as a derogation of state authority.

New style peace operations

UNEF, the prototype peace-keeping force, was small, had only light weapons, and a narrow, clearly defined mandate that was intended to separate the warring states. In contrast, ONUC had a complex mandate, high costs and heavy armaments. Like ONUC, the later UN operations in Namibia and Cambodia signified a clear involvement with the internal process of forming a state.

Namibia

The year 1990 brought a successful end to 44 years of UN pressure to achieve independence for the former German colony of Southwest Africa, more recently called Namibia. A mandated territory, administered by South Africa under the League of Nations, it was on the UN agenda since 1946, when the General Assembly rejected the mandatory's request to incorporate the territory. The positions taken subsequently by South Africa and the majority of the General Assembly led to the use of almost every possible means of pacific settlement of disputes. The fierceness of the General Assembly's position can be explained by the resentment that the South African policy of *apartheid* caused in most of the world. When the General Assembly declined in 1946 to allow South Africa simply to make Southwest Africa part of its realm, the government of South Africa was dealt a heavy blow. It renounced plans for annexation but declared it would administer the territory in the spirit of the mandate from the League. At the same time, it rejected requests from the General Assembly that Namibia be made a trust territory.

Political means to free Namibia from South African rule started in the General Assembly. In 1961, by a large majority, it proclaimed the inalienable right of the people of Namibia to self-determination and political independence. The General Assembly tried to organize voluntary coercive measures against South Africa. Since 1963, the Assembly repeatedly urged UN members not to supply South Africa with arms, military equipment, oil and oil products or do anything that would hamper the application of resolutions on Namibia. In the face of this pressure, about which the South African government expressed resentment, it acted in Namibia contrary to the wishes of the UN majority. The General Assembly pressed on by revoking the mandate of the League of Nations in 1966 and vesting formal authority over Namibia in a UN Council for Namibia.

An effort, that in the end turned out to be successful, began in 1978, when discussions took place on the future of Namibia among the five Western members of the Security Council – then Canada, France, the Federal Republic of Germany, the United Kingdom and the United States – who called themselves the 'Contact Group'. Consulting the South West African People's Organization (SWAPO) and the governments of states bordering South Africa, they developed a program based on free elections for the whole of Namibia as one political entity. The plan called for the appointment of a representative of the Secretary-General in the territory for a transitional period. The United Nations would supervise and control elections there and guard tranquility with a peace-keeping force. The South African government agreed to the plan in 1978. It envisaged a UN Transition Assistance Group (UNTAG) consisting of military and civilian personnel. that was set up to oversee the transition from South African rule to independence. Agreement was reached on an UNTAG force numbering 4,650 men, plus some 600 policemen and nearly 1,000 civilians and UN personnel – making it the largest UN force since the Congo operation. During 1989 and part of the following year, UNTAG fulfilled a successful function in overseeing the holding of the first free elections in Namibia, the repatriation of an estimated 80,000 refugees and the maintenance of law and order. Elections were held in November 1989, which resulted in a large victory of Sam Nujoma's SWAPO movement. In April 1990, Namibia gained formal independence and shortly thereafter it was admitted as member of the United Nations.

The case of Namibia illustrates both the weakness and the strength of the United Nations in managing political change. Though in the end the goal desired by the majority of UN members – Namibian independence – was reached, this was marginally due to UN activities. Forty-four years of UN dealing with the future of Namibia produced few concrete results, although it kept the issue on the international agenda. The crucial breakthrough in the negotiations occurred outside the formal UN process, in the context of the improved relations between the United States and the Soviet Union. Once agreement in principle had been reached, the United Nations, through the Contact Group and UNTAG, provided a useful channel to help to carry out the agreement.

Cambodia

The mass murders carried out in Cambodia by the Khmer Rouge in the beginning of the 1980s and the movement of many thousand refugees impelled action by the Security Council. It followed the model used for Namibia. In the UN Transitional Authority for Cambodia (UNTAC) some 20,000 military personnel and 2,400 civilians were set to work in 1991 in reorganizing the government and preparing for a free election.

As part of its mandate, UNTAC had the task of supervising the regrouping of three contending local military forces so as to end fighting. That was intended to protect the population so that elections could proceed. UNTAC accomplished its work of preparing for the election by personal contact and via radio programs. Using methods that pushed aside traditional notions of national sovereignty and emphasized human rights, UNTAC watched over relatively orderly elections in 1993 and then withdrew. Generally, UNTAC achieved reasonable but hardly complete success in a difficult mission. While little military force was used in Cambodia since then, the situation has hardly fully employed democratic methods or remained stable, although a functioning government has remained in place.

The UN missions in both Cambodia and Namibia illustrate the expansion of the Suez model of peace-keeping to include operations normally in the hands of established governments. The forces entered politically unsettled environments to ensure tranquility. They were accompanied by a large number of UN civilian personnel who assumed aspects of governing. In neither case was violent military action the primary means used to achieve the goals set out by the Security Council. In both cases much improvisation was required from both the UN personnel on the ground and their colleagues at UN headquarters.

Collective coercive measures

Despite the absence of a permanent military arm, the Security Council has twice approved patching together heavily-armed forces to end a breach of the peace. In a long line of more obscure situations, the Council approved economic and diplomatic sanctions that member governments carried out with mixed results. The first of the armed responses followed the attack in 1950 by North Korea on the Republic of Korea in the south. Neither of them were at that time UN members. The second involved the assault by Iraq on neighboring Kuwait in 1990.

In both instances, after the United States took the lead in the Security Council and in the field, it was authorized to command the forces that were assembled. They were heavily equipped to carry out extended field campaigns. The military action was accompanied by economic and political sanctions against the governments accused of violating the peace. Both actions, based on improvised forces, raised questions as to whether these were enforcement action as envisaged by the Charter and indeed whether they conformed to international law.

Korea

The extraordinary circumstances under which the Security Council responded to the North Korean attack lead to the conclusion that this was not a genuine exercise of collective security as envisaged by the Charter. At that time, the Soviet Union was boycotting the Council in order to protest the fact that the Nationalist government continued to represent China in UN organs, including the Security Council. The Nationalists had by then been driven off the mainland of China to Taiwan by the Communist government which the Soviet Union supported as the rightful Council member. Thus the absent Soviet Union could not veto the resolutions creating the UN military force under

United States command and operating under the UN flag. When the Soviet representative returned the next month, he vetoed any further decisions.

Before the end of 1950, the UN forces, led by the United States but including troops from South Korea and 15 other countries, had moved far into north Korea and then were driven back and narrowly missed defeat by the intervention of Chinese forces, officially called 'volunteers'. The next year, the UN forces, restored to strength, moved the battle lines to approximately the same position as when the conflict began. After the newly-elected American President Eisenhower intimated to the Chinese Communist government that nuclear weapons might be used, an armistice that was still in place in 2005 was agreed by North and South Korea and the United Nations Command.

Strictly speaking, the enforcement action in Korea hardly conformed either to the decision-making pattern of the Security Council nor to the more general concept of a standing force. The action did not, moreover, lead to permanent peace in the Korean peninsula. The question of unification of the divided country, on which the General Assembly had acted from 1948 onwards, still had not been resolved in early 2005. Meanwhile, with American protection the Republic of Korea developed as an industrialized country. The Communist government in North Korea oversaw a declining economy and UN agencies organized shipments of food to it so as to avoid mass starvation. Despite attempts in the UN system and via direct diplomacy, North Korea remained secretive, isolated and above all threatening because of a nuclear weapons program. It ejected IAEA inspectors and ignored the UN nuclear non-proliferation regime. Only with much resistance its government even agreed to talk with diplomats from China, Japan and the United States about reducing its nuclear programs. In 2005, it announced that it possessed nuclear weapons. The Korean peninsula remained divided into two heavily armed camps although in 1991, both Koreas were admitted as full UN members.

Iraq and the attack on Kuwait

The UN response to the sudden invasion by Iraqi forces in Kuwait in early August 1990 raised the expectation, so soon after the end of the Cold War, that at last the UN collective security system was working. Then the United Nations progressively endorsed the most forceful and far-reaching enforcement actions in its history – or for that matter, in the history of international organization. These included initially a wide range of economic, financial and diplomatic sanctions, intended to damage Iraq's war-making capacity and to isolate its government from possible allies. Later the Security Council authorized governments to use 'all possible means' – meaning military measures – to end the aggression against Kuwait. While the preponderant military force was contributed by the United States, 33 other countries joined it in aiding the expulsion of Iraqi forces from Kuwait in operations that began on 17 January 1991. Its military forces paralyzed by air, sea and land attacks, Iraq formally accepted a cease-fire on 6 April 1991. The UN forces halted without capturing the capital, leaving the government of Saddam Hussein in place in Baghdad.

Had the United Nations at last moved closer to the notion of collective security than in Korea? To what extent did the organization prove central to repelling what almost every government acknowledged was aggression?

Once the news arrived in New York that on 2 August 1990, Iraqi forces had invaded Kuwait, the Security Council immediately determined in Resolution 660 that a breach of the peace had occurred and demanded unconditional withdrawal. The Permanent Members of the Council all voted in favor of the resolution along with nine other members and one (Yemen) not participating. Earlier, after Iraq had claimed rights to certain petroleum resources exploited by Kuwait, a diplomatic encounter between the two governments had ended in failure. In line with the Charter procedure, the Security Council called upon the two parties to resume negotiations.

The disregard with which the government headed by Saddam Hussein met this resolution led the Security Council to act under Chapter VII of the Charter. It decided on Resolution 661 by a vote of 13 in favor with two abstentions to begin a program of economic and financial sanctions that would cut off Iraqi imports and exports, especially of oil; deprive it of access to resources abroad; and cut off any governmental assistance to the Baghdad government. That decision placed a legal obligation on all UN members. The Council set up a committee to oversee the application of sanctions. American forces and those of other coalition members quickly built up. Over the next nine months, the Council adopted 13 additional basic resolutions dealing with the situation in Kuwait. They were supplemented many times over the next seven years.

Once the Security Council decided that a breach of the peace had occurred, it was legally free to authorize the use of armed force to give effect to its decisions. The series of resolutions that led to that crucial moment in fact offered the Iraqi government repeated chances to return the situation to its prewar state. It refused to do so. A trip to Baghdad by the Secretary-General, acting under Security Council instructions, gave no result. In November 1990, the Security Council set a deadline of 15 January 1991 for Iraq to withdraw from Kuwait. If it were not to do so, the '...Member States co-operating with the Government of Kuwait...' were authorized to '...use all necessary means to uphold and implement...all relevant resolutions and to restore international peace and security to the area.' (UN Security Council Resolution 668) The entire series of resolutions to this point had had the support of the Permanent Members; on Resolution 668, China abstained, but 12 other governments voted in favor. Cuba and Yemen, frequent abstainers on earlier decisions, voted against Resolution 668.

By then, the United States had built up an enormous force in the area. It included some 400,000 troops in Saudi Arabia, a vast fleet of naval vessels in and around the Gulf and a huge air force. It was joined by lesser, but significant, contributions from France and the United Kingdom, among the Europeans, and from Egypt, Saudi Arabia and Syria from the Middle East, as well as a mixture of contributions from the 28 other allies. The Soviet Union offered no military cooperation but strongly supported the program adopted by the Security Council. Iraq replied contemptuously, threatening to spread any armed conflict to Israel and to use guided missiles, poison gas and, it hinted, nuclear weapons. Although some opinion leaders, especially in the United States, explicitly pinned their hopes on sanctions as a way to peace, the government of President George H.W. Bush in Washington decided to begin military action on 17 January 1991. It asserted that it and the other allies acted with UN authorization.

At first, only air and naval forces were engaged. Iraq used guided missiles against Israel and Saudi Arabia to little effect. The allied air force systematically destroyed the Iraqi command and control system. Then on 24 February, the allied force launched a ground attack from bases in Saudi Arabia. Despite the earlier blustering from Baghdad, Iraqi defenses immediately crumbled on contact with the allies, who halted their advance five days later with the Iraqis in full retreat.

In various respects, the decisions of the Security Council appeared to conform to the model of collective security under the UN Charter but in very important respects differed. On the political plane, it was clear that the actions of the Council were driven by the permanent members, strongly led by the United States. Back of the American position in the Council were President George H.W. Bush and his colleagues who repeatedly insisted that Saddam Hussein and his government threatened the peace. The obvious implication, sometimes openly stated, was that Saddam's government must be deposed. While the United Kingdom from the beginning and France later took parallel positions, the Soviet Union and China were more circumspect about intrusion into Iraqi affairs. The elected members of the Council were of course consulted in advance of the presentation of resolutions but usually only after the permanent members had reached a consensus in private. This leadership by the permanent members, begun with the decline of the Cold War, now gained a new, not altogether popular, prominence.

All of the Council's action were necessarily taken without the advice of the Military Staff Committee although it met twice in private sessions. Nor had any forces been organized or ear-marked in advance of the Iraqi invasion. Thus the Council had no ready military forces at its disposal. The entire military campaign was in fact organized under strong leadership, not to say dominance, by the United States, as had been the case forty years earlier in Korea.

At no time, however, did the Council appoint or give political directives to a UN commander or to a joint command of the sort established in the Korean case: the United States obviously opposed any such arrangements and prevailed without open dissent. Thus rather than the centralized source for politico-military policy implied by the UN Charter, the enforcement action against Iraq was based on decentralization and coordination. At the same time, the very wide support given to the Security Council by UN member governments and the broad spectrum of military response fitted with the notion that the world must unite against governments that breach the peace.

As the Iraqi forces in Kuwait staggered under the full force of the allied attack, the government in Baghdad accepted Security Council Resolution 660, which had demanded the unconditional withdrawal of its troops and resumption of pacific settlement, and retracted its annexation of the territory. Left behind was a looted city, hungry and displaced people and more than 500 burning oil wells. Unlike the Korea case, the Security Council then set out far-reaching conditions for a permanent cease-fire. These were contained in Security Council resolution 686, adopted on 2 March 1991 by a vote of 11 in favor with Cuba opposed and China, India and Yemen abstaining. Iraq agreed to carry out this resolution. To monitor the demilitarized zone which was established along the Iraqi-Kuwait border, the Security Council in Resolution 687 on 3 April 1991 created the UN Iraq-Kuwait Observation Mission (UNIKOM) which remained in place until 2003.

The conditions set out in resolutions 686 and 687 led to extraordinary penetration by an international organization into the Iraqi polity. As a direct result of the vast Iraqi military buildup and the threats made by Saddam Hussein and his associates, the Security Council demanded that Iraq dispose of all its chemical and biological weapons and ballistic missiles with a range of more than 150 kilometers. A series of inspection missions, fervently denounced and harassed by Iraq, uncovered unsuspected capacity to produce materials for such weapons. Step by step, Iraq was driven under UN supervision nearer full compliance with resolution 687, although repeated crises erupted over the mode of inspection.

Iraq was also held responsible for reparations for damages in Kuwait. To pay for this, a part of its sales of petroleum would be set aside under UN supervision. Only after more than four years of refusal, Iraq agreed to sell a relatively small quantity of oil under UN supervision in what was called the Oil-for-Food program to purchase food and medicine exclusively for its manifestly suffering population. Iraq was also ordered without satisfactory result to help with repatriation of displaced people.

The end of active fighting also impelled turbulent, sometimes desperate, measures to organize humanitarian assistance for an unanticipated mass of displaced persons and forced migrants. After a short-lived, confused uprising, a huge flight of Kurds, an often persecuted minority people in Iraq, into the mountains in Turkey, Iran and Iraq heightened the emergency. The Kurds in the Iraqi and Turkish areas were induced to return to their homes after the allies used military forces to provide a safety zone. Although this was not explicitly authorized by the Security Council, it impelled some enthusiasm about the possibilities of 'humanitarian intervention.' Moreover, the United States and some of its allies designated parts of north and south Iraq as 'no fly zones' in order to keep the Baghdad government from using military means to control its sometimes rebellious population.

Tight economic sanctions lasted until 2004. Furthermore, enough air and naval force, mostly American, remained nearby to take further military measures, should Iraq deviate too far from the cease-fire terms it had accepted. When an Iraqi assassination plot against President George H.W. Bush was reported in 1994, American planes carried out a punitive attack. Late in 1997 and early 1998, American and British forces again built up in the Persian Gulf to threaten Iraq after it interfered with UN arms inspectors. A threat of major hostilities eventually gave way, amidst much Iraqi bluster, to a compromise and postponement of any more use of force. The negotiations included a trip in early 1998 to Baghdad by Secretary-General Kofi Annan, who returned with an agreement negotiated with Saddam Hussein to allow further inspections under a somewhat altered formula.

After Iraq I

Whether or not the response to the invasion of Kuwait definitively tested the concept of collective security, the United Nations remained deeply engaged. A Security Council agent, the UN Special Commission (UNSCOM), probed deeply into the Iraqi armory and succeeded in uncovering and destroying a variety of missiles, stocks of conventional weapons and tanks, equipment that could be used for manufacture of chemical and biological weapons and evidence of some work on producing nuclear weapons. This work involved UNSCOM inspectors on the ground and cooperation with IAEA.

At every step of the way, the Iraqi government, still headed by Saddam Hussein, tried to obstruct the inspectors, even engaging in cat-and-mouse-tactics that, if they had not involved serious matters, could be described as fit for a television comedy. Reacting to semi-annual reports and other briefings, the Security Council almost always fully supported its commission, headed at first by an experienced Swedish ambassador and then by Richard Butler, a forthright Australian diplomat. But by 1999, the Iraqi government had not only reacted to its obligations to the Security Council with inventive, to say the least, information and strident demands for the end of embargoes but also had physically interfered with UNSCOM and then forced it to withdraw. Meantime, Butler had resigned and voiced blistering critiques related to his experiences.

If the UNSCOM phase had ended, so had the consensus that made possible the Security Council resolutions to reverse the Iraqi attack on Kuwait, to control Iraq's capacity to use weapons and to reiterate its support for the inspection and destruction program carried under its auspices. It took nearly a year for the Council to reach enough agreement to begin inspections again. In December 1999, it adopted resolution 1284, which created the UN Monitoring, Verification and Inspection Mission (UNMOVIC). It would carry on part of UNSCOM's work under new and narrower instructions and renewed, if unenthusiastic Iraqi consent. Hans Blix, former director of IAEA and sometime foreign minister of Sweden, was appointed to head it. Iraq held off permission for UNMOVIC to enter its territory until late September 2001, by which time a shocking event had changed the political background.

Terror attacks on the United States

On September 11, 2001, the killing of some 3,000 civilians and the destruction by aircraft highjacked by terrorists of the World Trade Center in New York, part of the American military headquarters at the Pentagon and the attempt to attack other buildings in Washington brought an immediate response from both the Security Council and the General Assembly. These made clear that self-defense against terrorist actions could be undertaken as if a classical interstate conflict had begun. That gave political, and probably legal, sanction for the United States' military campaign against the Taliban regime in Afghanistan, where the al-Qaeda terrorist network was then presumed to be headquartered.

The American-led forces within weeks, drove the Taliban government from power and the leadership of al-Qaeda, including Osama bin Laden, who was identified as its leader by President George W. Bush, disappeared. A special representative of the Secretary-General, Lakhdar Brahimi, contributed to the construction of an improvised governmental authority. American policy then foresaw the creation of a new Afghan government which by 2004 had held a national election. The United Nations resumed humanitarian activities, although it was unable to work in some disturbed regions. Meanwhile, American troops pursued terrorists, while an improved force, drawn largely from NATO countries, maintained a shaky security around the capital. In fact, the role of the Security Council and the associated UN apparatus remained limited and anything but leading.

Iraq II

A year after the September 11 terrorist attacks, in an address to the General Assembly, President George W. Bush reiterated an accusation that Iraq threatened the peace, because it defied the Security Council's demand to destroy weapons of mass destruction. In hardly veiled words, he warned that the United States, if necessary alone, intended to bring Iraq into conformity with UN policy. This began the complex series of steps to lead to the admission of UNMOVIC, resumption of inspection and eventually an American-mounted renewed military campaign that brought down the Saddam Hussein government.

Before that time, the UN involvement with Iraq continued with meetings and decisions in the Security Council and energetic inspections by UNMOVIC which was invited by Iraq to begin its work shortly after the September 11 attacks. The key Security Council decision came in November 2002 with the unanimous adoption of resolution 1441. This held that Iraq was in 'material breach' of earlier resolutions which had been taken under Chapter VII of the Charter. Iraq was told that it had 'final opportunity to comply' in disarming and that it would face 'serious consequences' if it interfered with inspections by UNMOVIC and IAEA. Meanwhile, the United States with the help especially of Great Britain began to prepare a military force that could be used against Iraq.

Before year's end, British Prime Minister Tony Blair in Parliament offered a 'dossier', based on intelligence, to support the claim that Iraq possessed weapons of mass destruction (WMD) and was prepared to use them. Early in 2003, U.S. Secretary of State Colin Powell, speaking in a high-level Security Council meeting, supported these claims and added more frightening details from intelligence reports. Meantime, UNMOVIC began producing a series of reports which indicated no discovery of WMD in Iraq, although the cooperation of the Iraqi government still remained unsatisfactory.

At the same time, it became ever clearer that the United States-led military buildup would soon reach a level permitting a heavy attack on Iraq. The U.S. government, moreover, claimed that Iraq had connections with the al-Qaeda terrorist movement. In the national political arena, some leaders demanded new reference of the situation to the United Nations, while the US government showed much reluctance to submit its decisions about Iraq to consideration by the Security Council. It insisted, rather, that inspection in the field proved nothing. Nevertheless, the United States and the United Kingdom, both reflecting demands voiced within their national forums, sought a new resolution to complement Resolution 1441 with more explicit authorization for the use of force. It soon became obvious that most Security Council members and many other governments, not part of the Council, that took advantage of the practice open to UN members to appear in debates, opposed such a resolution. They pleaded for continuing inspection by UNMOVIC and attempted to calm the building crisis. The United States and the United Kingdom and their supporters insisted that Resolution 1441 authorized the use of force but that it would be desirable to extend its reach.

On 19 March 2003, the United States and its allies began their military campaign against Iraq, beginning with heavy aerial bombardment. Within weeks, resistance by Iraqi forces disintegrated. The United States military forces began organizing a governing authority. By May, the Security Council agreed to the appointment of a Special

Representative of the Secretary-General, which signaled at least some renewed cooperation in Iraq on both humanitarian and political issues. Economic sanctions against Iraq were halted. But the direct involvement of the UN staff soon was reversed by the bombing of the UN building in Baghdad in August. It killed the UN Special Representative, Sergio Vieira de Mello, who had been UN High Commissioner for Human Rights and an experienced field official, and 22 others. Secretary-General Annan withdrew the UN staff until security was restored; until early 2005, only a skeleton representation was in place. The humanitarian activities which the Security Council had supported with encouragement from the Secretary-General operated only at a slow pace in most of the country.

The Security Council, meanwhile, denounced the attack on UN personnel and passed resolutions to support the creation of an elected Iraqi government. The elections took place in January 2005 with some UN assistance. In fact, the UN role during the transition from war through occupation to a new government was limited both by lack of security and unwillingness on the part of the United States to deepen international collaboration on Iraq.

Meantime persistent rumors of corruption and irregularity in the oil-for-food program that had preceded the second Iraq war gave rise to demands from some political personalities in Washington for Annan's resignation. The United States officially stated that it found no reason for Annan to step down. Before then, the Secretary-General created a special independent commission to investigate. By early 2005 a preliminary report confirmed some irregularities and two senior staff members who had been in charge were subjected to disciplinary action. It was clear, however, that leading persons in the Saddam Hussein government had been able to divert very large sums from oil sales intended for relief.

Frustrations in Middle East

A decade after the invasion of Kuwait, the destruction of the Taliban government and the aftermath of a second round of armed conflict in Iraq, the Middle East was anything but a stable, pacific part of the world. The first invasion of Kuwait, despite wide accord in the United Nations, itself had deeply disturbed the region. Although the Security Council meticulously avoided linking the Arab-Israeli dispute to what happened in Kuwait, nevertheless political groups and the governments in the area insisted that two issues were bound together. The

United States government, moreover, took advantage of the upset relationships in the area to take a series of initiatives in the Arab-Israeli dispute. A series of diplomatic maneuvers outside UN auspices led to the Oslo agreement in 1993 by which the Palestine Liberation Organization was able to organize a government for part of the occupied territories. That new Palestinian Authority, still restricted in function and scope until negotiations with Israel would be concluded, got considerable aid through the UN system. But a durable peace remained only a distant aspiration after the peace-minded Israeli government of Prime Minister Yitzhak Rabin, who had been assassinated by an extremist Israeli youth, was succeeded by more intransigent coalitions. The death in late 2004 of the head of the Palestine Authority, the veteran Palestinian leader Yasser Arafat, appeared to offer new diplomatic opportunities. At the same time, the unpopularity of the United States in the area raised questions about how it could exert the leadership that earlier had at times assisted negotiations. By early 2005, however, the Washington government was once more pressing for Palestine-Israeli accords, while Secretary-General Annan emphasized their necessity.

Uniting for peace

Using the Security Council and action under Chapter VII of the Charter is not the only conceivable route to the use of coercion to maintain peace. After it became obvious in the autumn of 1950 that decision-making in the Security Council could be frozen solid by a permanent member, the United States sought a way around the veto that was embodied in the 'Uniting for Peace' resolution (see Chapter 2). In essence, Uniting for Peace was intended to mirror the collective security system by substituting recommendations of the General Assembly for directives by the Security Council.

When the Security Council was prevented from acting because of a veto by a permanent member, any seven (later nine) members or a majority of the General Assembly could summon an emergency special session of the Assembly. This could meet within 24 hours. The procedure made it possible by a two-thirds majority to label a member as a violator of the Charter. From there, the Assembly could recommend coercive sanctions against the violator. The member states that could provide military forces in such circumstances were asked to set them aside for possible UN use. The use of these forces would be planned by a Collective Measures Committee of the General Assembly.

Adoption of the Uniting for Peace Resolution really signified a fundamental alteration of the UN Charter but not according to the formal provisions for amendment (Art. 108–109). Supporters of this resolution, however, denied that it violated the Charter. In any case, it was clear that Uniting for Peace could shift important functions in maintaining peace from the Security Council to the General Assembly. There, the United States and its allies could count on a majority until the growing new membership changed the political configuration.

Because of Soviet and other opposition initially, the Uniting for Peace procedure has been used only sparingly and occasionally. Later, the Soviet Union softened its position and began to accept the permissibility of some such activities by the General Assembly. At the same time, the United States had become more reluctant to trust the General Assembly. Meanwhile, the non-aligned countries repeatedly demonstrated the ability to dominate the General Assembly and summoning special sessions found some favor as a device to dramatize particular issues, such as those related to the situation in Palestine.

The role of the General Assembly always is conditioned by the use of the Security Council, which has varied a great deal. During the early 1960s, it was kept busy, but then a long eclipse ensued. Beginning about 1987, however, it began a new period of energetic activity that lasted well into the next decade. It was encouraged by growing cooperation between the United States and the Soviet Union that followed President Gorbachev's endorsement of the value of multilateral institutions. An ultimately unfruitful symbol of its resurgence was a meeting of the Council attended by heads of state or government in January 1992, when the newly-elected Secretary-General Boutros Boutros-Ghali took office. He was instructed to report on methods for strengthening the maintenance of peace, but UN member governments gave it only partial effect. Other studies followed, including one on peace-keeping in 2000 by Lakhdar Brahimi that foresaw administrative and policy reforms. Some of the Brahimi recommendations were carried out. As many issues remained unresolved. Secretary-General Annan took the initiative in 2003 to appoint a high-level commission to study ways of strengthening the organization generally; its far-reaching findings that included proposals for the expansion of the Security Council membership were to be discussed at a Security Council summit in 2005.

The development of Uniting for Peace, its occasional use and the variations in the political readiness of the Security Council to act often made the separation between its jurisdiction and that of the Assembly vague and unpredictable. The Security Council remained the readiest instrument for responding at once to crises. The General Assembly could more easily deal with long, slowly maturing political issues. Neither could be fully reliable, whatever the tactics, in a complicated, rapidly changing world political environment.

Hybrid forms of peace-keeping

After the general success of the expanded forms of peace-keeping in Cambodia, Mozambique and Namibia, the Security Council created missions which implied use of considerable force along with conciliatory mechanisms. The results were mixed, both in the short and longer term, and some produced much controversy in the governments that furnished troops and other resources.

Somalia

The collapse of a dictatorial government and violent encounters among local war lords led in 1991 to famine in parts of Somalia and refugees in the surrounding countries of northeast Africa. In the midst of the chaos and the fighting in much of the country, UN agencies and NGOs could not operate to help the thousands of hungry and homeless people. Dismal reports and television pictures preceded a decision by the Security Council to send out a peace-keeping force titled UNOSOM of some 500 soldiers from Pakistan.

The local chieftain promptly shackled UNOSOM to the harbor area of Mogadishu, the capital and principal port. After yet more television pictures of pitiable suffering, the United States government produced a new situation by sending a military force of 28,000 to Somalia. The Security Council endorsed this action as a means of bringing help. It decided to create UNOSOM II to include the Americans and add another 10,000 soldiers from elsewhere.

The new device for dealing with Somalia and its successors with similar duties no longer had the familiar character of a peace-keeping force. The Security Council chose enforcement under Chapter VII of the Charter as a means of reacting forcefully to breaches of a case-fire demanded from local Somali bands. The UN approach to fighting in Somalia therefore differed sharply from either the original peace-keeping model or that of Cambodia.

Despite its use of force to reply to violations of the peace, UNOSOM II witnessed new outbreaks during 1993. Its soldiers came under fire that killed some. This soon became a crisis after an American unit, acting outside the UN command structure, fell into an ambush that killed 18 men. The United States soon withdrew its troops, the largest component of the force. Discouraged by the American reversal, the Security Council ended the entire mission in summer of 1994. After that, despite continuing hazardous conditions and the absence of real governmental authority, NGOs and some UN agencies continued to supply help to Somali civilians.

Yugoslavia

The many-sided UN response to a turbulent situation in what had been Yugoslavia during the 1990s differed even more from the original model of peace-keeping than Cambodia or Somalia. Like the action in the Somalia, what was done in former Yugoslavia had a political back-lash in several countries contributing to the UN activities. It eventually brought the involvement of NATO, the Organization for Security and Cooperation in Europe (OSCE) and the European Union and left the United Nations with a less comprehensive task.

After news reports gave a shocking vision of fighting, atrocities, 'ethnic cleansing' and fleeing inhabitants within and outside the terri-tories that had made up Yugoslavia, the Security Council began in 1991 to approve a series of resolutions that eventually numbered far more than 100 to deal with an extraordinarily complex, mercurial situ-ation. Part of these envisaged a peace-keeping force with enlarged func-tions, while others fell under enforcement action of Chapter VII of the UN Charter.

Both the UN Secretary-General and the European Union negotiated with the parties. This led to the creation by the Security Council of a UN Protection Force (UNPROFOR), first in Croatia and then in Bosnia-Herzegovina. It included as many as 14,000 soldiers. The Council also set up a complicated system of economic sanctions against the off-ending parties. In Bosnia, UNPROFOR was ordered to protect relief convoys over the road but disposed of neither the authority nor the means to halt armed engagements.

As Slovenia and then Croatia had withdrawn from the former Yugoslav federation, that left Bosnia-Herzegovina as a disputed terri-tory in which Muslims, Croatian Catholics and Serbian Orthodox Christians had once lived side-by-side. The nationalistic tendencies in Croatia as well as Serbia, now the center of what was left of Yugoslavia, impelled communal fighting in Bosnia-Herzegovina as well as claims and counter-claims in the form of military action and diplomatic demands. The attention of the UN forces and the Security Council came to center there. House-to-house fighting in Sarajevo, the capital, and 'ethnic cleansing' elsewhere soon reduced the population to poverty and desperation. The capital, Sarajevo, and some other cities were, according to a Security Council order, to be protected as 'safe havens.'

In practice in the complex strife, sabotage and ethnic cleansing followed each time a sector changed hands. Bosnian Serbs, who organized what they called an independent state, gained special prominence for these tactics, but Croats and Bosnian Moslems hardly avoided them. UN human rights rapporteurs, another wing of the UN response, confirmed grave violations of human rights that included concentration camps, torture, rape of women and children and large-scale murders. Thin on the ground and lightly armed, UNPROFOR soldiers watched in frustration but had neither the orders nor the strength to interfere or to shelter the 'safe havens'. The resulting tens of thousand displaced persons came under the protection and care of the UN High Commissioner for Refugees whose resources could only partly match such demands.

From the outset of the conflict over Bosnia, its government pleaded for military protection from the Bosnian Serbs, who were led by Radovan Karadzič, who was later accused of war crimes. As the Bosnian Serbs had support from the rump Yugoslavia, whose President Slobodan Milosovič disposed of military force from the time of the Cold War, they managed greatly to extend their sphere of control. The Security Council added to an earlier arms embargo a sea blockade and a 'no-fly zone' which was under the surveillance of land-based NATO air forces. The United States stationed strong naval forces in the Adriatic for additional flights.

While these gestures helped only modestly, the United States made it clear that it had no intention of committing ground troops to any intervention in former Yugoslavia. The British and French governments, which had furnished the majority of UNPROFOR troops, made it equally clear that they would not send their lightly armed soldiers into action in what had to become a full-scale military engagement. Nor within the European Union was there any general agreement on further action. Meanwhile, outside of the United Nations, the member governments of NATO decided to employ some of their air power alongside UNPROFOR.

In 1995, the Security Council gave permission to NATO to carry out air attacks on targets in Bosnia, but these could take place only on request of UNPROFOR. Its commanders were hesitant, because every aerial action or other strong gesture led to hostage-taking of UNPRO-FOR soldiers by the Bosnian Serb forces. In one horrific incident in the so-called safe haven of Srbrnica, a light contingent of Dutch peace-keepers, its plea for air strikes refused by higher command, stood by while a Serbian battalion rounded up thousands of Muslim men from among those sheltering in a UN compound as well as elsewhere and later killed them in one of the worst violations of human rights in Europe after World War II.

In successive months, frustrating negotiations among the Bosnian Serbs, the Yugoslav government in Belgrade, the Bosnian government in Sarajevo and the Croatian government took place. In the mountains and valleys of Bosnia-Herzegovina, the conflict continued and the population sunk further under a blanket of misery.

At last, after heavy air attacks and the formation of a British-French-Dutch quick response force in 1995, an intermediary sent from Washington obtained a cease-fire by means of dividing conquered territories among the parties. It was followed by agreements under heavy American pressure among the parties at a marathon negotiating session in Dayton, Ohio. This brought at least a cease-fire to the territories and late in 1995 the end of UNPROFOR. It was replaced by a strong NATO entity, the Implementation Force (IFOR) with a mandate for one year. In turn, it was replaced by a smaller force in a Bosnia that regained at least a modicum of tranquility. The UN had only a narrow political role centered primarily around a small international police unit and the protection of human rights and humanitarian aid. Yet this marked the first instance of cooperation on the ground between NATO units and the United Nations.

Although no anticipated development, the concern with violations of human rights and the international humanitarian law led the Security Council in 1993 to a striking innovation. It was the creation of an *ad hoc* international criminal tribunal to try persons accused of genocide, crimes against humanity and war crimes in former Yugoslavia. Sitting in the Netherlands, the tribunal in 1995 accused a long list of persons, including Karadzič and his military commander, General Mladič, of crimes. The NATO command, however, declined to press for the arrest of the accused, but only to hold them if they were coincidentally encountered.

The former President of the former Yugoslavia, Slobodan Milosevič, was surrendered by the government to the Tribunal in 2002. Since then, he has appeared in lengthy sessions in his own defense. By the end of 2004, there was no certainty on whether or when he would be convicted of the crimes of which he had been accused. Towards the end of 2004, 105 accused had appeared in proceedings before the Tribunal; 53 accused were in custody, 20 arrest warrants had been issued against persons currently at large (including Karadzič and Mladič), 15 accused had been transferred to serve sentence and 11 more sentences had been pronounced. The Tribunal was supposed to wind up its operations in the course of 2008.

In 1998, a statute was adopted by a world conference in Rome for an International Criminal Court, also to be located in The Hague. The Court is mandated to deal with the crime of genocide, crimes against humanity, war crimes, and the crime of aggression (yet to be defined). The Statute entered into force on 1 July 2002. By early 2005 more than 110 states had ratified the statute. However, major states, such as the United States, China, Israel, India and Pakistan indicated that they did not intend to become parties to the Statute.

Rwanda

Rather as with Somalia and Cambodia, horrifying television reports from Rwanda called attention in 1994 to what is widely acknowledged as genocide. This wave of murder accompanied a civil war that the Hutu-dominated government in Kigali framed as an ethnic conflict with the Tutsi minority. An invasion by a Tutsi-dominated army in exile that trained mostly in Uganda turned it into an unmistakable civil war. A small UN observer mission there was almost at once withdrawn over the strenuous protests of its Canadian commander.

After some 800,000 persons mostly identified as Tutsis had been killed by government troops and their followers and 1.5 million others took flight, the Security Council mandated the organization of a peace-keeping force of 5,500 soldiers who were to come primarily from Africa. It took many weeks even to begin with partial manning, because the involved governments could not equip the force. Meanwhile, the invaders drove out the former government and took on the task of restoring order. At this point, more hundreds of thousands, now mostly Hutus, fled from their homes to find shelter mainly in Zaire.

There too a civil war soon broke out as the result of an uprising by a Tutsi-led guerrilla group in the east of the huge country. Within months, it ejected the government from the capital, where the dictatorial General Mobutu had long held sway, and replaced it with one led first by father Laurent Kabila and subsequently by his son . In the east, the Hutu refugees that included some of the leaders of the massacre of their Tutsi neighbors wandered from one temporary bivouac to the next. UNHCR sought to return these refugees while striving to bring them material assistance. The background of ethnic strife and the continued presence of Hutu military chiefs in their ranks made this work slow, frustrating and confused. By 2004, neighboring eastern Zaire, now renamed the Democratic Republic of the Congo, had been occupied at various times by soldiers from Rwanda, Uganda and Zimbabwe and enjoyed nothing like reliable stability despite the posting by the Security Council of a new UN peace force of some 15,000 soldiers. UN development agencies and NGOs were, however, able to return to limited work in an unsettled atmosphere.

Following the example of its action in the Yugoslav case, the Security Council in 1994 created a war crimes tribunal to try those accused of war crimes and genocide in Rwanda. The tribunal, located in Arusha, Tanzania, began working in 1995 but only slowly built up cases and trials. In addition to financial stringency, this tribunal was affected not only by internal administrative confusion but also an at best luke-warm attitude on the part of the Rwandan authorities.

Haiti

Increasing repression and the forcible ejection of the elected President Jean-Bertrand Aristide in 1991 by a military group that originated in the earlier dictatorship soon came to the attention of the United Nations. The Security Council oversaw a number of futile attempts that involved the Secretary-General and the Organization of American States, which was indignant over Aristide's exile, to restore the elected government. Eventually in 1993, Secretary-General Boutros-Ghali proposed to the Council that under Chapter VII it endorse 'all possible means', the formula applied in Iraq, to handle the situation in Haiti. The United States then landed troops in Haiti, a controlling junta withdrew and Aristide was restored to the presidential office.

The Council established a peace-keeping force (UNMIH) to take over from the American forces which withdrew within little more than a year. UNMIH then continued in place along with programs to buildup a new police force and a small, clean military arm. An election took place under the supervision of international observers in 1996. Despite crises and changes in government and changed UN formulas for its missions that remained on the island, it remained doubtful that Haiti would remain stable and able to deal with its aggravated economic and social and associated political difficulties. In 2004, Aristide was indeed again forced by local unrest and outside pressure into exile.

Central America

Unlike other instances of hybrid peace-keeping, the situation in Central America involved no sudden calamities for the people of the region. Rather, simmering, occasionally flaming, civil wars and steady violations of human rights that produced intermittent refugee movements brought about the involvement of the United Nations. The UN role became more prominent when the Nicaraguan civil war of the 1980s gradually ground down and the stream of refugees from violations of human rights in Honduras, Guatemala and El Salvador increased in visibility. It did not, however, include overt use of force as in Yugoslavia.

On the basis of regional treaties and diplomatic steps by the Secretary-General and staff members, as well as with support from the General Assembly, a UN observer mission for El Salvador (ONUSAL) was created in the early 1980s. Its task was to oversee conformity to human rights standards and the reform of the police and army on the heels of the election of a civilian government. For a decade earlier, hit squads emanating from the military had terrorized villages.

Other UN activities in the region included witnessing the validity of an election in Nicaragua that resulted in the peaceful replacement of the revolutionary Sandanista government with a more moderate presidency. UNHCR had a steady task in protecting and caring for refugees from the region, many of whom were returned to their homes. The UN Development Program offered coordinated support to the refugee program and also to the rebuilding of El Salvador economy.

The Security Council capitalized on these gains by extending and broadening the mandate of ONUSAL, which helped with the observation of more national elections. At the same time, it assisted the governments with improving human rights in Honduras and Guatemala. By the end of the 1990s, no peace-keeping mission was in the region although coordinated UN concern with development, human rights and refugees continued.

Second thoughts on peace-keeping

During the decade of the 1990s, when peace-keeping activities reached a high point, especially the wider forms of the enterprise also encountered increasing criticism. By the mid-1990s, a high point, nearly 80,000 military personnel were in action on behalf of the United Nations throughout the world. Some missions got little attention from the media, such as those in Angola or Georgia. Others were of a bigger scale, larger than anything before in the history of international organization.

Most of these UN engagements, however, did not deal with inter-state conflicts as envisaged by those who wrote the UN Charter. Rather, the peace-keepers were occupied with civilian fighters, ethnic conflicts and humanitarian missions in social and physical disasters.

The existence of so many peace-keeping ventures evidenced some confidence in what they could accomplish. But their establishment and instructions followed no coherent pattern with regard to when and how they should be used. Even the report, *Agenda for Peace*, put together by Secretary-General Boutros-Ghali at the request of a Security Council meeting of heads of governments in 1991, produced no unified, defined approach by national governments. Some cynical observers even alleged that the multiple peace-keeping missions had more to do with shedding national responsibilities than with clear-minded proceedings and goals. In any case, peace-keeping ventures produced their own share of political controversies in national capitals as well as in UN organs.

The inherently contentious political content of most peace-keeping decisions was deepened by the way in which the UN Secretariat led them. A tiny few UN officials were saddled with a rapid expansion of tasks along with slender financial resources. The earlier, relatively straight-forward, sharply defined missions gave way in the 1990s to increasingly complex demands and goals. Some of the new peace-keeping, as in Somalia and to some extent Yugoslavia, involved direction of actual war-making. For this, the UN staff had never been equipped. Since then, however, both the Secretariat facilities for military counsel and for political analysis have been augmented as part of a reorganization mounted by Secretary-General Annan.

What occurred in Somalia and in Yugoslavia had raised new doubts, especially in military circles, about the worth of any UN peace-keeping, old or new style. Some of the skepticism was rooted in the command and control functions in the peace-keeping incidents. Unease about the peace-keeping operations impelled Secretary-General Annan in 2000 to appoint a commission led by Lakhdar Brahimi, a senior Algerian ambassador with much experience in UN affairs, to investigate practices and their direction and to recommend changes. The commission urged more precise, workable mandates and better analytical facilities in UN headquarters, as well as other reforms. Some of these were put into practice by the Secretary-General, but others depended on commitments by member governments in the Security Council and elsewhere in the UN structure.

Although the Secretary-General had the formal command of ventures that were not based on Chapter VII of the Charter and appointed the field command, officers of national units often sought advice or permission from their own governments before carrying out UN orders. The United States, which furnished the most important military elements in Somalia and Haiti and had been the UN command in Korea and Iraq I, insisted that American soldiers should never serve under foreign military command. This conformed to doctrine in the United States forces and to demands from the U.S. Congress. It also meant that American elements were not available for service on the ground in some of the most trying peace operations.

The use of military units in UN operations, moreover, ran up huge bills compared to normal budgets. In some years, peace-keeping operations cost more than the rest of the UN budget. In the five years before 1995, for instance, the cost of peace-keeping increased by a factor of eight. These costs were hardly met by contributions from member governments, but those of rich lands were assessed considerably higher percentages than the rest. That led to increasing criticism from the United States and West European governments that, as earlier, opposed increases in the UN budget and criticized UN costs generally. Furthermore, the United States adopted laws in 1995 that led to a reduction of the American contribution. As the United States and some other countries lagged in paying up their obligatory contributions, peace-keeping, successful or not, helped build up the financial crisis that eternally pressed on the United Nations.

Limits and potentials in maintaining peace

More than 50 years of experience with pacific settlement of disputes and nearly that much with peace-keeping forces can be summed up in a few rather solid conclusions. The first of them consists of two generalizations that color all the rest. First, the settlement of international disputes, and even cooling them off, remains a slow process in which the time-honored methods of diplomacy figure large. The second is that the pacific settlement mechanism that includes Chapter VI of the UN Charter, the activities of the Secretary-General and the political atmosphere developed especially by the General Assembly still depend mainly on willingness of disputants to use it. Other conclusions include the following:

1. The use of peace-keeping forces links to what Hammarskjöld called 'preventive diplomacy' – using the UN and especially the Secretary-General to prevent the worsening of a dispute and its broadening into a great power confrontation. In fact, preventive diplomacy and peace-keeping require some cooperation, or at least acquiescence from governments disposing of important military and economic power. During the Cold War, this meant especially from the United States and the Soviet Union; later China, Germany and Japan were often added to the list. They must define their interests in such a way as to keep their distance and also to allow the Security Council to bring the peace-keeping force into being. UNEF fulfilled these conditions. ONUC did at first, but the later discord demonstrated how damaging increasing demands for influence by the great powers, each of whom backed an opposed camp in the internal strife, could become both to peace-keeping and the leadership of the Secretary-General.

2. If the United Nations actually does use force (as in Korea or Kuwait and to some extent in Somalia and Yugoslavia), it has to be strong enough to accomplish its aim quickly. If it does not, its credibility declines and the operations suffer. In case force is used, the Secretary-General may be excluded from substantial participation. If he is given substantial responsibility, he has to have acceptance by the Security Council or the General Assembly of his own interpretation of his authority. That means the Secretary-General has in some manner to maintain the confidence of the majority of members, including some with broad influence, in his decisions. The principles Hammarskjöld set out for his policies still offer a benchmark for peace-keeping. Moreover, the Secretary-General uses these principles as a basis for negotiations with the disputants and the contributing governments that resemble. His task then is that of a governmental leader or a very senior diplomat, rather than that of an international civil servant whose every move must be approved. He has, for example, to

- assemble contributions to a military force;
- arrange for its safe passage;
- obtain permission from the disputants for its emplacement;
- find a means of financing the operation;
- appoint a commander;
- provide political and administrative backup;
- and explain the progress, or lack of it, to the Security Council.

Moreover, the Secretary-General may step into swampy political ground in selecting from offers of forces. Hammarskjöld barred the use of great power troops. Later, however, British troops were kept on in Cyprus to help with peace-keeping, French soldiers served in UNIFIL, and Soviet and Eastern European military men have taken up UN duties in the Middle East and in Yugoslavia and American troops made up most of the initial force in Haiti. Nevertheless, the host governments must consent to the presence of any foreign troops, the choice of which may pose a crucial issue.

3. Several important legal problems concerning peace-keeping remain unsolved. The first of these concerns the degree of obligation that rests on member states after decisions to set up a peace-keeping force are taken by either the General Assembly or the Security Council. Then, if a government does provide troops, it is not clear whether it has the right to withdraw them without consent from the UN organ responsible for the force. Finally, the right of a government, on whose territory a peace-keeping force is deployed, to end its operation is not clear. An agreement is worked out between the host country and the UN that defines some of these rights, but unanticipated political reasons easily reopen uncertainties.

4. UNEF and, even more, UNFICYP and UNIFIL illustrate how temporary arrangements in international politics have a tendency to continue so long as to seem permanent. The presence of a buffer between warring parties can indeed help to maintain international peace but does not necessarily resolve the dispute so that further outbreaks can be avoided permanent. Thus, peace-keeping differs from peace-making.

Arms control and weapons of mass destruction

The authors of the UN Charter thought that the creation of stable international society would reduce the need for national armament. To the degree that the Security Council could insure international peace and security, the chances would increase for world-wide arms control. Thus, disarmament – or at least arms control – was set out as principal aim of the new organization.

Few concepts have occupied so much UN time and effort and delivered so fragmentary results as arms control and disarmament. With the exception of treaties on nuclear non-proliferation and the control of arms on the seabed, almost all international agreements on armaments until Gorbachev's vast alterations of Soviet policy concerned secondary issues. Before and after that, the great powers tended to keep their negotiations outside of the UN framework. Actual control of the general level of armaments through an international organization, thus, remains a distant ideal. Meanwhile, the fire power of national governments, even those of poor countries, increased as never before.

However limited the results in terms of the overall arms control issue, both the General Assembly and the Security Council have made a long series of gestures towards carrying out their duties under Articles 11 and 28 of the UN Charter. Under them, the General Assembly may consider general principles of maintaining peace, including disarmament and arms control; the Security Council has responsibility for setting up a system of regulation of armaments.

Almost immediately after its establishment, the United Nations began exploring possibilities of arms control. Equally soon, it appeared that the Soviet Union and the United States would not accept regulations that reduced their military strength or its further development. So long as those attitudes prevailed, UN efforts would be limited to formulation of general principles, furnishing a forum for discussing the problem and striving for limited arms control agreements.

The early, tone-setting debates took place in the Atomic Energy Commission, established in 1946, by the General Assembly, and in the Commission on Conventional Armaments, set up in 1947, as the result of an initiative by the Security Council. In both these limited-membership bodies, efforts to create effective control systems were frustrated by the attitude of the major powers and the Cold War. Both organs were dissolved in 1952 and replaced with the UN Disarmament Commission, to which all UN members eventually belonged; it reported to the General Assembly. Besides, in 1961, the General Assembly set up the Eighteen-Nation Disarmament Commission with the hope that this smaller body could organize a workable system of arms control. Seven years later, it too disappeared and all discussions were carried in a new UN Conference on Disarmament in Geneva. It reports to the General Assembly and remains the most important global forum for debating trends in arms control and disarmament. In the 1990s, its agenda included the banning of nuclear weapon testing; the end of nuclear proliferation and dismantling of weapons; prevention of a nuclear war; preventing the use of outer space for nuclear arms; effective security for non-nuclear powers from the use of nuclear weapons; control of new kind of weapons of mass destruction and radiation weapons; a general program of disarmament; and transparency with regard to arms.

In addition, the General Assembly has summoned three special sessions, in 1978, 1982 and 1988, on disarmament. These stimulated a great deal of public attention and adopted a series of resolutions that fueled more discussion in the General Assembly without reaching much the desired goal.

Non-proliferation

Taking the position that the spread of nuclear weapons endangers the world, the General Assembly in 1968 approved the text of the treaty to limit further proliferation. The treaty had the backing of both the Soviet Union and the United States. It came into effect in 1970 for the states that ratify it. It was extended in 1995 for an indefinite period. The treaty obliges nuclear states not to furnish such weapons or means of making them to non-nuclear powers. Moreover, the nuclear powers pledged to develop security guarantees for non-nuclear signatories and to negotiate on nuclear and other disarmament. Altogether more than 180 governments, including China and France which long hesitated, have adhered to the treaty. Yet a number of countries which could be assumed to have such weapons, including, Israel, India, Pakistan and Brazil, have declined to accept the treaty. North Korea withdrew its earlier ratification and in 2005 claimed that it had nuclear weapons.

Preparation of the non-proliferation treaty led to the SALT and later the START talks between the Soviet Union and the United States with a view to limiting armaments on both sides. These began outside the UN framework and by the 1990s produced quite real reductions in arms in Europe. In 1991, after a decade of talks, the American and Soviet presidents signed an agreement to reduce the number and type of nuclear weapons in their arsenals. Parallel negotiations between NATO and the Warsaw Treaty Organization also achieved considerable success. In these circumstances, UN discussions may have helped keep governments that did not take part in the European talks better informed and able to submit their reactions. Thus, the UN disarmament approach at least helped in forming a political atmosphere that favors arms reduction.

Ban on nuclear testing

A treaty to ban all testing of nuclear devices was for years a controversial proposal in the General Assembly. It was finally adopted in 1996 and by the following year was accepted by some 150 governments. Before the General Assembly approval in 1996, a limited test-ban treaty was in effect for much of the world, but even it had not prevented much-criticized atmospheric tests in 1995 by France and China. These attracted so much popular opposition they probably encouraged the adoption of the UN comprehensive test ban treaty.

Demilitarized and nuclear-free zone

The notion of forbidding dangerous nuclear activities in several defined places has won the support of the General Assembly. One of these is outer space and another Antarctica. Specific treaty provisions covering both of these were recommended by the General Assembly and have entered into force for signatories. A UN convention is also in force to prohibit the emplacement of nuclear weapons on the deep sea bed. The General Assembly also has recommended treaties barring nuclear weapons in Latin America, while 12 South Pacific states developed a treaty, endorsed by the General Assembly in 1986, to limit nuclear weapons and testing activities. Similar attempts have been made with regard to the Indian Ocean, Africa and the Middle East and East Asia.

Chemical and biological weapons

Since 1975, a convention approved by the General Assembly has been in force to prohibit the manufacture or use of biological weapons, although some of the main potential users have never acceded to it. An earlier convention, dating from 1925 and supervised by the International Committee of the Red Cross, bans the use of chemical weapons. In the early 1990s, complex negotiations led to a convention consolidating early laws. It forbids the production, possession, stockpiling and distribution of chemical weapons. The majority of UN members have signed but not some of those few suspected of continued reliance on chemical weapons.

A related topic of control concerned prohibiting the use of landmines directed against personnel. It was the object of a world-wide campaign, supported by some governments but led by NGOs, that received the Nobel Peace Prize in 1997. In that year, an international convention on the prohibition of anti-personnel mines was concluded. It entered into force in 1999. Parties to it undertake never under any circumstances to use such mines or to develop, produce and trade in them. Moreover, they undertake to destroy all anti-personnel mines and report on the measures they have taken. By 2004, there were 141 states parties to the Convention, excluding, however, such major powers as the United States, the Russian Federation and China.

Altogether these conventions form a web of controls on important aspects of arms control. Ratifying states accept obligations to respect these controls. Yet it is obvious that they did not extend far enough to stem an enormous arms race that continued almost without pause from the end of the Second World War to the late 1980s. Responsibility for either the arms race of the lack of control over armaments can hardly be laid at the UN door. Only national governments, acting on their own or jointly, can stop producing or buying weapons or using them. The United Nations offered a forum for negotiation and discussions. These provide reference points for national policy. If the results were modest, so were the intentions of leading governments with regard to the UN process.

Conclusion

Very soon after the establishment of the United Nations, it was clear that the system of collective security as envisaged failed to operate. Attempts to use the organization to maintain peace, moreover, raised the query as to whether the system could work at all or, if it did work, would produce satisfactory results.

The proximate cause of the failure of collective security – a system that calls for the use of coercion when the Charter is violated – lay in the antagonistic relationship and view of the world of the Soviet Union and the United States. These two great powers could most easily sustain the costs of ignoring the United Nations and the collectivity of states it implied. If either of them had started a war against the other, the United Nations would have been brushed aside as futile. When one or other supported a party to a conflict, the organization encountered great difficulty in delivering the promises of its Charter.

Sometimes, however, the United Nations produced useful results during violent conflicts. On occasion, it used coercive methods or the suggestion of ultimate coercion. An international force was mounted in Korea, according to the decision of the Security Council and with support from the General Assembly. The United Nations did assemble the needed support for UNEF. The superpowers agreed to open the ONUC chapter; it closed with forceful measures. They and their fellow governments employed the organization in the Iran-Iraq war and in ending the Afghanistan invasion. The Security Council acted to give legitimacy to the US-led effort to turn back the Iraqi invasion of Kuwait. The United Nations achieved its aim in Namibia without the use of force (see above). It helped in the struggle over Zimbabwe's independence (see Chapter 5). It had a role in adjusting the politics of Central America at the end of the 1980s. At least it called attention to the massive violations of human rights in Yugoslavia, even if it could not prevent them, and established war crimes tribunals to judge suspects from Serbia/Montenegro and Bosnia-Herzegovina and Rwanda. In fact, the UN presence was hardly ever entirely absent, and sometimes was leading, in dealing with a long series of international conflicts.

Yet the accent in maintaining the peace through the United Nations never was on the use of force. The entire system, rather, depended almost always on peace-making and peace-keeping by consent. No UN army ever existed and perhaps never will. Even had there been such a force at the disposal of the Security Council, its use would be intended to return the parties to the methods of pacific settlement. It seems likely to remain so as long as national governments dispose of armed forces and the doctrine that they make their own decisions.

In fact, it would be difficult to find a single member state whose government would under all circumstances respect Article 2 (4) of the UN Charter which forbids the use of force against the territorial integrity and independence of any other state. Moreover, any government can try to defend its use of force under the self-defense provisions of Article 51. These facts ensure that maintaining peace has to depend on the cooperation and consent of governments. In case of a conflict, the best reaction from the point of view of keeping the peace usually would be to stop the fighting. If the disputants discern that neither can fully achieve its goal, then they can perhaps be brought to settling their dispute or at least not to spread it to other countries. Peace-keeping forces usually signal that a great majority of governments in fact supports an end to fighting and a resumption of pacific settlement. This signal gains intensity by the fact that military units may be employed for non-coercive purposes, as was the case with UNEF and with UNFICYP.

The good offices and mediation of the Secretary-General, which again in the late 1980s began to achieve the prestige of Hammarskjöld's time, relies exclusively on non-coercive approaches. One way or another, the parties to conflicts have found ways to accede to the Secretary-General's suggestions. Kofi Annan, moreover, reorganized the staff to give more efficient accent to systematic evaluation of political developments and to useful responses to conflicts and humanitarian emergencies.

If fundamental conflicts among UN members and among their people remain, perhaps the time gained by peace-keeping and other methods of pacific settlement could ultimately resolve more conflicts. If not, at least in the short run, human lives have been spared and even more misery avoided.

5
Human Rights and Decolonization

The contemporary concern for human rights is inextricably linked to their violation by the German National Socialists as well as the weak reaction from abroad from 1933 until their defeat in World War II. The inhumanity of the Nazis and their allies, including the Italian Fascists before the war, culminated in an explicit program to exterminate Jews, gypsies, homosexuals and other 'subhuman species', especially in the German occupied territories. One of the purposes of the newly established United Nations was to see to it that this was never to happen again.

Unlike the League of Nations Covenant, the UN Charter contains specific articles on human rights. One of the principal purposes of the organization (UN Charter Art. 1, 3) is to achieve international cooperation to promote and encourage respect for human rights and fundamental freedoms for all without distinction as to race, sex, language, or religion. Accordingly, an elaborate set of powers and aims is set out by the UN Charter. The General Assembly initiates studies and make recommendations to governments (Article 13). To further the general welfare, the organization was enjoined to promote universal respect for, and observance of, human rights and fundamental freedoms for all without distinction as to race, sex, language or religion (Article 55). Its members pledge themselves with the organization to take joint and separate cooperative action for this purpose (Article 56). The Economic and Social Council (ECOSOC) may make recommendations for the purpose of promoting respect for, and observance of, human rights and fundamental freedoms (Article 62, paragraph 2). This general authority was supplemented with the specific requirement that the Economic and Social Council organize a commission for the promotion of human rights (Article 68). A related aim of the Trusteeship System is to encourage respect for human rights and fundamental freedoms (Article 76).

For the first time in history, the United Nations formulated fundamental human rights for all mankind. Earlier efforts had been only on a national scale, as in post-revolutionary France and in the newly independent United States. Building on these national standards, the ambitious new UN work began in 1946, when the Commission on Human Rights was created. Its presiding officer for the first few years was Eleanor Roosevelt, the widow of the United States President – a powerful personality in her own right. The Economic and Social Council instructed the new commission to develop proposals for:

- an international bill of rights;
- international declarations or conventions relating to civil liberties, the status of women, freedom of information, and similar matters;
- the protection of minorities; the prevention of discrimination on grounds of race, sex, language, or religion;
- any other matter concerning human rights.

The Commission on Human Rights meets annually for six weeks. Enlarged over the years, it includes representatives of 53 states, elected for three-year terms by the General Assembly. They are elected according to the following political-geographical distribution: Africa: 15; Asia: 12; Latin America and the Caribbean: 11; Eastern Europe: 5; Western Europe and other states: 10. It has a broad mandate touching on any matter relating to human rights. The Commission carries out studies, usually drafted by rapporteurs or by the Office of the High Commissioner for Human Rights in Geneva, which is a division of the UN Secretariat. It drafts international instruments relating to human rights for ratification by governments. It also undertakes special tasks assigned by the General Assembly or the Economic and Social Council. It investigates allegations of violations of human rights, and receives and processes communications related to such violations.

Under what is called the '1503 procedure', the Commission deals in closed meetings with confidential communications about violations of human rights. Private complaints are discussed first in the Sub-Commission on the Promotion and Protection of Human Rights. If that body concludes that there seems to be 'a consistent pattern of gross and reliably attested violations of human rights', it refers the complaint to the Commission, which may then investigate further. The fact that such complaints are dealt with may have a certain corrective effect, the more so because it is common practice that the chairman of the Commission will announce, after the meeting, the names of the states that have been discussed under the 1503 procedure.

In its public meetings, the Commission may discuss human rights situations in all parts of the world. ECOSOC resolution 1235 (adopted in 1967) allows both members and non-members of the Commission to call attention to violations of human rights anywhere. This may lead to resolutions with recommendations to be submitted to ECOSOC and to the General Assembly. It may also lead to further study of the problem, for example by a working group or special rapporteur. The latter possibility has been widely used by the Commission by the appointment of rapporteurs on several countries. These have included in the past such countries as Afghanistan, Iran and Iraq. Nowadays they include Belarus, Burundi, the Democratic Republic Congo, Myanmar/Burma, North Korea, and the Occupied Palestine Territories. Independent experts deal with Afghanistan, Haiti, Liberia, Somalia, Sudan, and Chad, while the Secretary-General has appointed personal representatives on Cambodia and Cuba.

Furthermore, the Commission has appointed rapporteurs on special themes, such as summary and arbitrary executions, torture, religious intolerance, mercenaries, freedom of opinion and expression, the independence of judges and lawyers, the sale of children, child prostitution and child pornography, contemporary forms of racism, racial discrimination and xenophobia, violence against women, internally displaced persons, missing persons in the Former Yugoslavia, and toxic wastes. Working groups deal with the problem of involuntary disappearances and with arbitrary detention. Their reports are discussed by the Commission in public meetings. Increasingly, the Security Council asks rapporteurs to submit their reports to it.

The Commission may invite representatives of non-member states or liberation movements to take part in its deliberations on a nonvoting basis. UN Specialized Agencies and certain other intergovernmental organizations also may take part in discussions on topics of concern to them. Finally, a unique feature of the Commission on Human Rights is that representatives of non-governmental organizations (NGOs) with consultative status are seated on the floor of the Commission. They have the right to address the Commission, and to have written statements circulated as UN documents.

The Commission also takes up the annual reports of the Sub-Commission on the Promotion and Protection of Human Rights. Its

26 members are selected in their personal capacity, although some retain rather close relations with their governments. Notwithstanding its name, the Sub-Commission deals with studies on a broad range of human rights, which it submits to the Commission. The Sub-Commission has also an important role in the initial phase of the earlier-noted 1503-procedure.

In the past, tensions developed between the two bodies. Many members of the Commission held that the Sub-Commission should not make pronouncements on the human rights situation in specific countries (as it used to do) but limit itself to its task of preparing studies for consideration by the Commission. Although they may have a formal point, as government representatives, they use their status to deplore the fact that certain members of the Sub-Commission, who are often both human rights experts and activists, tend to favor victims of human rights violations. But the Sub-Commission has also received criticism from academics, who have argued that it should focus its energies on existing implementation procedures, helping the treaty bodies with studies they cannot do themselves and suggesting countries with urgent human rights problems that have not previously been the subject of adequate attention under the 1235 public procedure. In 2000, the Commission decided that the Sub-Commission could henceforth only deal with country situations that were not being dealt with by the Commission itself. Decisions to undertake studies were subjected to a more rigid system of approval. Since then, tensions between the two bodies have considerably decreased.

Apart from the controversial content of its agenda, the Commission has often been the butt of criticism for the customary choice of its presiding officer. As the membership of the Commission is elected by the General Assembly on the basis of geographical criteria, the routine diplomatic practice of rotation has put representatives of known violators of human rights in the chair of presiding officer. This stimulates charges that UN members are guided more by cynicism than by the Charter in handling human rights issues.

The Universal Declaration of Human Rights

By adopting the Universal Declaration of Human Rights on 10 December 1948, the United Nations took its first capital step of practical importance in the field of human rights. Drafted by the Commission on Human Rights, the Declaration was accepted by the General Assembly by 48 votes in favor, none against and eight abstentions (the Soviet

Union, Byelorussia, the Ukraine, Poland, Czechoslovakia, Yugoslavia, Saudi Arabia and South Africa). Not legally binding, its preamble proclaims it a 'common standard of achievement' for all peoples and all nations. It has become the foundation for establishing obligatory legal norms to govern international behavior with regard to rights of individuals. It has shifted some of the emphasis of international law from its concern exclusively with the state to greater attention to individual people. It has inspired and stimulated thinking and the formation of private groups, and has served as a model for national constitutional protection of persons.

Roughly three categories of rights can be distinguished in the Universal Declaration. First, certain articles relate to the physical and spiritual integrity of the human person. These rights include that of life; the prohibition of slavery or servitude, torture, cruel, inhuman or degrading treatment or punishment; arbitrary arrest, detention or exile; and freedom of thought, conscience and religion. The second category concerns political life, including the right to freedom of opinion and expression; and peaceful assembly and association and participation in government, directly or through freely chosen representatives. Finally, the Declaration includes social, economic and cultural rights, among which are social security; free choice of employment; just and favorable conditions of work; protection against unemployment; rest and leisure; education; and participation in the cultural life of one's community.

The rights set forth in the Declaration have such deep attractiveness everywhere in the world that few political leaders would admit simply to disregarding them. Most of the individual civil and political rights are familiar as behavioral norms for Western governments, even when practice violates them. Many non-Western states tend to give more emphasis to the importance of social, economic, and cultural rights – sometimes at the expense of civil and political rights. Some developing countries claim a need first to provide the necessities for human survival, such as food, clothing, and shelter. Until such basic needs are met, the argument goes, guaranteeing fundamental civil and political liberties is bound to take second place. Some repressive regimes even defend their violations with the claim that they cannot allow the luxury of civil and political rights so long as the population suffers from underdevelopment. This argument is patently fallacious: it has never been demonstrated that the curtailment of civil or political rights does contribute to economic development. Nor is there any reason to assume that the right not to be tortured or to have a fair trial for an alleged criminal offense interferes with economic development in such countries as Libya or Liberia but does not in the United States. The curtailment of civil rights may contribute mainly to the preservation of the oppressive government itself!

From such arguments both the strength and weakness of the Declaration can be inferred. The document settles no legal obligations on the UN membership. That partly explains why the General Assembly adopted it with relative ease, although the effect of the then recent annihilation of people by the Nazis should not be underestimated. It also helps to explain why many governments that voted for it have in fact done little to give it effectiveness. Furthermore, in 1948, few African and Asian states were members or even independent. Had they been, perhaps other aspects of human rights would have been emphasized. An example is the right of all peoples to self-determination, mentioned as a principle (not a right) in the UN Charter, but not cited in the Declaration. It is, however, contained in the two human rights covenants of 1966, which are binding as legal obligations on the governments that ratify them (see further below).

No government has ever publicly dissociated itself from the Declaration, and indeed the General Assembly, the Secretary-General and other parts of the UN system have repeatedly underlined its significance. Specific reference to it is made in such important resolutions as the Declaration on the Granting of Independence to Colonial Countries and Peoples of 1960, the Declaration on the Elimination of All Forms of Racial Discrimination of 1963; and the Declaration on the Protection of All Persons from Torture and Other Cruel, Inhuman or Degrading Treatment or Punishment of 1975. In 1968, the first World Conference on Human Rights adopted the Proclamation of Teheran in which the Universal Declaration was proclaimed as stating a common understanding of the peoples of the world concerning the inalienable and inviolable rights of all members of the human family and constituting an obligation for the members of the international community. In the Final Declaration of the second World Conference on Human Rights, which was held in Vienna in 1993, the Universal Declaration was named the source of inspiration and the basis for the United Nations in making advances in standard setting as contained in the existing international human rights instruments. Secretary-General Annan has insisted that promotion of human rights should penetrate every UN activity in reforming the system.

In addition to its influence in many national constitutions and on UN policies, the Universal Declaration has inspired the creation of a wide net of new international rules. In the form of multilateral treaties, they have been ratified by a large number of governments and give evidence of the increasing attention that international law pays to individual persons. A topic that has benefited from profound treatment is discrimination and the protection of minorities, for which the Commission on Human Rights originally established its Sub-Commission in 1947. In studies and special reports, the Sub-Commission laid the foundation for preparing a Convention on the Elimination of All Forms of Racial Discrimination that was adopted by the General Assembly in 1965 and to which 169 states have acceded (2004). The Convention established a committee on the elimination of racial discrimination that meets twice a year and reports annually to the General Assembly. The Committee examines the information placed before it by states parties to the convention. From time to time, it comments upon particular situations involving racial discrimination or draws them to the attention of the General Assembly. So far, only 45 states have recognized the competence of the Committee to deal with communications from individuals within the jurisdiction of those states and to prepare proposals and recommendations in regard to such communications.

The international covenants on human rights

The most comprehensive development of the Universal Declaration can be found in the two international covenants on human rights, adopted by the General Assembly in 1966, after extended drafting exercises by the Commission on Human Rights and consultations with governments. These two covenants deal respectively with economic, social and cultural rights, and with civil and political rights.

Like the Universal Declaration, the covenants carry the mark of the political context of their time of birth. The then new influence of the Afro-Asian states led to an emphasis in both documents on the right of all peoples to self-determination. Furthermore, the covenants state that all peoples may, for their own ends, freely dispose of their natural wealth and resources without prejudice to any obligations arising from international economic co-operation that is based on the principle of mutual benefit and international law. 'In no case,' the Covenant on Economic, Social and Cultural Rights proclaims, 'may a people be deprived of its own means of subsistence.' Thus the former colonial countries insisted that nations should be able to govern their own political and economic destinies without imperialistic control.

The covenants further include most of the other rights mentioned in the Universal Declaration, omitting, however, the right to property, the right to nationality, and the right to seek and enjoy asylum. The rights that are mentioned, are given stricter legal form and developed further than in the original document.

In the Covenant on Economic, Social, and Cultural Rights, articles set out the right to work and to fair wages and equal pay for work of equal value. In particular, women are guaranteed conditions of work not inferior to those enjoyed by men. The right of everyone to form labor unions and to choose which he will join is also guaranteed. The document spells out the right of each person to an adequate standard of living for himself and his family. This standard includes food, clothing, and housing. Other rights included in this Covenant cover:

- the enjoyment of the highest standard of physical and mental health;
- the right of everyone to education;
- the right of everyone to take part in cultural life and to enjoy the benefits of scientific progress and its applications; and
- the right to social security, including social insurance.

The classical rights appear in the Covenant on Civil and Political Rights. These include the right to life; to liberty and security of person; to freedom of thought, conscience and religion; to hold opinions without interference; to freedom of expression; and to peaceful assembly. The Covenant specifically forbids torture or cruel, inhuman, and degrading treatment or punishment. Persons arrested by the state have the right, when they are held, to be informed of any charges. A person detained on a criminal charge must be brought promptly before a judge or other authorized officer of justice and tried within a reasonable time or else released. Freedom of movement is also dealt with. Anyone lawfully within the territory of a state is entitled to liberty of movement. Everyone is entitled to leave a country, including his own. The Covenant defines the conditions under which exceptions ('derogations') may be made to the exercise of these rights.

Each of the covenants establishes a method of supervision of compliance by governments. The Covenant on Economic, Social and Cultural Rights requires that parties periodically furnish reports to the UN Secretary-General on the measures they have adopted and progress made in achieving the observance of the included rights. These reports are submitted to the Committee on Economic, Social and Cultural Rights, a committee of eighteen individual experts, which was established in 1985 by the Economic and Social Council. This Committee considers the national reports and submits its findings to ECOSOC for consideration. It may make recommendations of a general nature on these matters to the relevant organs of the Organization. Under the provisions of this Covenant, individuals may not complain directly to an international body about violations of these rights. The Covenant serves as a standard of aspiration and means of judging progress toward a broad list of economic, social, and cultural benefits.

The Covenant on Civil and Political Rights provides for a special permanent supervisory organ. This is the Human Rights *Committee* (to be distinguished from the *Commission* on Human Rights) that consists of 18 persons of high moral character and recognized competence in the field of human rights. Nominated by governments, they serve in their personal capacity. The parties to the Covenant must submit reports to the Committee on any national measures to give effect to the relevant rights and on the progress made in the enjoyment of those rights. A specific authorization obliges the Committee to deal with complaints by a state that another has failed to fulfill its obligations. This procedure is limited to states that have recognized in advance the competence of the committee; so far, this procedure has never been used. Finally, if it adheres to an optional protocol, a government allows its subjects to communicate to the Committee that they are victims of violations by that state of any rights set out in the Covenant. So far, 104 states have acceded to this Optional Protocol (2004). The Committee, after determining that the communication is admissible under the Protocol, must bring it to the attention of the government concerned which is obliged within six months to submit written explanations or statements clarifying the matter and the remedy taken. The Committee then considers the communication in light of all available information and forwards its views to the government and the individual concerned. Over the years, the Committee has built up an important body of case law and has formulated a number of general recommendations that constitute an important source of interpretation of many substantive articles of the Covenant.

Capital punishment, though not explicitly forbidden in the Covenant, is limited to the most serious crimes in accordance with the law in force at the time the crime was committed. It shall not be imposed for crimes committed by persons below eighteen years of age and shall not be carried out on pregnant women. In 1989, the General Assembly, by a vote of 59 in favor, 26 against, with 48 abstentions, adopted a second optional protocol, against the death penalty. States that become parties to it are bound not to carry out executions. Only a limited exception is permitted: states may make reservations when accepting the Protocol, allowing them to use the death penalty 'in time of war pursuant to a conviction for a most serious crime of a military nature committed during wartime'. The large number of votes against (including China, the United States and most Middle Eastern countries) and abstentions shows that abolition of the death penalty is still a controversial issue. The Second Optional Protocol is adhered to by 50 states (2004).

Both human rights covenants were unanimously adopted by the General Assembly and recommended to the members for accession on December 16, 1966. Both entered into force in 1976. By 2004, 152 states had ratified the Covenant on Civil and Political Rights; 92 states had ratified the first Optional Protocol. The other Covenant has been ratified by 149 states. As for the United States, President Carter submitted the covenants for advice and consent to the Senate, which ratified the Covenant on Civil and Political Rights in 1992, with a large number of reservations, interpretations and 'understandings', which greatly limits its impact. In 2001, China ratified the International Covenant on Economic, Social and Cultural Rights. In 1998, it signed, but it has so far not ratified, the International Covenant on Civil and Political Rights.

No UN member, whether a party to the covenants or not, complies with *all* obligations to protect human rights. A steady stream of reports from such non-governmental organizations as Amnesty International, the International Commission of Jurists, and Human Rights Watch brings to light numerous violations of fundamental human rights, especially in the civil and political realm, in many countries. The UN Commission on Human Rights also deals with a full agenda of alleged violations. In recent years, it has looked into charges against among others Afghanistan, Burundi, Cambodia, Equatorial Guinea, Haiti, Indonesia, Iran, Iraq, the Former Yugoslavia, Myanmar, Rwanda, Sudan, the Democratic Republic Congo, and the Occupied Palestine Territories. Many governments have failed during certain stages of the investigation, to cooperate. One of the grounds they adduced was that it intervened in their domestic affairs. Such refusals obviously hamper, but do not prevent, the gathering of evidence.

Whether parties to the covenants or not, governments usually pay lip service to their provisions and the Universal Declaration. They also take the trouble to react to the Commission's critical comments. These UN documents, it can be argued, constitute an accepted normative framework of which governments are conscious. At the same time, the reality of governmental behavior tends to be covered with a great deal of symbolism, a strong feature of UN activity in the field of human rights in particular. For example, as early as 1950, the General Assembly declared December 10 of each year as Human Rights Day, when special attention should be paid to human rights in countries throughout the world. The General Assembly named the period 1973–83 the 'Decade Against Racial Discrimination', 1983–1992 was the 'Second Decade against Racial Discrimination', and 1993–2003 was the third such decade. In 1995 a start was made with the 'Decade for Human Rights Education' and 1998, when the fiftieth anniversary of the Universal Declaration of Human Rights was celebrated, was again a year of human rights. Such symbolic actions – and even the very rhetoric of the Universal Declaration itself – have some meaning, for they keep alive the consciousness of the concept and focus attention of various groups and individuals on aspects of human rights violations. The symbols cannot, of course, replace actual observance by national governments of the obligations of the covenants.

Other human rights activities

In addition to the Universal Declaration and the two covenants, which cover human rights in general, over the years the General Assembly has adopted a large number of declarations and conventions with regard to specific subjects. One of the first was a declaration that the principles, including the prohibition of crimes against humanity, applied by the Nuremberg Tribunal in trying German war criminals after World War II, are part of international law. This was followed by the adoption in 1948 by the General Assembly of the Convention on the Prevention and Punishment of the Crime of Genocide (the deliberate eradication of a people or their culture) that came into force in 1951. In 1968, the General Assembly adopted a Convention on the Nonapplicability of Statutory Limitations to War Crimes and Crimes against Humanity, two of the laws enforced at Nuremberg; it came into force in 1970.

Discrimination on the basis of sex has also received significant attention. The Convention on the Political Rights of Women won the approval of the General Assembly in 1952. In 1967, it adopted a declaration calling for the abolition of all rules, laws, regulations, and customs that discriminate against women, and their replacement with legal protection; states are supposed to report regularly on their progress in executing the provisions of the declaration. In addition, governments were urged in 1962 to accede to a convention regulating minimum age and consent to marriage. In 1979, the General Assembly adopted the Convention on the Elimination of All Forms of Discrimination against Women. The Convention provides for a supervisory committee whose 23 members are elected in their personal capacity by the states, 177 as of 2004, that are party to the Convention. This Committee, which meets annually for a period of three weeks, considers the reports submitted by the states parties on the legislative, judicial, administrative or other measures that they have adopted to give effect to the provisions of the Convention. The Committee reports annually through ECOSOC to the General Assembly and may make suggestions and general recommendations based on the examination of reports and information received from the states parties. Furthermore, no less than four world conferences have been held on the improvement of the position of women; the most recent one was held in 1995 in Beijing.

Another topic that has involved much activity by the General Assembly, relates to the protection of rights of individual persons who are subject to arrest or detention. It supplemented long-standing treaty law by adopting a new convention on the abolition of slavery, the slave trade, and practices similar to slavery in 1956. The Declaration against Torture or Cruel, Inhuman or Degrading Treatment or Punishment adopted in 1975, was also followed in 1984 by a binding convention against torture, which has been ratified by 136 states as of 2004. A committee of 10 expert members considers the reports that state parties to the Convention submit every four years on the measures they have taken to give effect to their undertakings under the Convention. If the Committee receives reliable information which appears to it to contain well-founded indications that torture is being systematically practiced in the territory of a state party, it may designate one or more of its members to make a confidential inquiry, if necessary including a visit to the territory, in agreement with the state party. The Committee will transmit its findings to the state party on a confidential basis. It may decide, after consultations with the state party concerned, to include a summary account of the result of the proceedings in its annual report. A complaints procedure by states or individuals is only possible if the state concerned has explicitly recognized this competence of the Committee. This has been done so far by 41 states (for state complaints) and 39 states (for individual complaints). Furthermore, an optional protocol is under preparation that would allow regular visits by the Committee to places where people are being detained, along the model of the European Convention for the

Prevention of Torture. This would vastly increase the possibilities of the Committee to supervise the observance of the treaty obligations. There is, however, considerable doubt whether many states would be prepared to accept the extended obligations under such an optional protocol.

In 1979, the General Assembly adopted an eight-article code of conduct for law enforcement officials, and in 1981, a declaration on the elimination of all forms of intolerance and of discrimination based on religion or belief. In 1959, the General Assembly adopted a declaration on the rights of the child, which was followed some thirty years later, by a binding convention on that subject. The latter Convention has been ratified by 192 states, a record number. This Convention also provides for a supervisory committee of ten independent expert members. The Committee considers the reports that state parties must submit every five years on the measures they have adopted which give effect to the rights recognized in the Convention. The Committee reports through ECOSOC to the General Assembly. The most recent international human rights convention is the one for protection of migrants and their families that was adopted in 1990 and entered into force in 2003. This Convention has now been ratified by 27 state-parties.

High Commissioner for Human Rights

In 1993, the General Assembly, acting on a recommendation of the second World Conference on Human Rights, decided to establish a UN High Commissioner for Human Rights. This official has the principal responsibility for UN human rights activities and carries out the tasks assigned to him by the competent bodies of the United Nations. The Commissioner coordinates all activities in the promotion and protection of human rights and heads what used to be known as the UN Centre for Human Rights. In 1997, it was joined with the secretariat of the High Commissioner to become the Bureau of the High Commissioner for Human Rights. In 1994, the Ecuadorian diplomat José Ayalo Lasso was appointed as the first High Commissioner. He was very active in paying diplomatic visits to states and excelled more in practising quiet diplomacy than in publicly denouncing human rights violations. He was succeeded by the former Irish President, Mary Robinson (1997–2002). She acted as a sort of 'conscience of mankind' by publicly expressing herself about the importance of the promotion of human rights in general and the role of certain violating states in particular. Thereby she provided moral support to victims of human rights violations, which made her not popular among offending governments. During his brief functioning in 2002–03, her successor, the Brazilian diplomat Sergio Vieira de Mello, focused on management problems. He was killed while on a mission for the UN Secretary-General in Iraq. The present High Commissioner, the Canadian judge, Louise Arbour, who was appointed in 2004, has indicated that she will give high priority to the reform program of the Secretary-General and to technical assistance.

The Office of the High Commissioner is responsible for providing services to the Commission on Human Rights and most of the treaty bodies and for the functioning of the special rapporteurs and the working groups. It is also responsible for the implementation of the technical cooperation program, the maintenance of field offices and the organization of international conferences on human rights and other international gatherings. For all of these tasks, the Office receives far too little funding and therefore has a permanent shortage of sufficiently qualified personnel.

The Israeli-Occupied Territories

Since 1968, a Special Committee to Investigate Israeli Practices Affecting the Human Rights of the Population of the Occupied Territories meets at Geneva and New York and holds hearings in cities of States close to the occupied territories that have concentrations of Palestinian refugees. Israel has so far not agreed to the General Assembly's request that it permit the Committee to visit the occupied territories to make on-the-spot investigations. Israel has also repeatedly been criticized by NGOs for excessive use of force by law enforcement officers and for holding Palestinians in administrative detention without charge or trial. While there is reason for serious concern about these human rights violations, the amount of attention paid to such abuses by Israel by UN organs as compared to other countries, seems more motivated by political considerations than by the quantity or nature of the abuses.

Specialized Agencies

In addition to the instruments and activities mentioned so far, a great many recommendations and conventions bearing on human rights have been adopted by Specialized Agencies. The International Labor

Organization (ILO) and the UN Educational, Scientific, and Cultural Organization (UNESCO) have been especially active. The conventions that they have adopted often involve supervision of national behavior by relevant international organizations and, especially in the case of the ILO, violations can lead to embarrassing publicity and even painful sanctions.

The International Criminal Court

Governments approved a statute in 1998 for an International Criminal Court, to be located in The Hague. The Court will deal with the crime of genocide, crimes against humanity, war crimes, and the crime of aggression (yet to be defined). The statute builds on precedents created by the Nuremberg and Tokyo war-crimes tribunals and the *ad hoc* criminal tribunals on Yugoslavia and Rwanda established by the Security Council (see chapter 4). A complaint by any ratifying government, the Security Council or the independent prosecutor, who is provided for in the Statute, will trigger exercise of the jurisdiction of the court. It will hear, however, cases only when national systems of justice are ineffective or unavailable.

The statute entered into force on 1 July 2002. By winter 2004, the statute was signed by 139 states and 97 had ratified it. However, important states, such as the United States, China, Israel, India and Pakistan, have indicated that they do not intend to participate. The United States even concluded bilateral treaties with a number of states by which these committed themselves not to render United States citizens to the court for trial.

The right of self-determination

The right of self-determination of all peoples and all nations, as mentioned in the common article 1 of the two international human rights covenants of 1966, has been widely interpreted as laying down in the form of a binding treaty the right of colonized people to political independence. It symbolized as it were the result of a political struggle that had begun already before and gained strength during and after World War II.

Most of the present UN members are former colonies that gained political independence through direct or indirect involvement of the United Nations. In 1945, more than 750 million people lived in non-self-governing territories of various kinds. By 2004, in a world that had undergone rapid growth of its population, fewer than two million lived in the remaining seventeen dependent territories. Perhaps the colonies would have gained their independence during the past 60 years in any case, but the involvement of the United Nations helped to maintain explicit legitimacy of the process and to keep it in most situations relatively peaceful.

The mandates system under the League of Nations was strictly limited to the colonies of the defeated states, Germany and Turkey that became mandates of Great Britain, France, Belgium and Japan. The future of the colonial empires held by the victors in World War I remained their business. Even during World War II, many leaders regarded the idea that some international supervision should apply to all colonies, as totally unacceptable. During the early stages of drafting the UN Charter, the British government in particular stoutly opposed the idea that the new organization should deal with the future of colonies. Prime Minister Winston Churchill exclaimed that he would never consent to the 'fumbling fingers' of 40 or 50 governments prying into the life of the British Empire. He had not become prime minister, he declared, for the purpose of presiding over the dissolution of the empire.

Nevertheless, the spirit of the times proved contrary to the continuation of colonial empires. The UN Charter sets out self-determination of peoples as a principle (Article 2, paragraph 1). Other sections seek to promote the welfare of non-self-governing people and to move the former League of Nations mandates along to eventual independence (Chapters XI and XII). However, in 1945 few people envisaged the pace by which the colonial empires were to be almost dissolved in a little over two decades.

Declaration on non-self-governing territories

At the insistence of the United States and the Soviet Union, the San Francisco Conference inserted a 'declaration regarding non-self-governing territories' into the UN Charter as Chapter XI. This declaration laid on administering states the duty of ensuring the political, economic, and social advancement of the territories they administered. Moreover, the administering powers were enjoined to develop self-government, to take due account of the political aspirations of the people, and to assist them in the progressive development of their free political institutions. An effort to include political data in the reports was turned down. This was, then, not an actual declaration of independence: the goal was self-government.

The Trusteeship System

The UN Trusteeship System took over from the League of Nations mandate system, assuming responsibility for the remaining territories that had not reached independence. To the former League mandates were added colonies taken from Italy and Japan after the Second World War. States also had the right to place other territories under the supervision of the system, but none were added by this means. In practice, the system became a stepping-stone to independence. Before that time, it was intended to promote the political, economic, social, and educational advancement of the inhabitants of the trust territories. But beyond the aims of the League system, the new one also was charged with progressive development toward self-government or independence, as appropriate to the situation in the lands, based on the freely expressed wishes of the people concerned.

Two of the former mandated territories of the days of the League of Nations never became part of the Trusteeship System. The British mandate of Palestine was excluded because of the dispute between the Jewish and Arab populations that eventuated in the establishment of Israel in 1948. The other territory, Southwest Africa, was long administered by South Africa as an integral part of its territory. It remained the subject of continuing dispute between that country and the United Nations until it finally was granted independence in 1990 as the state of Namibia (see Chapter 4).

With the independence of ordinary trust territories, the role of the Trusteeship Council as a supervisory organ is now a thing of the past, although in recent years there have been calls to give it a renewed role within the UN system on other issues such as the protection of the environment. It used to consist of an equal number of administering and non-administering powers, always including the permanent members of the Security Council. It considered reports submitted by the administering states, accepted and examined petitions from the inhabitants of the trust territories, and decided on whether progress had been made toward the goals of the system. It sent missions to the territories, which observed the situation and interviewed officials and inhabitants about every three years.

Declaration on Granting of Independence

Altogether, 30 former non-self-governing and trust territories became independent between 1945 and 1960. Yet, the African and Asian states became increasingly impatient with regard to setting dates for the independence of the remaining territories. They turned their attitudes into action when the General Assembly in 1960 adopted a 'Declaration on the Granting of Independence to Colonial Countries and Peoples' (Resolution 1514(XV)). This document proclaimed the need to end colonialism quickly. It claimed that alien subjugation of a people denied human rights and violated the UN Charter. It demanded immediate steps to transfer power to the people of non-self-governing territories on the basis of the *right* to self-determination. It also directed its fire against any attempt to disrupt the national unity of the territories, by which was meant a policy of 'divide and rule' by colonial powers.

The imposition of economic sanctions

The case of Rhodesia/Zimbabwe deserves to be recalled as, in 1966, it was the first time in the history of the United Nations that the Security Council ordered limited economic sanctions under Chapter VII of the UN Charter. This was in reaction to the Unilateral Declaration of Independence (UDI) from the United Kingdom, the formal governor, proclaimed the year before by the white minority government of Ian Smith. The Security Council characterized the situation in Rhodesia as a threat to the peace, requiring correction. When limited sanctions failed to dislodge the Smith-government, the Council, in 1968, extended them to include all exports and imports, except for educational and medical supplies and, in special circumstances, foodstuffs. Most UN members complied with the order of the Security Council, except for Portuguese Mozambique and South Africa, both of which bordered Rhodesia. Moreover, traders in Western countries evaded the boycotts, sometimes by putting false labels on Rhodesian tobacco, the most lucrative export. The General Assembly repeatedly urged the Security Council to strengthen the sanctions system by extending it to the two non-complying regimes. The Council refused to do so or to employ military means, probably because of the great cost and the huge effort of blockading the coastlines and scattered ports of the two territories that gave access to the sea to landlocked Rhodesia.

The sanctions against Rhodesia did levy costs upon its white minority government. But it endured 14 years and contrived to evade some of the effect of the boycotts. Its own industry thrived in an effort to replace missing imports. The execution of sanctions was seriously sabotaged by noncompliance and by halfhearted measures on the part of some UN members, which hardly contributed to the prestige of the Security Council. The establishment of independent Zimbabwe in 1979, under a government with a majority of black ministers, was more due to the success of the struggle of black guerrilla-fighters than to that of UN-imposed economic sanctions.

East Timor (Timor Leste)

When the former Portuguese colony of East Timor declared itself independent in 1975, it was invaded and occupied by Indonesian forces. Its annexation by Indonesia was, however, never recognized by the United Nations. During the next 24 years, a military campaign of pacification caused the loss of lives of hundreds of thousands of civilians. In August 1999, the UN supervised a referendum, which resulted in political independence. During the next two years anti-independence militias, presumably supported by Indonesia, conducted indiscriminate violence. In 2002, under strong international pressure, along with a UN-sanctioned Australian-led peace force, Indonesia gave up its involvement in the territory, which as an independent state then became a UN member.

Remaining colonial issues

One of the remaining colonial issues is the territory of Western Sahara, a former Spanish colony on the west coast of Africa. The Spanish colonial administrator left long ago, but the future of the territory has remained in dispute between the Kingdom of Morocco on the one hand, and the Polisario movement, supported by Algeria, on the other. Polisario claims independence for the territory, which is largely held by the Moroccan army. Sporadic fighting has not helped to solve the issue. Since 1995, preparations have been made, under the guidance of a UN-mission (MINURSO) for a referendum whereby the inhabitants will be able to choose between independence and joining Algeria. Although special representatives of the Secretary-General have tried repeatedly to make progress, their frustration has led to repeated 'rescheduling' of the referendum, which to this date has not yet taken place, due to procrastination, especially on the part of the Moroccan government.

In the case of the Falkland Islands (Malvinas) the question of whether it is a colonial issue, is itself a matter of dispute. Governed by the United Kingdom since 1833, Argentina has continually claimed that the islands are part of its national territory. The United Kingdom placed the islands on the UN list of Non-Self-Governing Territories in 1946, while Argentina expressed its reservations regarding sovereignty. Negotiations took place between 1965 and 1982 between the United Kingdom and Argentina, which did, however, not solve the matter of sovereignty. In

April 1982, Argentinean armed forces invaded and occupied the islands. The Security Council demanded an immediate end to the hostilities, the immediate withdrawal of Argentine forces and urged that negotiations take place in order to find a diplomatic solution to the dispute. In the end, a military confrontation led to the defeat of Argentina. The British Government has taken the position that the wishes of the 2000 inhabitants, mainly of British descent, who want to retain their ties to the United Kingdom, should prevail. The General Assembly has repeatedly urged Argentina and the United Kingdom to resume direct negotiations on all aspects of the future of the islands.

Gibraltar, which is also governed by the United Kingdom, is a somewhat similar case as the Falkland Islands, but Spain has been less insistent in recent years in its demand for transfer of sovereignty.

The General Assembly continues to pay attention to the future of six territories administered by the United Kingdom: Anguilla, the Cayman Islands, Montserrat, Bermuda, the Turks and Caicos Islands, and the British Virgin Islands. It has also adopted resolutions on the territory of New Caledonia in the western Pacific Ocean, in response to disturbances that have taken place on that island, which is formally part of metropolitan France. With regard to Guam, a territory held by the United States, the General Assembly has declared that the military bases on the island could become an impediment to decolonization.

Apartheid

The release of Nelson Mandela, the leader of the African National Congress – the main opposition group in South Africa – in 1990, after 27 years of imprisonment, led to the first multiracial elections in 1994. Mandela was elected as the first black President of South Africa, which brought *apartheid* officially to an end. These developments had been preceded by a long-time struggle by the United Nations against *apartheid*.

UN bodies have spent more effort dealing with the policy of *apartheid* in South Africa than with any other issue of human rights. During most of its sessions since 1946, when India first lodged a complaint about discriminatory legislation directed against South Africans of Indian origin, the General Assembly has pronounced itself on the issue. Obviously related to the General Assembly's opposition to racial discrimination generally, *apartheid* attracted focused international attention, because it stood as the only deliberately created, legally based system of racial discrimination in the world.

Apartheid as such figured on the UN agenda since 1952, following the legal codification of older South African practices of discrimination and their extension in accordance with the doctrines of the government formed by the white-only National Party after its electoral victory in 1948. Attempts to change the *apartheid* system ran the gamut of UN methods, ranging from diplomacy and legal steps to coercive programs.

At first, the General Assembly sought to deal with complaints against South Africa by diplomatic negotiations. South Africa rejected these approaches, claiming that its racial affairs were a domestic matter under Article 2 (7) of the UN Charter. The General Assembly reacted with annual resolutions of increasingly strident character. It strongly condemned South African behavior and defined *apartheid* as 'a crime against humanity'. It urged other UN organs to exclude South Africa from international meetings and conferences. The General Assembly denounced efforts to turn the all-black 'home lands', which South Africa claimed as centers of several cultural groups that made up the majority of its population, into independent states. Governments, the Assembly insisted, should break off all cultural, educational, scientific, and sporting contacts with South Africa. Rather, support should be given to the suppressed South African blacks and to liberation movements. Since 1962, UN efforts were sparked by a Special Committee against *Apartheid*, supported by a Center against *Apartheid* in the UN Secretariat. Legal approaches were represented by the General Assembly's adoption of an international convention on the suppression and punishment of the crime of *apartheid* (1973) and a convention against *apartheid* in sports (1985).

Increasingly, the General Assembly demanded by large majorities that South Africa be coerced into adopting a different racial policy. The Assembly repeatedly asked the Security Council to deal with *apartheid* as a threat to international peace and security and to take necessary measures, including sanctions, to force South Africa to adhere to international standards. It also asked the Security Council to consider the expulsion of South Africa from the United Nations. These demands were reiterated in lengthy texts adopted each autumn. Beginning in 1979, the South African delegation was excluded from the General Assembly on the grounds that its credentials were invalid.

At the same time, the Security Council became increasingly sensitive to the disturbances and friction caused in the southern African region by policies of *apartheid* and supporting actions by South Africa. The Sharpeville incident, in which South African police killed 67 and wounded 186 blacks, propelled *apartheid* into the Security Council in 1960. Accepting part of the argument so stridently put forward by the General Assembly, the Security Council concluded that the situation in South Africa, if unchanged, might endanger international peace and security. It called on South Africa to end *apartheid* and instructed the Secretary-General, in consultation with the South African government, to take adequate measures to uphold the purposes and principles of the UN Charter. Eventually, the Security Council decided on a mandatory arms embargo that prohibited any state from providing South Africa with arms and military equipment for police use. It also banned co-operation with South Africa in nuclear development. Then, after the turbulent uprising in 1976 in the black township of Soweto, the Security Council reacted to the death of several hundred people by condemning the South African Government and calling on it to end *apartheid* because of its effects on peace. Since then, the Security Council took up South African raids on the neighboring countries, including Lesotho, Mozambique, and Angola, issuing condemnations and warnings. But the Council never adopted proposals for stronger economic and military sanctions, because the Western countries declined to support such actions. Between 1966 and 1989, South Africa made lightning military raids into the surrounding territories. However, these ended when a United States sponsored agreement was reached in 1989, under which Cuban soldiers were withdrawn from Angola, and South Africa promised to grant independence to the territory of Namibia.

The end of *apartheid* was in the first instance not due to UN pressure but to domestic opposition. However, that opposition has benefited from the international political and moral support it received both through the United Nations and outside.

Conclusion

Given the controversial, not to say revolutionary, aims of the human rights activities of the United Nations, no simple assessment of what has been done can be given. In terms of the goals set out in the UN Charter and elaborated over the years, the human rights programs have had both successes and failures.

The most positive result of the human rights programs is undoubtedly the creation of international standards for the treatment of human beings all over the world. Common criteria now exist for judging whether human beings enjoy fundamental human rights. The

United Nations can claim the accomplishment of making the norms sufficiently concrete so that it is possible to determine where and when they are violated. All governments accept human rights norms in principle, if not in practice. By paying at least lip service to this idea, they also implicitly accept the assumption that a limited world community exists. Moreover, NGOs rely on these very norms to take governments to task and remind them of whatever moral or legal obligations they have assumed.

A second positive outcome can be demonstrated in the remarkable increase in information that UN organs collect and distribute on the performance by states in the field of human rights. A vast reporting network includes the Commission on Human Rights, its special rapporteurs, various committees, some of the Specialized Agencies, the member-states themselves in their national reports, and various publications by UN organs. These efforts are again supplemented by extensive information gathering by NGOs.

Both the process of creating norms and the monitoring of the performance of states have encouraged the active participation of NGOs, such as Amnesty International, the International Commission of Jurists, Human Rights Watch, and others. They constantly demand more effective enforcement and protection of human rights. They attempt to influence the United Nations directly through persuasion and indirectly through the member governments. An example of successful collaboration between one such organization, Amnesty International, and the UN system, can be found in the adoption by the General Assembly in 1984 of the Convention against Torture and Other Cruel, Inhuman or Degrading Treatment or Punishment. This Convention condemns acts of torture as a denial of fundamental rights and of UN purposes, and urges states to take measures against such violations. Similarly, relief organizations have been active partners of the UN High Commissioner for Refugees in his efforts to succor those who flee from massive denial of their rights. These private organizations, such as Catholic Relief Services or the International Rescue Committee, have helped to spread consciousness of the international norms for human rights.

Yet, the UN performance in supervising and controlling the actual performance of states in the human rights field must be accounted as much less positive than the formulation of norms. Even when violations of human rights can be pinpointed as to time and place, this does not necessarily ensure that UN organs will deal with them in an objective manner. Some of the worst offenders in the field of human rights are members of the Commission on Human Rights, where their representatives make pious statements. Whether or not a case will be considered by a UN organ, depends more on political factors than on the nature of the alleged violation. The *apartheid* policies of South Africa or human rights violations by the Israeli forces in the Occupied Territories unfailingly figured highly on the agenda, while at the same time dramatic violations taking place in such countries as China or Iraq long time remained unchecked by UN action. Only after Idi Amin was removed from power in Uganda were his government's murderous transgressions of human rights norms publicly taken up in UN forums. The same is true of the massive scale killings by the regime of Pol Pot in Cambodia. Within the Commission on Human Rights, debates have a predominantly political character, as governments try to defend their behavior and accuse others of wickedness. In fact, complaints about violations of human rights often become the vehicle for denouncing political opponents. It is not completely without reason that some observers have accused the United Nations of applying a double standard.

The United Nations can, moreover, neither effectively punish nor reward governments for their degree of compliance with human rights standards. Incentives to secure compliance in fact are practically unavailable. The Security Council has the right to act only when it is convinced that a violation of human rights threatens international peace and security. Not all violations in fact can clearly be considered as endangering the peace. Furthermore, enforcement action under Chapter VII of the Charter may be too heavy an instrument to be appropriate. In any case, the powers that command the veto in the Council, have shown much reluctance to undertake sanctions. Voluntary sanctions remain an option, but these have never worked well. Finally, enforcement actions may bear more heavily on those who already suffer than on those who cause the difficulties. For example, economic sanctions against South Africa would have seriously affected the majority population of blacks while whites might be better able to protect themselves. Nevertheless, African nationalists used strongly to favor sanctions for want of more effective means for ending *apartheid*.

Despite the difficulty of securing a high level of compliance with human rights norms, the importance of UN activities in this field should not be underestimated. The ideas on which such work are based may take on a life of their own, just as did the French Declaration on the Rights of Man and the Citizen and the Bill of

Rights of the United States Constitution. They matured over decades, slowly entered law and practice, and eventually became the actual limit on the behavior of governments. The human rights norms developed within the framework of the United Nations may well be on a similar path.

With regard to the right of self-determination, the United Nations has been a major channel through which independence for former colonial territories has been effectuated. In many cases, such as Indonesia, Libya, Angola, Mozambique, and East Timor, the UN role has significantly facilitated the decolonization process. As this process in its classic sense has been virtually completed, most of this is now a matter of history.

Yet, even remaining situations that have colonial overtones can cause international concern, as in the case of the Falkland Islands, New Caledonia and Western Sahara. The answer to the question of 'what constitutes a nation' is important for the way in which the struggle for national self-determination presents itself. Many ethnic minorities view themselves as actual or potential nations. Illustrations are offered by secessions, such as Biafra, which tried unsuccessfully to secede from Nigeria in 1967, and Bangladesh that broke off from Pakistan in 1971. More recently, ethnic minorities in such diverse countries as Ethiopia, Sudan, the Russian Federation, Former Yugoslavia, India (Sikhs), Spain (Basques), Turkey, Iran and Iraq (Kurds) and Israel (PLO) have based their claims for independence on the right to self-determination. The fight for national self-determination has continued in a form somewhat different from earlier years. As there are only few overseas territories still governed by Western European or American rulers, the issue of self-determination is increasingly faced by governments from inside their own territories. Most governments are aware of this danger to the territorial integrity of their states. The claim of ethnic minorities to self-determination and eventual independence is the new form in which the struggle against colonialism presents itself. The classic form of colonialism may be over, but a related, new form has developed: the actual or perceived oppression of ethnic minorities. This has become one of the dominant problems the world is facing.

6
Cooperation for Economic and Social Progress

Far more time, effort and money in the UN system go into cooperation to promote economic and social progress than into any other endeavor. More than 80 percent of the personnel of the global agencies, including the United Nations itself, work on issues concerning a higher level of general welfare for the world's people. A huge list of programs covers practically every human preoccupation from the condition of the world environment down to better methods of drying dishes in outdoor tropical kitchens. The vast scope of these programs has generated an organizational tangle so complex that, some observers have concluded, it is beyond either understanding or management. Yet all of it is intended to contribute, and arguably to some extent does, to '..the creation of conditions of stability and well-being which are necessary for peaceful and friendly relations among nations...' (Art. 55, UN Charter) If so, its slow, long-term course contrasts sharply with the crisis atmosphere of the conflicts taken up in the Security Council, but the issues may be no less important to the future of mankind.

The UN system approaches economic and social problems through four main avenues:

- Collection and distribution of information about the economic and social situation in the world.
- The establishment of practical programs of assistance to governments and through them to their people.
- The negotiation of binding international conventions or agreements, such as the 1988 UN Convention against Illicit Traffic in Narcotic Drugs and Psychotropic Substances.

125

– The adoption of non-binding resolutions, declarations, and recommendations to guide member states in their policies so that the results of cooperation may be maximized.

The United Nations has devoted much effort to the elaboration of operational programs for economic development. Loans apart, the UN system mounts more than 10,000 development projects per year. Reaching to 150 countries, these programs, like so much that the UN system undertakes, assist governments and only occasionally reach without intermediaries the people who are intended ultimately to benefit. To this emphasis more recently was added the control and treatment of AIDS, malaria and tuberculosis. Together, they involve commitments of money, people's work, and hope on a scale never before reached by international agencies.

Global conferences

Although the notion of international conferences to deal with common problems can be traced back at least to the public international unions of the 19th century (see Chapter 1), as well as to smaller networks of scientific and intellectual collaborators, the technique of concentrating the attention of governments on specific issues gradually became a keener instrument. Most of the gatherings originate in discussions carried on in the normal machinery of the UN system and are then prepared by special committees. The outcome has further added to the conceptual equipment and organizational devices available for global cooperation. A list of some of the most important recent conferences makes their salience to contemporary global issues clear (see Table 6.1).

Table 6.1   UN-originated world conferences

1963 – UN Conference on the Application of Science and Technology to
        Developing Countries, at Geneva.
1964 – UN Conference on Trade and Development, which led to the establishment
        by the General Assembly of UNCTAD as a permanent body, at Geneva.
1971 – conference on Industrial Development, at Vienna.
1972 – conference on the physical environment, which set up the UN
        Environment Program, at Stockholm.
1974 – conference on world food issues, which set up the International Fund
        for Agricultural Development and the World Food Council, at Rome.
1974 – conference on world population issues, at Bucharest.
1976 – conference on human settlements, which established the Nairobi-based
        Habitat, a UN body, at Vancouver.

Table 6.1   UN-originated world conferences – *continued*

1976 – conference on employment, income distribution, social progress, and the
      international division of labor, at Geneva.
1977 – conference on water, at Mar del Plata, Argentina.
1978 – conference on primary health care, at Alma Ata, Soviet Union.
1977 – conference on desertification, at Nairobi.
1979 – conference on agrarian reform and rural development, at Rome.
1979 – conference on refugees in southeast Asia, at Geneva.
1980 – conference on UN decade for women, at Copenhagen.
1981 – conference on the development of the least developed countries, at Paris.
1981 – conference on new and renewable sources of energy, at Nairobi.
1981 – conference on international assistance to refugees in Africa, at Geneva.
1981 – conference on Kampuchea (Cambodia), at Geneva.
1982 – conference on the exploration and peaceful uses of outer space, at Vienna.
1984 – conference on population, at Mexico City.
1987 – conference on cooperation for peaceful uses of nuclear energy, at Geneva.
1987 – conference on drug abuse and illicit traffic, at Vienna.
1990 – summit conference on children, at New York.
1992 – conference on environment and development, at Rio de Janeiro.
1993 – world conference on human rights, at Vienna.
1994 – international conference on population and development, at Cairo.
1995 – world conference on social development, at Copenhagen.
1995 – fourth world conference on women, at Beijing.
1996 – second conference on human settlements (Habitat), at Istanbul.
1996 – world conference on food, at Rome.
2001 – world conference against racism, racial discrimination, xenophobia
      and related intolerance, Durban, South Africa.
2002 – international conference on financing for development, at Monterrey,
      Mexico.
2002 – world summit on sustainable development, at Johannesburg.
2003 – world summit on the information society, at Geneva.

Such meetings, many of which are attended by a large number of governmental heads, end with the adoption of a program of action. This sets out goals and programs for both the UN system and member governments. Increasingly, too, such conferences are attended by representatives of transnational non-governmental organizations – as many as 30,000 for some events. Along with government representatives, they become active publics. Follow-up sessions to assess the results frequently are summoned. Discussions in UN organs refer to them as bench marks and standards.

A comprehensive list of conferences would also include those called for the purpose of approving the text of international conventions, such as those on the law of the sea, on the ban on military land-mines, establishing the International Criminal Court as well as follow-up conferences on the how the earlier programs were applied. Furthermore, the UN General Assembly from time-to-time holds thematic meetings related to special subjects, such as AIDS or the Millennium Summit, attended by heads of governments, in 2000. Increasingly, NGOs and other transnational organizations take part. A related device is the proclamation of years or decades dedicated to a particular cause, such as an international year of youth.

In all cases, the subject matter of the conferences also forms part of the agenda of the General Assembly and usually of the Economic and Social Council. While the conference method presumably promotes the awareness of government officials and interested publics and stimulates the work of the UN system, critics suggest that it results in one-time spectacles that raise false expectations and that programs of action often remain dead letters.

Economic and social data

All the organizations in the UN system collect, process and publish masses of data on the economic and social situation in member countries and in the world generally. They also assist in improving the quality of available material. Generally speaking, statistical data are furnished by member governments. It could hardly be otherwise, for a national census, for example, involves great costs and a large organization of collectors. Such costs could not be paid by an intergovernmental organization, even though it might offer technical assistance. Other kinds of data, such as descriptions of natural resources, may result from development projects supported by the UN system. The UN Secretariat, as well as those of other agencies, includes a statistical office to analyze and present the constant flow of data that reaches it.

Statistical and survey material provide an essential basis for programming any kind of development or discerning trends. Without such information, cooperative programs would simply be stabs in the dark. Moreover, governments depend on such publications in order to keep track of the context of important transactions, such as international trade in commodities or the transport of persons. The data also provide important raw material for academic analysis of economic processes and social evolution. They also serve private businesses that make sectoral forecasts for their own use. Increasingly, statistics and other survey materials have been subjected to standardization and, in some instances, correction.

Among the annual surveys published by the United Nations is the *World Economic Survey*. From their own vantage points, three other agencies of the UN system, the World Bank, the IMF and UNCTAD, publish analogous documents; the Bank's annual *World Development Report* has been especially influential. UNICEF produces its own analysis of the state of the world's children. UNDP now turn its data into an analytical report on human development. They are complemented by and based on periodical statistical collections, such as the UN *Statistical Yearbook* and the monthly *Statistical Bulletin*.

Although the analytical reports may err on the side of caution, they nevertheless sometimes create controversy because one national governmental bureau or another disagrees with their conclusions or has serious doubts about their quality. Further, the fact that governments provide most statistical data published by the UN system means that reporting is sometimes open to manipulation for nationalistic purposes or is based on dubious methodology or deficient collection facilities. Full correction of such distortion lies beyond the capacity of the UN system. Nevertheless, the publications from the UN system are among the most reliable global social and economic data.

Reduction of poverty

Although from its earliest conception, the United Nations has been associated with encouraging economic development, this took on new dimensions with a growing realization that not only were large parts of the world population poor but also were growing relatively poorer. The incidence and consequences of poverty repeatedly were underlined by the General Assembly and in studies carried out by the secretariats of organizations in the UN system. Although development activities based on flows of official financing grew rapidly, they have never breached the rather narrow limits imposed on them both by major donor governments and by the conditions under which recipient authorities would accept aid. Neither experts nor governments, moreover, have been able to mark out highly reliable paths to development. Consequently, both economic theories of development and practical measures still generate controversy.

The activity within the development apparatus put together by the General Assembly reflects changing approaches and time periods. Some of it began early in UN history, while other pieces were added as styles changed. It included a phase of anti-capitalism, favored by many of the new governments in the former colonies; by the early 1980s, this had much diminished. All of the activity, too, connects in some manner with the broader UN system that includes the World Bank, the IMF, the World Food Program (WFP), and the specialized agencies. All parts of this system compete for scarce financial, intellectual, and other resources. Sectoral ministries of governments collaborate with different agencies for specific purposes and are both agents and objects of competition. In no case, however, do member governments receive unrestricted financial grants or supplies; every agency in the UN system insists on defined programs and projects worked out jointly with the recipient government. Nor does the total cost of development programs begin to approach in value the military aid programs that have been offered by various national governments. Furthermore, in recent years, the flow of capital from private sources in developed countries has greatly exceeded official development aid.

Technical assistance

During World War II, the main sponsoring governments of the United Nations organized the UN Relief and Rehabilitation Administration (UNRRA) to meet some of the most urgent human needs in the allied territories that were liberated from German and Japanese occupation. In order to stimulate war-damaged economies, UNRRA offered advice on reconstruction and some equipment along with foodstuffs and relief supplies. This approach was a precursor of technical assistance offered later by the United Nations. In fact, as early as 1948, it responded to a request from Haiti for advice on modernizing its whole economy.

The UNRRA and initial UN experiences joined both governments of poor and rich states. The poor wanted help, while the rich held that a secure world required productive economies. This led to the creation in 1948 of the UN Expanded Program of Technical Assistance (EPTA) by the General Assembly. By letting contracts for the execution of specific projects to the Specialized Agencies, which already provided some modest help to governments, EPTA was intended to enlarge and coordinate technical assistance in the whole UN system. Its approach sought economic development mainly through upgrading the skills of national governmental service, through better administrative techniques and planning, and through the provision of experts for short periods to help solve specific problems. This program met at least some of the demands of the poor countries for assistance and fitted well with post-colonial needs.

After unsuccessful exploration of a large capital grant agency, which the rich countries declined to fund, the General Assembly established the (first) UN Special Fund in 1958 to support longer-term projects that were expected to eventuate in investment. An inventory of natural resources or a training scheme for middle managers would be examples of such projects. The organization was merged with EPTA by the General Assembly in 1965 to form the UN Development Program (UNDP) which is still a principal UN operational agency for development. It relies on voluntary contributions from member governments and, like its forerunners, engages other organizations in the UN system and the UN Secretariat as its contractors. Its programs for 2004–5, including those with other organizations, could call on various resources totaling $3.5 billion, although programs in progress were far less.

To a steady drumbeat of criticism from the developing countries, each year more numerous, about what they saw as inadequate funding, the level of contributions has mounted. In 1950, EPTA began with $20 million, a mere shadow of contemporary outlays. Inflation and the growing needs of the developing countries and especially the poorest lands, however, moderate the significance of this growth.

Although the size of UNDP, its omnipresence in the developing countries and the variety of projects undertaken represents a unique accomplishment, it is nevertheless only one of the intergovernmental agencies that now operate. The World Bank towers head and shoulders above small UNDP grants by providing long-term, low-interest 'soft loans' for development and well as higher-interest, self-liquidating loans. The Bank also undertakes technical assistance projects, sometimes as a UNDP contractor, but more often on its own account. On technical assistance, it has outspent UNDP since 1982; its project lending, some of which grows out of technical assistance, exceeds $15 billion dollars annually. Furthermore, other multilateral sources of technical assistance, such as the European Union, also offer increasing shares of the total available aid.

Technical assistance now aims at cooperative efforts and matching financing, although the poorest countries are excused from most local costs. Projects are mounted only after a formal request is made by the receiving government, which must have drawn up a definite plan that includes a training element. UNDP reports that a majority of its projects now leads to further investment from both public and private sources.

Aside from complaints that UNDP falls far short of the needs of developing countries, the organization has attracted both praise and criticism. Probably incontrovertible in some instances, this criticism can in part be understood as resulting from UNDP's responsiveness to developmental choices made by recipient countries. Added to this is the complexity of operating a field program in a varied world. Furthermore, it has no foolproof doctrine for stimulating development, any more than the recipient governments or the World Bank do. In addition, it must counter the centrifugal force of intergovernmental agencies – its principal executing partners – that have their own mandates and limited willingness to submit to centralized control.

Cooperation among the more than 130 UNDP offices under Resident Directors at the field level, representatives and staff of other organizations in the UN system, the World Bank and the IMF, and officials of the host governments has not always been optimal. Moreover, donor governments and NGOs acting on their own mount development projects. The different organizational bases encourage differing points of view about the same goals of development. Conflicts have to be ironed out in a negotiating process that sometimes causes great impatience among the officials of the host country. Sometimes technical experts fail to adapt to local conditions at their posts or act in ways that the local culture rejects. Sometimes they are insufficiently briefed or inappropriately trained. The central bureaucracy of UNDP was in fact organized without much expectation of the several waves of expansion that have taken place since the 1960s and has also been subject to the parsimonious financing provided to most international agencies.

The effective authority over general policy in UNDP was placed by the General Assembly in the hands of a Governing Council, made up of the representatives of 48 countries. The operations of UNDP are led by its Administrator, who is chief executive officer. This construction has resulted in the expansion of services administered by the UN system and brought about cooperation on a larger scale with the World Bank and also the European Union. It nevertheless was neither intended as a centralized command post nor has it developed such a character.

In addition, the Governing Council, which functions under the authority of the Economic and Social Council and the General Assembly, also supervises the limited grant agency, the UN Capital Development Fund, set up in 1966; the UN Population Fund (UNFPA) (see below); the UN Volunteers, set up in 1970 (see below); and some additional programs, such as assistance in the fields of science and technology, and some trust funds for special purposes, such as the UN Development Fund for Women. UNDP Resident Directors also oversee the actual projects, report back on their programs, take on occasional special assignments and try to help shape bi-lateral and multi-lateral projects into a coherent whole. Consequently, its original complexity only increased with the larger scope of its program.

UN Population Fund

Although the UN system has long shown an interest in demographic developments, for the first two decades its members could rarely agree on practical programs affecting population growth; yet it was understood by all that such growth intimately related to development. In 1966, the General Assembly began the construction of the UN Fund for Population Activities, which later became the present UN Population Fund (UNFPA). By 2003, it could credibly propose a biennial budget, contributed mainly by governments, of more than $640 million. Its work reflects the links among population growth, development and deterioration of the global environment.

UNFPA supports national governments in collecting basic population data, in applying knowledge of population dynamics to training and development planning, family planning services, policies beyond family planning and information and education programs. Ironically, the United States, a prime mover in establishing UNFPA, has declined to contribute to the agency since 1985 because of contested assertions that it supported abortions and coercive family planning in China.

UN Capital Development Fund (UNCDF)

The idea of a fund that could make financial grants to the developing countries is nearly as old as the United Nations Itself: so is the chilly opposition from most donors. Yet the General Assembly in 1966 decided that existing sources of capital assistance, then rare, should be supplemented by a UN Capital Development Fund (UNCDF). It concentrates on grants and long, low-interest loans, especially for community development in the least developed countries. Resources gradually grew until in 2003–2004 some $130 million was available.

UN University (UNU)

Based on the notion that advanced research and training could materially help the world to learn more about maintaining peace and assist developing countries to advance, the UN University got approval of the General Assembly in 1973. It is an autonomous UN organ and is financed by government and private contributions. Strongly supported by Japan, it has a central office in Tokyo a chain of more than a dozen research and training centers and programs in locations in Asia, Europe, Africa and Latin America. Although it does not grant degrees, it has offered advanced training to thousands of persons, published a wide range of research and sponsored conferences and scholarly networks.

UN Volunteers (UNV)

This modest part of UNDP, set up in 1970, seeks to tap the vigor of youth in constructive opportunities to help with national development by means of international cooperation. In 2004 more than 5000 volunteers served in more than 130 lands.

UN Children's Fund (UNICEF)

A veteran among the assistance mechanisms, UNICEF has always enjoyed the support and attention of member governments and of non-governmental organizations. It also has acquired a reputation as a well-administered, alert organization. UNICEF was established by the General Assembly in 1946 to provide special aid to children who had suffered from World War II. Its earliest tasks involved provision of supplies and services for direct relief, which eventually became less pressing. Its new tasks, reflecting what its staff had learned, included support to governments for developing long-term programs for health improvement, social welfare and teaching, with special reference to children, pregnant women and nursing mothers. It frequently acts in cooperation with other agencies, especially WHO and UNDP. It was a primary international actor in bringing relief to the displaced people along the Thai border after the genocidal activities of the *Khmer Rouge* government in Cambodia in the late 1970s and has been active in many other human disasters.

UNICEF operates on a biennial budget of more than $680 million to support operations in 2004–05 when it will be able to call on total resources of some $3 billion. It operates from 285 country offices as well as its New York headquarters. Some $400 million of its resources comes from the private sector, including such direct income as the sale of greeting cards and other collections managed by national UNICEF committees. Its policies are set by a 41-member Executive Board on which different regions of the world are represented.

UN Conference on Trade and Development

More than any other agency in the UN system, UNCTAD acts as the interest group for the Third World. Its original rationale included a distinctive analysis of underdevelopment associated with Raul Prebisch, who was Executive Secretary of the UN Economic Commission for Latin America (ECLA). His approach contended that advanced development takes place in certain economic centers while countries on the periphery grow dependent. The periphery suffers from declines in the terms of trade, the price levels for their production as related to their imports. This dependency can be changed, said Prebisch, by changing the terms of trade in favor of the developing countries.

This view greatly appealed to developing countries with single major exports, such as Ghana with its cocoa crop. The Prebisch view made its way through the UN machinery and resulted in a three-month conference in Geneva in 1964, despite steady skepticism on the part of the developed countries. The conference sought a counterweight to the 'rich man's clubs,' in and outside of the UN system, as well as to the disappointment with the Economic and Social Council (see below). Consequently, the 1964 meeting was turned into a permanent organ of the General Assembly, to be called UNCTAD. It includes a Trade and Development Board and a permanent secretariat. Every three or four years, UNCTAD meets in a general conference, usually marked by sharp controversies between developing and developed countries. The board meets in the interim. The formal purposes are to:

- Promote international trade so as to encourage development.
- Formulate and give effect to policy principles on international trade.
- Stimulate action in the UN system to reach multilateral agreements on trade, especially to stabilize commodity prices.
- Serve as a center for harmonizing trade and related policies of governments and regional groupings.

It would achieve its main goals by bargaining among three groups of UN members – the developed, the then socialist countries and the developing countries. The device of dividing UNCTAD into negotiating units created the 'Group of 77', the original developing countries at UNCTAD I in Geneva.

The Group of 77 tries to present a common policy. This is not easy as its membership has grown by another 50 governments. Many of the G-77 differ in their interests, as a comparison of Nepal and Mexico would indicate at once. Furthermore, the group includes high income oil producers and newly industrialized countries at various stages of development. The 30-odd poorest countries have gradually been singled out for special treatment. Despite differences, the Group gradually manifested strength in other international meetings. Its members tried to hang together because of the conviction that they must do so in order to achieve anything at all. Gradually, the significance of G-77 has waned as individual developing countries form alignments that reflect their particular interests on an issue.

Even if few governments proclaim much satisfaction with the concrete results from UNCTAD, it has offered an institutional service to the developing countries. Its meetings encourage them to formulate their economic views more precisely. Moreover, the UNCTAD Secretariat has adapted to an 'interdependence' approach that gives attention to 'northern' interests. UNCTAD publications provide a basis for continuing interchanges between rich and poor countries and project a critical light on what the developing world regards as the orthodoxies of the IMF and the World Bank.

UNCTAD also presents critical opinions on the progress of negotiations on reductions of tariffs and obstacles to trade under the auspices of the General Agreement on Tariffs and Trade (GATT) which has been replaced by the World Trade Organization (WTO). UNCTAD has also promoted the drafting or revision of agreements among producer and consumer countries to regulate trade and price of cocoa, rubber, coffee, tin, olive oil, sugar, wheat, and tropical timber. In 1980, after years of negotiations, both developing and developed countries agreed to establish a Common Fund for Commodities. It would finance buffer stocks of commodities in international trade during times of low demand. When demand increased, the stocks could be used, thus helping to stabilize price levels. In practice, its provisions operate only to a limited degree.

Meanwhile, the end of 1990 had a special significance for GATT. This agency, spun off the abortive attempt in 1948 to create an International Trade Organization, had drastically lowered tariffs for most world trade and helped to control some non-tariff barriers. Its contracting parties, now more than 100, had been through seven rounds of negotiations in 1986, when a new one was launched in a session in Uruguay. The Uruguay Round developed severe controversies over free trade for services, such as banking and insurance, and especially for agricultural products. As the issues were complex and the negotiating process in GATT slow and painstaking, with major traders such as the United States and the European Union, pitted against each other, a successful outcome eventually emerged in 1994. With the conclusion of Uruguay round, the GATT parties set up a World Trade Organization to continue on a permanent basis outside the UN system with a broad agenda to promote free trade.

New International Economic Order

The UNCTAD approach to economic change begins with the assumption that the working of the world economy could be changed by deliberate governmental action. Even though GATT and the IMF program look towards a world economy free of central direction, the notion of directed – or at least guided – policy colors the approaches of other UN agencies. The first two 'Development Decades', proclaimed by the General Assembly, reflect the popularity of a global, directed approach to the world economy. The high point of this approach was reached during the aftermath of the oil embargo of 1973, related to the Israeli-Arab war. In the following year, the sixth special session of the General Assembly demanded a New International Economic Order (NIEO).

While the oil crisis was an immediate cause, deeper reasons for this attempt to direct a vast change in the world economy could be found in the anguish of the developing countries and their increasing sophistication and solidarity. They pushed their program of action, seeking NIEO, through a controversial Assembly session in which the developed countries repeatedly proclaimed opposition. Essentially, the developing countries took the oil crisis as an opportunity to validate and advance their program which contained familiar elements: expansion of producers' associations (with the example of the Organization of Petroleum Exporting Countries (OPEC) in mind); linking prices of imports in developing countries to exports from them; reform of the international monetary system; and free exercise of full permanent sovereignty over natural resources (which implied a right of nationalization).

This was followed by a Mexican-sponsored proposal of a Charter of Economic Rights and Duties of States, which was adopted by a vote that showed overt opposition or significant abstention by almost all developed countries. This polarization moderated somewhat by September 1975, when both the developing countries and the United States and some of its friends came to the seventh special session of the General Assembly with a more cooperative attitude. This led to the adoption of a resolution covering a negotiating framework for application of NIEO measures in the UN system. The resolution also affirmed a target of 0.7 percent growth of gross national product of developed countries as their portion of assistance; this had long been sought by the poorer lands.

Yet, with the somber international economic situation of the subsequent years and the rise of a strong free market philosophy in the United States and other developed countries, the momentary grouping around the notion that common difficulties could be overcome with international cooperation soon drained away. NIEO had no vitality by the beginning of the 1990s. Several positive elements did, however, emerge. These include broader activities by the World Bank and the IMF, the creation of a general system of tariff preferences to benefit the developing countries, increased capitalization for the World Bank and IMF where the developing countries increased participation, and some parts of the not-yet-operative law of the sea convention. Some of its more radical ideas about reforming world trade lived on in the non-governmental anti-globalization movements of the early 21st century.

The global environment

The political differences between wealthy and poor countries that NIEO dramatized also play a part in the rise to prominence of environmental issues. While some of the leaders of the developing countries strove with endless zeal for industrialization, groups within the developed countries, driven by NGO activity, sought to rein in increasing use of energy and natural resources. The startling dispersal of radioactive material from the breakdown of a power nuclear reactor at Chernobyl in the USSR in 1986, the disclosure of unrestrained dumping of toxic wastes in Africa and other developing areas, the connection between population growth and desertification, and the rapid cutting of the tropical rain forest all contributed to the new understanding. So too did the evidence of the destruction of the ozone layer and the possibility of global warming as a result of the use of fossil fuels. The UN system was in various ways involved in all of this and at various times led the way to augmented consciousness of the importance of the global environment to all human endeavor.

Gradually, governments of both developed and developing countries came to accept that the world environment was seriously threatened by despoliation of the natural environment. Yet considerable strife emanated from fears in developing countries that their efforts to lift their levels of well-being would be impaired. Although the UN system decided to make room for environmental considerations with the creation of the UNEP in 1972, it was only as the 1990s approached that the issue reached the top of the international agenda.

Even though UNEP is small compared with the World Bank or FAO, its staff of some 500 professionals and its 58-country Governing Council adroitly took advantage of growing concern among many publics about threats to the environment. A key statement of global concern came with the report in 1987 of the World Commission on Environment and Development, which was set up by the General Assembly and headed by the then Norwegian Prime Minister, Gro Harlem Brundtland. Its report, titled *Our Common Future*, linked the environmental safeguards with a series of recommendations for 'a new era of economic growth' that is both socially and environmentally sustainable. The heads of all agencies in the UN system, including the World Bank and the IMF, then gathered to emphasize that all development projects must help to sustain rather than harm the environment. This was followed by UNEP's own report to the General Assembly on how to proceed.

One outcome was the summoning of a UN Conference on the Human Environment, 20 years after the first environmental conference in 1972, in Rio de Janeiro, not far from the threatened Amazon basin. The conference took up climate change; management of international traffic in dangerous wastes and products; protection of fresh water resources and of the oceans; combating deforestation, desertification and drought; preservation of biological diversity; integration of biological and developmental concerns to improve living standards; and protection of health.

The conference adopted the Rio Declaration on Environment and Development, a program of action entitled 'Agenda', and a statement of principles on the management, conservation and sustainable development of all types of forests. Two conventions were opened for signature at Rio and later came into effect in ratifying countries. That on climate changes aims at stabilizing omissions of carbon dioxide and other greenhouse gases to prevent the 'greenhouse effect.' Its ideas were extended into a practical program in Kyoto protocol that came into force in 2005. The second convention deals with biological diversity and seeks sustainable use of all the species of the earth and the ecosystems of which they are a part.

As a concept for international action, concern with the environment has merged with economic development. Throughout the UN system, development projects are vetted for environmental effect. Other projects have to do directly with environmental promotion but are linked with economic outcomes. The convention on global warming has especially far-reaching effects as it implies reduction in the use of fossil fuel in, for instance, the automobile-based American economy and in emissions from inefficient electrical power generating plants in Russia and China. UNEP keeps watch on developments in these fields and publishes reports and statistics about them. Furthermore, transnational NGOs, such as Greenpeace, make much of violations of standards and some come into direct, even violent, conflict with governments when they interfere with movements of radioactive materials.

Refugees and disasters

Organized international concern with refugees dates back to the early days of the League of Nations. Only after World War, when millions of displaced persons in Europe and Asia roamed across the path of the victorious armies, did the scope of assistance and protection operations reach a large scale. Since then, in several organizational forms the United Nations has tried to cope with refugees.

The principal organizational instrument since 1951 has been the UN High Commissioner for Refugees (UNHCR), which was originally created by the General Assembly as a temporary agency. It rests on a renewable General Assembly resolution and the UN Convention on the Status of Refugees (1951), which now has 130 adherents. The sudden outflow of Hungarian refugees after the suppression of a rebellion against oppressive Communist rule in 1956, saw UNHCR assisting with the handling and eventual resettlement of some 200,000 people. With the passage of years, even the Hungarian government expressed its gratitude.

Since then, UNHCR has been on the scene, first to protect the human rights of people outside of their own countries with a well-founded fear of persecution, and then to offer material assistance, wherever forced migrations occur. In 1990, it was responsible for aid to some four million refugees from Afghanistan, some two million from Ethiopia and other hundreds of thousands who appear in the wake of repression or violence elsewhere. Its estimates of refugees who could claim help, aside from displaced persons within their own countries, reached more than 17 million in 2004. With its budget of some $950 million for 2004 and the constraints of working through national governments, it clearly could not reach every refugee.

In other humanitarian disasters, the UN structure also has responded. As a device to signal and organize responses to a humanitarian emergency, the system has the services of a UN Secretariat department, now headed by an Under-Secretary-General. This helps to mobilize resources from many quarters and to back up UNHCR and WFP. And for extraordinary humanitarian emergencies, such as the droughts in Africa during the 1980s and the situation of the Cambodians who fled their country during the depredations of the Pol Pot government in the late 1970s, the UN has organized special operations to bring food, shelter and other services. In all such emergency operations, WFP has been a principal source of food aid. Originally conceived as a means to funnel surplus food so as to promote development, WFP now claims to be the world's largest humanitarian agency with programs in 81 countries and in 2004 a budget of $3.2 billion.

Although refugees and victims of man-made disasters supposedly need only short-term attention, more than one incident has turned into a long-term concern. The fate of the refugees from the Arab-Israeli war of 1948 can be taken as a clear example of this transformation. More than one-and-one-half million people, by the late 20th century almost all of them children and grandchildren of the original refugees, received some sort of assistance from the UN Relief and Works Agency for Palestine Refugees (UNRWA). It was organized to care for refugees until they could return to what is now Israel. In the Arab countries, where large numbers of refugees live, governments have usually avoided merely absorbing them. Most of the budget for UNRWA camps, schools and other services is covered by contributions from the Western countries, including never less than 25 percent from the United States. Most of the UNRWA employees in fact are drawn from the refugee ranks, while the organizational headquarters was removed to Vienna after fighting engulfed Beirut in the early 1980s.

With the Oslo agreement of 1995, Israel and a new Palestinian authority led by the veteran liberation fighter, Yasser Arafat, UNRWA turned to assisting the new Palestine entity. But the quick breakdown of the Oslo agreement into renewed violence, including suicide bombings in Israel and deep armed incursions into some UNRWA camps and other Palestinian neighborhoods in response once more engaged the organization in emergency services.

Narcotics drug control

Control of the traffic in narcotic drugs is one of oldest items on the international agenda. An interlocking system of international conventions and control organs dates back to before the First World War. The League of Nations supervised the system and developed it further. The United Nations took over the League's tasks and formed a narcotics drugs commission under the wings of the Economic and Social Council. These bodies have led several phases of revisions of existing laws and the establishment of expert organs, including research laboratories, as part of the UN Office on Drugs and Crime, located in Vienna. WHO joins the effort by identifying substances that need control. That office also sponsors development programs to substitute licit crops for the plants that produce raw material for illegal traffic, such as opium and cocaine. Application of the international rules, however, remains in the hands of national authorities. The national efforts to reduce illicit traffic range from negligible to strenuous.

AIDS

The main source of international leadership to cope with the growing spread of AIDS (Acquired Immune Deficiency Syndrome), as might be expected, was WHO. By 1990, it had mounted a program of assistance to more than 125 countries and worked with national committees in 155 lands. The General Assembly gave strong endorsement to the program in 1987, when for the first time it urged support on a health issue, and has since then discussed somber reports from WHO. UNDP and the World Bank have adjusted their projects to support the WHO's Global Program on AIDS, which by 1990 had available more than $100 million in voluntary funds. Meanwhile, even with the gross under-reporting of cases characteristic in some countries, there was evidence that more and more people had begun to understand the sexual nature of the transmission of the disease and to respond to preventive information made available via WHO through national governments.

However quickly the HIV/AIDS program had internationalized attention to the pandemic, some of the main donor governments, cheered on by NGOs, replaced the WHO-directed efforts in 1996 with a new, interagency office. The UNAIDS program enlisted not only WHO but also UNDP, UNICEF, UNFPA and others in a joint effort that was intended by the main donors to remedy shortcomings in the original program. This reflected dissatisfaction on the part especially of the United States in the work of the then WHO Director-General.

By 2004, UNAIDS had in effect brought the HIV/AIDS pandemic, then affecting an estimated 40 million people, onto the system-wide agenda of the United Nations. In the background were 20 million deaths from the disease and evidence that women were being infected more quickly than men. Governments, the UN system agencies and others could draw on a novel UN-sponsored Global Fund to Fight AIDS, Tuberculosis and Malaria that identified the great killers in the developing countries, for practical projects. The Global Fund had actually received some $3 billion while much more was pledged. The donors included foundations that put up some $150 million and 53 governments.

Conventional economic, social and cultural cooperation

The mushrooming growth of UN operations to support economic and social development, to promote the general welfare and to protect the environment combine improvisation, imagination, dire need, political compromise and timidity and a shortage of resources. These programs derive from older forms of organized international activity. These continue to be applied, day-in and day-out, and ultimately affect the newer programs.

For all its shortcomings and futile ambition, the NIEO demonstrates how old forms can still be used to express ideas that otherwise would hardly have come to the surface. It had a basis in the familiar form of a recommendation by an international deliberative body. All members of the United Nations are pledged to take joint and separate action to effect to recommended plans for promoting the general welfare (Art. 56, UN Charter). If the majority of governments vote for a recommendation, it is a modest assumption (that often fails to become actual) that the governments will follow policies that they approve at the international level.

Relying on national governments to cooperate by giving practical effect to agreed policies is a method that reaches back through the League of Nations to the middle of the 19th century. It starts with the assumption that some problems, such as the spread of an epidemic disease, affect all states and that their cooperation is obviously in their self-interest. Each cooperating country carries out the general international policy with its own resources. This basic notion gradually grew more sophisticated and came to include the drafting of a long series of international conventions on specific subjects, such as controlling international trade in women and children. Scholars, too, elaborated theoretical concepts to explain the increasing practical international cooperation.

The conceptual line that has had the most influence on the creation of international institutions and their programs was developed by the 'functionalist' writers. A leading inspiration to some of the theorists of our time was David Mitrany, an English academician and adviser to multinational business. He wrote his best-known book, *A Working Peace System*, at the formative stage of the post-World War II institutions. Mitrany argued that transnational cooperation springs out of technological development. Conventional politicians may impede or distort such cooperation, but they do not manage it. The web of technical cooperation, which was illustrated during both world wars by the highly successful international collaboration among civil servants, engineers, and scientists of the victors, eventually becomes so dense that it delimits the action of the state. Technical experts can agree, no matter what conventional politicians think. Therefore, the real world is shaped by technological imperatives. The cooperation thus bred eventually will 'spill over' into what is now regarded as political areas.

The functionalist argument has served as an important justification for separating the functions of the specialized agencies in the UN system from the central organization, at least for day-to-day operations and technical recommendations. It also supported additional attention to technical cooperation, especially as its worth in several fields had been proven during by the League of Nations.

The notion that an efficient international system requires cooperation on technical subjects has found expression in the complex organizational structure of the United Nations. The set of agencies and deliberative bodies, some of which are discussed earlier in this chapter, develops policy recommendations covering an endless series of topics with respect to economic, social, cultural, education, health, and related problems, as set out in Article 55 of the Charter. The UN Secretary-General and his staff prepare studies for the system and make proposals, either on their own initiative or with the cooperation of governmental representatives. The Economic and Social Council, discussed in Chapter 2, has the formal assignment of giving central direction.

In the hope of assembling the best technical advice, ECOSOC has created a series of commissions, composed of specialists nominated by their governments. A few similar commissions existed under the League of Nations, where, however, specialists were appointed in their personal capacities, not as governmental nominees. The ECOSOC commissions cover such subjects as statistics, population, the status of women, and development planning, as well as human rights and narcotic drugs, mentioned earlier. In addition a long list of even more specialized advisory bodies, such as the Committee on Crime Prevention and Control, offer their advice.

Along with promoting cooperation on specific topics, ECOSOC has also set up a more decentralized system along regional lines. A set of commissions offers advice to governments and limited services to governments in their regions. These bodies include the UN Economic Commission for Africa (headquarters in Addis Ababa), the Economic Commission for Asia and the Western Pacific (Bangkok), the Economic Commission for Europe (Geneva), the Economic Commission for Latin America and the Caribbean (Santiago, Chile) and the Economic Commission for Western Asia (Baghdad). Assisted by small staffs, drawn mostly from their own regions, these deliberative organs have scored some success but remain the subject of debate, both in regard to the validity of the regional principle and their claims to speak for regions. Yet they sometimes help stimulate economic and foster regional standards. At the height of the Cold War in Europe, the Economic Commission for Europe was one of the few places where a few cooperative and constructive relationships between the two sides could carry on.

Despite the elaborate institutional structures and the early welcome accorded to functionalist ideas, many member governments complain that the decentralized UN system lacks both sharpness and responsiveness. The specialized agencies and the World Bank and IMF duly submit reports to ECOSOC, the formal coordinator, but then tend to go their own ways. ECOSOC and its system of developing general policy recommendations remains what it has been: it is secondary in immediate impact, as compared with the practical programs and ambitious aspirations encouraged by an unprecedented degree of international organization.

7

The 21st Century: a Changing UN

As the world changes, so does the United Nations. As the 21st century opened, the United Nations had experienced a brief euphoric period when in the Iraq war of 1991 collective security appeared to work for the first time as planned. An active new Secretary-General had offered apparently acceptable prescriptions for strengthening the UN capacity to maintain peace. But Secretary-General Boutros-Ghali soon suffered from the debacle in Somalia and growing frustration from important American political elements. Although his successor in 1997, Kofi Annan, brought new energy to his office and then presided over considerable enthusiasm at the high-level Millennium General Assembly, the terrorist attacks of 11 September 2002 and the buildup to the second war in Iraq once again brought confusion and widespread gloom to the atmosphere.

Only for a short time after the apparent success of collective security in 1991 could the United Nations enjoy wide support among almost all governments. It was then harder facilely to denounce the United Nations as simply a bureaucratic, useless, spend-thrift organization. The memory had dimmed of the moment in 1983 when a departing deputy representative of the United States talked of moving the United Nations headquarters from New York, while the American delegation stood 'down at the dockside, waving ...a fond farewell as [it] sailed into the sunset.' That was the time of the Kassebaum Amendment, originating in the U.S. Senate that ordered a cutback of American contributions to the UN budget from 25 to 20 percent unless a system of weighted voting was introduced for financial decisions. A series of economy measures that affected the UN system years later followed from Washington and pinched increasingly. That was also the time when the ultra-conservative Heritage Foundation, claiming in 1984 that 'a world without a United Nations could be a better one', reached its greatest influence on the Reagan White House. That same year, the United States, later followed by the United Kingdom and Singapore, withdrew from UNESCO, criticizing it for mismanagement and 'politicization.' It seemed then only a matter of time before the United States would depart from the United Nations itself.

By 1990, all of this seemed to have undergone a marked change. The United States government had obviously revised its attitude, especially where the Security Council was concerned. Its crucial role in giving legitimacy to the American-led armed response to the invasion of Kuwait by Iraq brought new prestige to the organization. A renewed faith in the future of the then 45-year-old organization appeared in the remarks of government leaders. In issues of international peace and security, the United Nations soon was employed as never before. The Security Council dispatched missions to Cambodia, to Somalia and Rwanda and assumed some hesitant role in dealing with the consequences of the disintegration of Yugoslavia. The first two of these began with a high level of engagement, including troops from several sources.

The services of the Secretary-General once again took on special significance and complemented much activity by the Security Council. Pérez de Cuéllar had had a serious role in ending the eight-year war between Iraq and Iran. He and his agents negotiated the departure of Soviet troops from Afghanistan. Through UNTAG, the organization supervised the decolonization of Namibia. Boutros-Ghali came into office in 1992 in the wake of the new spirit but soon had to cope with the continuing consequences of the financial stringency and the arrears in contributions, especially on the part of the United States.

Iraq had become the center of a second burst of UN activity in 1990, when the invasion of Kuwait ordered by President Saddam Hussein in August was promptly found by the Security Council to breach the peace. A series of 12 increasingly determined resolutions culminated at the end of November with a resolution that permitted UN members to use 'all appropriate means' – tantamount to expressly authorizing military force – to secure the withdrawal of Iraq if it had not done so by 15 January 1991. Of paramount importance was the fact that the collective security system appeared successfully to be facing its supreme test.

Improved relations between the Soviet Union and the United States provided an essential foundation for decision-making. Unlike the days of the Cold War when their rivalry paralyzed the Council, now they were not only cooperating closely but doing so in regard to a variety of issues. That formed a nucleus from which decisions could emerge, although it was not a guarantee of eternal harmony either between the two former antagonists or the other members of the Council.

Collective legitimization

Creation of a broad consensus about permissible behavior for governments constitutes a foremost task for any diplomacy and especially of the procedures in multilateral organizations. As the variety of situations bearing on peace and security reaches towards the infinite, the constant reinterpretation and adaptation of the basic norms of the UN Charter is necessary. Once a consensus – or even a near-consensus – emerges, it can be used to give the actions of a government an explicit stamp of legitimacy.

'Collective legitimization' is what Inis Claude has called this function. It sets the conditions under which violence in international relations may be acceptable. For example, the military operations of the United States to help South Korea after the attack by North Korea in 1950, received broad approval in the United Nations. Although the United States had the military power to carry on by itself, that government thought it prudent to garner the international recognition that its actions were permissible and worthy of general support. The international reaction in 1991 to Iraq's seizure of Kuwait would be another case in point.

Collective legitimization depends entirely on whether the UN member governments form opinions on a particular issue that add up to something approaching unanimity. When there is wide division, seeking legitimization is hopeless; this is another way of saying that the government that arbitrarily embarks on violent actions, or other hurtful practices, cannot expect automatic or any approval at all from the rest of the world. A clear example can be found in the Vietnam War of the 1960s and the early 1970s. The United States made no real effort vainly to seek UN support.

In the recent past, the Afro-Asian states often have been in a better position than the western countries to line up support from the majority of the United Nations for their independently-decided military actions. To some extent, this explains the backing given by a majority of the General Assembly to 'wars of liberation' in such places as the Portuguese African colonies, Rhodesia/Zimbabwe, and Namibia. It also relates to the support given the Palestine Liberation Organization

(PLO). The definition of aggression adopted by the General Assembly in 1974 (UN Res. 3314 (XXIX)) explicitly excludes such wars.

Thus, the United Nations can be used to produce some judgment as to the permissibility of military operations that probably could not have been stopped in any case. Actions that some governments might view as aggression can thus also sometimes be turned into operations with collective legitimization. This was the case in the first UN armed action against Iraq but certainly not in the second Iraq war.

The Soviet Union

For many years, the Soviet Union had taken a reserved or negative attitude towards the United Nations. While carefully protecting its autonomy of action, it opposed constructive initiatives that others could accept. Its position was symbolized by the nickname – Mr. Nyet – given longtime Foreign Minister Andrei A. Gromyko, who cast many vetoes in the Security Council in the course of a few years. The Soviet Union usually objected to expanding UN activities and, like the United States, was critical of the expenditures and the level of salaries paid to UN staff members. It consistently resisted the use of peace-keeping forces and refused to pay part of its obligatory, assessed contributions. It eventually boycotted the first two Secretaries-General, Lie and Hammarskjöld, and provokingly proposed weakening the office by turning it into a 'troika,' named after a three-horse Russian sleigh.

With Mikhail Gorbachev's ascension to power, the Soviet approach changed drastically. In 1987, he published a major article in the Soviet press on his views about the UN and followed it with a similar speech to the General Assembly. He pleaded for closer multilateral cooperation within the UN framework. Wider use should be made of UN military observers and peace-keeping forces in disengaging warring troops and observing cease-fire and armistice arrangements. States should be encouraged to cooperate within the UN framework in combating international terrorism.

Other proposals by Gorbachev referred to closer cooperation among states to establish both economic and ecological security. The UN role in the field of human rights should be strengthened and a special fund for humanitarian cooperation should be created. The role of the International Court of Justice should be upgraded and the international community should encourage the Secretary-General to undertake good offices, mediation, and reconciliation.

Even if Gorbachev's proposals were hardly original or revolutionary in echoing the provisions of the UN Charter, they were put forward as a comprehensive package by the leader of a major power. Moreover, it was a power that had shown little enthusiasm for an active United Nations and had opposed some of the very programs, such as genuine promotion of human rights, that now were praised. Soviet participation in UN bodies promptly turned from reserve to staunch defense of the United Nations. Its representatives began making numerous proposals to strengthen the organization. After Gorbachev's removal from power, however, the Soviet Union and its successor, Russia, gradually began emphasizing narrower definitions of its interests. By 2004, the government of Vladimir Putin made it clear that it had redefined its UN policy and was especially sensitive about any decision that implied restricting national decisions.

The Five Policemen

If for a few moments in the 1990s, the permanent members of the Security Council seemed to act as the great power 'policemen' as Franklin Roosevelt had wanted, the UN security system still operates under serious structural limitations that have been understood from the beginning. Nothing can be done if one of the five 'policemen' behaves cynically or casts the veto for irrelevant or selfish purposes or uses force. Furthermore, under the veto-protected Charter, to change the rigid composition of the permanent members would be possible only under exceptional circumstances. Besides that, the system has never had the standing military forces foreseen in the Charter, so that even an agreed response to a breach of the peace still demands much unpredictable improvising.

A possibly even greater political drawback of the system began to surface after the revival of the Security Council. Elected members and all of the rest of the UN membership may chafe under the governance of the Big Five. Some grumbling became audible, especially from the middle powers, such as Canada, that normally furnish peace-keeping components. Academic studies and UN committees had long made suggestions of formulas for revising the Council. In 2003, Secretary-General Annan named a high-level commission to examine reforming the entire UN system including the Security Council. In its report late in the next year, the commission proved unable to find unanimity on changing the Security Council and recommended a choice of two patterns of enlargement, neither of which envisaged depriving any of the permanent five of 1945 of its veto or adding more veto-wielders.

The participation and services of the middle powers in the United Nations has had a rather special character. Among middle powers Canada, Netherlands, Sweden, Norway, and from the developing countries, India, Nigeria and Pakistan have made considerable military contributions to peace-keeping. Middle power participation also supported the build-up of the military force facing Iraq after its invasion of Kuwait. Even without permanent places at the Security Council table, Germany and Japan, which have been openly seeking permanent seats on the Council, have used their financial resources to bolster peace-keeping operations.

Echoing the restiveness among the middle powers, other smaller powers have more than once indicated that their interests were not sufficiently taken into account. Apprehension about domination by the great powers dates back to the San Francisco Conference, when the unanimity rule was discussed and the smaller powers lost the fight to eliminate it. Thus, while an application of the concept of the five policemen may help to maintain international peace and security, it may eventually involve costs in terms of international consensus.

The Third World

Most of the governments of the poor countries of Africa and Asia place the abolition of poverty, the need to catch up with the economic level of the major industrialized lands and more recently controlling HIV/AIDS ahead of maintaining international peace and security in distant locations. For the countries of the South, the momentary cooperation between the United States and the Soviet Union did not rank as stunning progress. On the contrary: it aroused some fear that a 'new world order', referred to by President George H.W. Bush in a speech to the General Assembly in 1990, would be established at the expense of the low-income countries. Third World countries would no longer be able to use the East-West competition for footholds in Africa and Asia to their own advantage: it would no longer be possible to play off the United States against the Soviet Union. The New International Economic Order (NIEO) glimmered farther away than ever.

Despite these fears and suspicions, the Afro-Asian majority at the beginning of the 21st century still regarded the United Nations as one route to their goals, even if at times it served only a symbolic purpose and a means of keeping issues alive. And at an increasing pace in such African upheavals as those in Sierra Leone, Cote Ivoire, Liberia and eastern Congo, the UN mechanisms for maintaining peace were employed, sometimes with strong neighborly participation.

The United States

From the point of view of the United States at the Millennium, much had changed to its advantage both within and without the United Nations. Most of the countries in Eastern Europe had left the Soviet orbit, all of them, except for Belarus, had rejected central planning and state socialism and were in the process of installing market economies of the Western type – as the United States had always advocated. The re-unification of Germany was widely understood as a victory for the West and for democracy. The changes meant that the Soviet Union would dissolve and leave Russia as a possible partner.

The immediate worldwide response to the Iraqi invasion of Kuwait took the form of overall support for US-led political and military measures. In the autumn of 1990, the United States headed an unlikely alliance, consisting of its NATO-partners, its former Soviet enemies and a sizable group of Arab and other Third World countries. As this alliance was founded partly on the basis of resolutions adopted by the Security Council, the overall approach of the United States to the United Nations became very much more favorable than in the recent past. The government in Washington showed clear signs of wanting to channel more of its international activities through UN bodies. The Congress began to release funds to pay up the delinquent American contributions to the United Nations. The United States without much fanfare later rejoined UNESCO as did the United Kingdom and Singapore.

The shock of the al-Qaeda attacks on American targets in September 2001 had immediate repercussions in the United Nations. The response of the Security Council stoutly backed American plans to use its force and that of many other volunteering countries to attack the al-Qaeda base in Afghanistan. With the Taliban government in Afghanistan quickly pushed out of control, UN agencies soon resumed their humanitarian programs in the parts of the Afghanistan that were peaceful. A senior representative of the Secretary-General was on hand in Kabul to assist in rebuilding a viable state.

By 2004, almost all of this warm cooperative spirit had evaporated under the impact of the decision of the George W. Bush's government to proceed to war with Iraq whether or not the Security Council gave its consent. The United States claimed that the Iraqi government threatened peace with its presumed stock of weapons of mass destruction and connections with al-Qaeda. It impatiently dismissed the results of UN inspection and destruction of weapons in Iraq. The dramatic presentation of these claims by Secretary of State Colin Powell in the Security Council early in 2003 convinced only a handful of governments, among which the most important was the United Kingdom. Despite widespread demands from other governments and publics, when the Security Council failed to approve immediate use of the vast force that the United States had been emplacing around Iraq, the second war there began. The United Nations and especially the Security Council had been trumped by the growing unilateralism on the part of the United States. It remained unclear how much collaboration with the UN system would be resumed by the United States, but there was no doubt at all that important segments of public opinion in the United States would oppose much return to the sunny moments of 1990 and 1991.

The Secretary-General

The role of the Secretary-General was particularly braced by the new attitude of support for the United Nations in 1990.

Secretary-General Hammarskjöld once enunciated a conception of his office that clearly demonstrated how the divisions of opinion about the place of the United Nations in world politics restrict the functioning of the organization. He declared that the United Nations should rely on, and give voice to, the policies of the small powers that had little ability to resist the actions of the great. He viewed his office as the protector of the 'general interest.' The great powers, especially the Soviet Union, understood this notion as reducing their influence. The smaller powers, bound by their own nationalistic notions, were hardly eager to surrender their policies to an activist secretary-general, even if he claimed to be impartial. U Thant and Kurt Waldheim both tried to stand as persuasive presences in international politics, but Thant failed in restraining the United States from its policies in Vietnam and Waldheim found no way to project his organization into a durable centrality in the Middle East, the 1973 oil crisis, or the hostage-taking of US embassy personnel in Iran in 1979–80.

During the second term of Javier Pérez de Cuéllar as the 1990s opened, the office seemed to have regained some of its former influence in international affairs, especially with regard to peace and security. He made skillful use of the opportunities offered by the international context. His good offices, either in person or through personal representatives, contributed to the resolution of such already-mentioned issues as the war between Iraq and Iran, the withdrawal of the Soviet Union from Afghanistan, improved security in Central America and the independence of Namibia.

Yet it proved too early to talk of a permanent reversal of fortunes for the office of Secretary-General. The élan with which Boutros-Ghali took the post in 1992 soon flared out under the impact of the flaccid reaction to the Rwanda genocide and the fumbling approach of the Security Council to the disintegration and violence in former Yugoslavia. In both of these instances, the Secretary-General became a lightning rod for criticism, especially in the United States, whose government used its veto to hold his tenure to one term.

Kofi Annan rebuilt and even expanded the prestige of the office of Secretary-General. He undertook reforms of the Secretariat that built on his own experience as a staff member as well as on Boutros-Ghali's successes and frustrations. Using the occasion of the new millennium and a session of the General Assembly at a very high level – said by some to be the greatest gathering of heads of state and government in history – to present the draft of a Millennium Declaration. It was accepted with praise and set out the direction the organization was to take in the new century. Unlike many such policy documents, this one included quantitative indicators of progress and a review process. He was able to convince the United States to pay much of its arrears in financial contributions and generally improved communication with Washington – even to the point that some UN insiders thought it had become inappropriately close.

Yet the fragility of relations with Washington had hardly built up to solid confidence in the United Nations. The failure of the Somalia mission included a crisis in public opinion after the death of American soldiers in an ill-starred raid undertaken under orders outside of UN command channels. It was followed by a review of multinational engagement by the Clinton government that eventuated in a new accent in Washington on national decision-making. Without concerted explanation by the government, the United Nations was widely blamed in American mass media for the debacle.

Kofi Annan openly pointed out that the United States failed to follow mandatory UN procedures by engaging its force in Iraq without the sanction of the Security Council. He later remarked in a BBC radio interview carried over the whole world that in his opinion the war was illegal. After the attack in Baghdad which killed mission chief and other members of the Secretariat, Annan withdrew his staff. Although the United States gingerly sought renewed support from the UN system for its plan to hold elections in Iraq and to phase out its own military engagement, Annan hesitated to order a full-scale resumption of activities there. He did, however, send technical advisers from the UN electoral service office to help the Iraqi provisional government prepare for the election scheduled for January 2005. Although Annan generally employed 'correct' diplomatic relations with the United States, the Bush government unmistakably chilled the relationship with him and his organization. Meanwhile, some segments of American opinion heaped scorn on the United Nations. Nor did the comments overlook the fact that Annan's second term would end in 2006, hardly too far away to think of his future and a successor.

As the United States dramatically demonstrated with its veto of a second term for Boutros-Ghali, it could condition who would hold the office in the future. Nevertheless, a good deal of the future of the Secretary-General would depend on whether enough highly motivated and able staff people can be appointed. In the recent past, the prestige of the office suffered from the fact that recruitment to the UN Secretariat gave priority to 'as wide a geographical basis as possible' over 'the highest standards of efficiency, competence, and integrity', reversing the order set out in the Charter (Article 101(3)). This practice arises from pressure from the member governments to obtain appointments for their nationals and also from electoral campaigning by candidates for the office. The salaries offered, moreover, were not attractive to some of the best candidates from developed countries.

The specialized agencies

Along with the United Nations as the central organization, the various other agencies of the UN family also make up an active, probably indispensable, element in organized international relations. The several technical and operational agencies associated in the UN system form a varied picture. Some of the smaller organizations go about their daily activities in a quiet, disciplined and quite effective manner. Little is heard of political controversy at UPU, the International Civil Aviation Organization (ICAO), ITU, WMO, the International Maritime Organization (IMO) and the World Intellectual Property Organization (WIPO). Their useful function in today's world comes closest to what

David Mitrany once called 'technical self-determination.' At the same time, their utility is no guarantee that the winds of political controversy can never disturb them.

The two big financial agencies, the World Bank and its daughters, and the IMF, remain strong, independent and generally respected institutions. Because their system of weighted voting allows the main capital-contributing governments to set the tone of the discussions in these Washington-based agencies, they have avoided the peril of 'politicization.' The management of the Bank and Fund remain highly technocratic, with a strong reliance on market forces and, compared to other agencies, relatively little democratic control. Their staff policies are primarily based on qualitative considerations rather than geographical distribution. The skills of these organizations, however, do not protect them from the accusation, especially from the poor countries, that they are guided by an ungenerous attitude. This implies that they allow a preference for financially sound economic policies to override those of a social and humanitarian nature. This criticism poses a dilemma, for, without practices acceptable to the international banking community, they could not raise the funds needed for their operation; but with them they leave their member-clients unsatisfied.

The 'Big Four' specialized agencies, UNESCO, WHO, FAO and ILO, all have felt the lash of criticism, culminating in accusations of mismanagement and 'politicization.' The term is used mostly by western governments when they find the forums of the specialized agencies used for controversial proposals not to their liking. Applications for membership by the Palestine Liberation Organization (PLO) offer a case in point. As membership in the United Nations itself remains unattainable because of the likelihood that the United States and perhaps others would veto the application in the Security Council, Arab governments have tried on several occasions to open seats for the PLO in UNESCO, WHO and FAO. These attempts set off bitter political debates with the United States announcing that it would cut off its considerable financial contributions to these organizations and thus threaten their very existence.

The United States not only withdrew from UNESCO, as mentioned, but from the ILO in the 1970s. It returned to the latter soon afterward. The United States and some other governments also levied accusations of inefficiency and bureaucracy against FAO, but withdrawals like those affecting UNESCO did not follow. The organizations continued to function, but there is little doubt that this is an issue of 'politicization' with a long life.

Some of these difficulties have a structural origin, given the powerful and secure positions held by the chief executives of most of the specialized agencies. They can act as if they were princes in their own fiefdoms with little outside control over their activities and positive support from their own constituencies within national governments. Neither ECOSOC nor the General Assembly effectively can direct what the agencies do. Given the variety of motives that plays in the selection of the chief executives of the specialized agencies and even some of the organizations, such as UNICEF and UNCTAD, that report to the General Assembly, the difficulty of coordinating the system seems likely to persist.

Yet these difficulties should not be overdramatized, no matter what impression an occasional crisis produces for the headline readers of the international press. The specialized agencies serve and are likely to continue to serve as a bedrock of information, skills and cooperation in their fields. They offer genuine services in such activities as the combat by WHO against transmissible diseases, including AIDS; the search for an end to hunger in the world by FAO; the setting of labor standards by ILO; and the promotion of literacy and scientific networks by UNESCO. It would indeed be hard to imagine a world that would not be worse off without them.

The UN in the 21ˢᵗ century

Before the new century was a decade old, the United Nations clearly was changing in the ways it operated internally, in the support it received from its members, and in the expectations it meets and the functions it served. Its aims were reformulated and its methods modernized under the impact of internal and external criticism. Striking as this was, it owed little to the manifold proposals for structural reform that had been discussed for years and almost never put into practice. Members of the organization were far from agreement on proposals for such changes as weighted voting in the General Assembly, associate membership for micro-states, expansion of the membership of the Security Council, abolition of the veto or the establishment of a stable financial basis for the UN. Nevertheless, approaching 60 years after its founding, the United Nations not only existed but showed capacity to revive its appeal, undertake the slow diplomatic process of reform and even at times to gain new strength.

Fifty national governments founded the United Nations in 1945. Since then, nearly three times that many have joined the organization, most of them one-time colonies that are now independent. With almost no exceptions, all governments in the world consider it of importance to belong. They find uses for the organization to satisfy some of their policy needs and in seeking international cooperation and peaceful negotiation of differences. Most of them complain of its shortcomings, as well, and sometimes with good cause, as this volume has tried to point out. Despite that, there is every reason to expect that the United Nations will continue as a usually indispensable, if only occasionally decisive, factor in the international politics of the 21st century.

Appendix: Charter of the United Nations

WE THE PEOPLES OF THE UNITED NATIONS DETERMINED
    to save succeeding generations from the scourge of war, which twice in our lifetime has brought untold sorrow to mankind, and
    to reaffirm faith in fundamental human rights, in the dignity and worth of the human person, in the equal rights of men and women and of nations large and small, and
    to establish conditions under which justice and respect for the obligations arising from treaties and other sources of international law can be maintained, and
    to promote social progress and better standards of life in larger freedom,

AND FOR THESE ENDS
    to practice tolerance and live together in peace with one another as good neighbours, and
    to unite our strength to maintain international peace and security, and
    to ensure, by the acceptance of principles and the institution of methods, that armed force shall not be used, save in the common interest, and
    to employ international machinery for the promotion of the economic and social advancement of all peoples,

HAVE RESOLVED TO COMBINE OUR EFFORTS TO ACCOMPLISH THESE AIMS
Accordingly, our respective Governments, through representatives assembled in the city of San Francisco, who have exhibited their full powers found to be in good and due form, have agreed to the present Charter of the United Nations and do hereby establish an international organization to be known as the United Nations.

CHAPTER I

PURPOSE AND PRINCIPLES

Article 1

The Purposes of the United Nations are:
1. To maintain international peace and security, and to that end: to take effective collective measures for the prevention and removal of threats to the peace, and for the suppression of acts of aggression or other breaches of the peace, and to bring about by peaceful means, and in conformity with the principles of justice and international law, adjustment or settlement of international disputes or situations which might lead to a breach of the peace;

2. To develop friendly relations among nations based on respect for the principle of equal rights and self-determination of peoples, and to take other appropriate measures to strengthen universal peace;
3. To achieve international co-operation in solving international problems of an economic, social, cultural, or humanitarian character, and in promoting and encouraging respect for human rights and for fundamental freedoms for all without distinction as to race, sex, language, or religion; and
4. To be a centre for harmonizing the actions of nations in the attainment of these common ends.

Article 2

The Organization and its Members, in pursuit of the Purposes stated in Article 1, shall act in accordance with the following Principles.
1. The Organization is based on the principle of the sovereign equality of all its Members.
2. All Members, in order to ensure to all of them the rights and benefits resulting from membership, shall fulfill in good faith the obligations assumed by them in accordance with the present Charter.
3. All Members shall settle their international disputes by peaceful means in such a manner that international peace and security, and justice, are not endangered.
4. All Members shall refrain in their international relations from the threat or use of force against the territorial integrity or political independence of any state, or in any other manner inconsistent with the Purposes of the United Nations.
5. All Members shall give the United Nations every assistance in any action it takes in accordance with the present Charter, and shall refrain from giving assistance to any state against which the United Nations is taking preventive or enforcement action.
6. The Organization shall ensure that states which are not Members of the United Nations act in accordance with these Principles so far as may be necessary for the maintenance of international peace and security.
7. Nothing contained in the present Charter shall authorize the United Nations to intervene in matters which are essentially within the domestic jurisdiction of any state or shall require the Members to submit such matters to settlement under the present Charter; but this principle shall not prejudice the application of enforcement measures under Charter VII.

CHAPTER II

MEMBERSHIP

Article 3

The original Members of the United Nations shall be the states which, having participated in the United Nations Conference on International Organization at San Francisco, or having previously signed the Declaration by United Nations of 1 January 1942, sign the present Charter and ratify it in accordance with Article 110.

Article 4

1. Membership in the United Nations is open to all other peace-loving states which accept the obligations contained in the present Charter and, in the judgment of the Organization, are able and willing to carry out these obligations.
2. The admission of any such state to membership in the United Nations will be effected by a decision of the General Assembly upon the recommendation of the Security Council.

Article 5

A Member of the United Nations against which preventive or enforcement action has been taken by the Security Council may be suspended from the exercise of the rights and privileges of membership by the General Assembly upon the recommendation of the Security Council. The exercise of these rights and privileges may be restored by the Security Council.

Article 6

A Member of the United Nations which has persistently violated the Principles contained in the present Charter may be expelled from the Organization by the General Assembly upon the recommendation of the Security Council.

CHAPTER III

ORGANS

Article 7

1. There are established as the principal organs of the United Nations: a General Assembly, a Security Council, an Economic and Social Council, a Trusteeship Council, an International Court of Justice, and a Secretariat.
2. Such subsidiary organs as may be found necessary may be established in accordance with the present Charter.

Article 8

The United Nations shall place no restrictions on the eligibility of men and women to participate in any capacity and under conditions of equality in its principal and subsidiary organs.

CHAPTER IV

THE GENERAL ASSEMBLY

COMPOSITION

Article 9

1. The General Assembly shall consist of all the Members of the United Nations.
2. Each Member shall have not more than five representatives in the General Assembly.

FUNCTIONS and POWERS

Article 10

The General Assembly may discuss any questions or any matters within the scope of the present Charter or relating to the powers and functions of any organs provided for in the present Charter, and, except as provided in Article 12, may make recommendations to the Members of the United Nations or to the Security Council or to both on any such questions or matters.

Article 11

1. The General Assembly may consider the general principles of co-operation in the maintenance of international peace and security, including the principles governing disarmament and the regulation of armaments, and may make recommendations with regard to such principles to the Members or to the Security Council or to both.
2. The General Assembly may discuss any questions relating to the maintenance of international peace and security brought before it by any Member of the United Nations, or by the Security Council, or by a state which is not a Member of the United Nations in accordance with Article 35, paragraph 2, and, except as provided in Article 12, may make recommendations with regard to any such questions to the state or states concerned or to the Security Council or to both. Any such question on which action is necessary shall be referred to the Security Council by the General Assembly either before or after discussion.
3. The General Assembly may call the attention of the Security Council to situations which are likely to endanger international peace and security.
4. The powers of the General Assembly set forth in this Article shall not limit the general scope of Article 10.

Article 12

1. While the Security Council is exercising in respect of any dispute or situation the functions assigned to it in the present Charter, the General Assembly shall not make any recommendation with regard to that dispute or situation unless the Security Council so requests.
2. The Secretary-General, with the consent of the Security Council, shall notify the General Assembly at each session of any matters relative to the maintenance of international peace and security which are being dealt with by the Security Council and shall similarly notify the General Assembly, or the Members of the United Nations if the General Assembly is not in session, immediately the Security Council ceases to deal with such matters.

Article 13

1. The General Assembly shall initiate studies and make recommendations for the purpose of:
   a. promoting international co-operation in the political field and encouraging the progressive development of international law and its codification;
   b. promoting international co-operation in the economic, social, cultural, educational, and health fields, and assisting in the realization of human

rights and fundamental freedoms for all without distinction as to race, sex, language, or religion.
2. The further responsibilities, functions and powers of the General Assembly with respect to matters mentioned in paragraph 1 (b) above are set forth in Chapters IX and X.

Article 14

Subject to the provisions of Article 12, the General Assembly may recommend measures for the peaceful adjustment of any situation, regardless of origin, which it deems likely to impair the general welfare or friendly relations among nations, including situations resulting from a violation of the provisions of the present Charter setting forth the Purposes and Principles of the United Nations.

Article 15

1. The General Assembly shall receive and consider annual and special reports from the Security Council; these reports shall include an account of the measures that the Security Council has decided upon or taken to maintain international peace and security.
2. The General Assembly shall receive and consider reports from the other organs of the United Nations.

Article 16

The General Assembly shall perform such functions with respect to the international trusteeship system as are assigned to it under Chapters XII and XIII, including the approval of the trusteeship agreements for areas not designated as strategic.

Article 17

The General Assembly shall consider and approve the budget of the Organization.
1. The expenses of the Organization shall be borne by the Members as apportioned by the General Assembly.
2. The General Assembly shall consider and approve any financial and budgetary arrangements with specialized agencies referred to in Article 57 and shall examine the administrative budgets of such specialized agencies with a view to making recommendations to the agencies concerned.

VOTING

Article 18

1. Each member of the General Assembly shall have one vote.
2. Decisions of the General Assembly on important questions shall be made by a two-thirds majority of the members present and voting. These questions shall include: recommendations with respect to the maintenance of international peace and security, the election of the non-permanent members of the Security Council, the election of the members of the Economic and Social Council, the election of members of the Trusteeship Council in accordance with paragraph 1 (c) of Article 86, the admission of new Members to the

United Nations, the suspension of the rights and privileges of membership, the expulsion of Members, questions relating to the operation of the trusteeship system, and budgetary questions.
3. Decisions on other questions, including the determination of additional categories of questions to be decided by a two-thirds majority, shall be made by a majority of the members present and voting.

Article 19

A Member of the United Nations which is in arrears in the payment of its financial contributions to the Organization shall have no vote in the General Assembly if the amount of its arrears equals or exceeds the amount of the contributions due from it for the preceding two full years. The General Assembly may, nevertheless, permit such a Member to vote if it is satisfied that the failure to pay is due to conditions beyond the control of the Member.

PROCEDURE

Article 20

The General Assembly shall meet in regular annual sessions and in such special sessions as occasion may require. Special sessions shall be convoked by the Secretary-General at the request of the Security Council or of a majority of the Members of the United Nations.

Article 21

The General Assembly shall adopt its own rules of procedure. It shall elect its President for each session.

Article 22

The General Assembly may establish such subsidiary organs as it deems necessary for the performance of its functions.

CHAPTER V

THE SECURITY COUNCIL

COMPOSITION

Article 23

1. The Security Council shall consist of fifteen Members of the United Nations. The Republic of China, France, the Union of Soviet Socialist Republics, the United Kingdom of Great Britain and Northern Ireland, and the United States of America shall be permanent members of the Security Council. The General Assembly shall elect ten other Members of the United Nations to be non-permanent members of the Security Council, due regard being specially paid, in the first instance to the contribution of Members of the United Nations to the maintenance of international peace

and security and to the other purposes of the Organization, and also to equitable geographical distribution.
2. The non-permanent members of the Security Council shall be elected for a term of two years. In the first election of the non-permanent members after the increase of the membership of the Security Council from eleven to fifteen, two of the four additional members shall be chosen for a term of one year. A retiring member shall not be eligible for immediate re-election.
3. Each member of the Security Council shall have one representative.

FUNCTIONS and POWERS

Article 24

1. In order to ensure prompt and effective action by the United Nations, its Members confer on the Security Council primary responsibility for the maintenance of international peace and security, and agree that in carrying out its duties under this responsibility the Security Council acts on their behalf.
2. In discharging these duties the Security Council shall act in accordance with the Purposes and Principles of the United Nations. The specific powers granted to the Security Council for the discharge of these duties are laid down in Chapters VI, VII, VIII, and XII.
3. The Security Council shall submit annual and, when necessary, special reports to the General Assembly for its consideration.

Article 25

The Members of the United Nations agree to accept and carry out the decisions of the Security Council in accordance with the present Charter.

Article 26

In order to promote the establishment and maintenance of international peace and security with the least diversion for armaments of the world's human and economic resources, the Security Council shall be responsible for formulating, with the assistance of the Military Staff Committee referred to in Article 47, plans to be submitted to the Members of the United Nations for the establishment of a system for the regulation of armaments.

VOTING

Article 27

1. Each member of the Security Council shall have one vote.
2. Decisions of the Security Council on procedural matters shall be made by an affirmative vote of nine members.
3. Decisions of the Security Council on all other matters shall be made by an affirmative vote of nine members including the concurring votes of the permanent members; provided that, in decisions under Chapter VI, and under paragraph 3 of Article 52, a party to a dispute shall abstain from voting.

PROCEDURE

Article 28

1. The Security Council shall be so organized as to be able to function continuously. Each member of the Security Council shall for this purpose be represented at all times at the seat of the Organization.
2. The Security Council shall hold periodic meetings at which each of its members may, if it so desires, be represented by a member of the government or by some other specially designated representative.
3. The Security Council may hold meetings at such places other than the seat of the Organization as in its judgment will best facilitate its work.

Article 29

The Security Council may establish such subsidiary organs as it deems necessary for the performance of its functions.

Article 30

The Security Council shall adopt its own rules of procedure, including the method of selecting its President.

Article 31

Any Member of the United Nations which is not a member of the Security Council may participate, without vote, in the discussion of any question brought before the Security Council whenever the latter considers that the interests of that Member are specially affected.

Article 32

Any Member of the United Nations which is not a member of the Security Council or any state which is not a Member of the United Nations, if it is a party to a dispute under consideration by the Security Council, shall be invited to participate, without vote, in the discussion relating to the dispute. The Security Council shall lay down such conditions as it deems just for the participation of a state which is not a Member of the United Nations.

CHAPTER VI

PACIFIC SETTLEMENT OF DISPUTES

Article 33

1. The parties to any dispute, the continuance of which is likely to endanger the maintenance of international peace and security, shall, first of all, seek a solution by negotiation, enquiry, mediation, conciliation, arbitration, judicial settlement, resort to regional agencies or arrangements, or other peaceful means of their own choice.

2. The Security Council shall, when it deems necessary, call upon the parties to settle their dispute by such means.

Article 34

The Security Council may investigate any dispute, or any situation which might lead to international friction or give rise to a dispute, in order to determine whether the continuance of the dispute or situation is likely to endanger the maintenance of international peace and security.

Article 35

1. Any Member of the United Nations may bring any dispute, or any situation of the nature referred to in Article 34, to the attention of the Security Council or of the General Assembly.
2. A state which is not a Member of the United Nations may bring to the attention of the Security Council or of the General Assembly any dispute to which it is a party if it accepts in advance, for the purposes of the dispute, the obligations of pacific settlement provided in the present Charter.
3. The proceedings of the General Assembly in respect of matters brought to its attention under this Article will be subject to the provisions of Articles 11 and 12.

Article 36

1. The Security Council may, at any stage of a dispute of the nature referred to in Article 33 or of a situation of like nature, recommend appropriate procedures or methods of adjustment.
2. The Security Council should take into consideration any procedures for the settlement of the dispute which have already been adopted by the parties.
3. In making recommendations under this Article the Security Council should also take into consideration that legal disputes should as a general rule be referred by the parties to the International Court of Justice in accordance with the provisions of the Statute of the Court.

Article 37

1. Should the parties to a dispute of the nature referred to in Article 33 fail to settle it by the means indicated in that Article, they shall refer it to the Security Council.
2. If the Security Council deems that the continuance of the dispute is in fact likely to endanger the maintenance of international peace and security, it shall decide whether to take action under Article 36 or to recommend such terms of settlement as it may consider appropriate.

Article 38

Without prejudice to the provisions of Articles 33 to 37, the Security Council may, if all the parties to any dispute so request, make recommendations to the parties with a view to a pacific settlement of the dispute.

CHAPTER VII

ACTION WITH RESPECT TO THREATS TO THE PEACE, BREACHES OF THE PEACE, AND ACTS OF AGGRESSION

Article 39

The Security Council shall determine the existence of any threat to the peace, breach of the peace, or act of aggression and shall make recommendations, or decide what measures shall be taken in accordance with Articles 41 and 42, to maintain or restore international peace and security.

Article 40

In order to prevent an aggravation of the situation, the Security Council may, before making the recommendations or deciding upon the measures provided for in Article 39, call upon the parties concerned to comply with such provisional measures as it deems necessary or desirable. Such provisional measures shall be without prejudice to the rights, claims, or position of the parties concerned. The Security Council shall duly take account of failure to comply with such provisional measures.

Article 41

The Security Council may decide what measures not involving the use of armed force are to be employed to give effect to its decisions, and it may call upon the Members of the United Nations to apply such measures. These may include complete or partial interruption of economic relations and of rail, sea, air, postal, telegraphic, radio, and other means of communication, and the severance of diplomatic relations.

Article 42

Should the Security Council consider that measures provided for in Article 41 would be inadequate or have proved to be inadequate, it may take such action by air, sea, or land forces as may be necessary to maintain or restore international peace and security. Such action may include demonstrations, blockade, and other operations by air, sea, or land forces of Members of the United Nations.

Article 43

1. All Members of the United Nations, in order to contribute to the maintenance of international peace and security, undertake to make available to the Security Council, on its call and in accordance with a special agreement or agreements, armed forces, assistance, and facilities, including rights of passage, necessary for the purpose of maintaining international peace and security.
2. Such agreement or agreements shall govern the numbers and types of forces, their degree of readiness and general location, and the nature of the facilities and assistance to be provided.
3. The agreement or agreements shall be negotiated as soon as possible on the initiative of the Security Council. They shall be concluded between the Security Council and Members or between the Security Council and groups

of Members and shall be subject to ratification by the signatory states in accordance with their respective constitutional processes.

Article 44

When the Security Council has decided to use force it shall, before calling upon a Member not represented on it to provide armed forces in fulfilment of the obligations assumed under Article 43, invite that Member, if the Member so desires, to participate in the decisions of the Security Council concerning the employment of contingents of that Member's armed forces.

Article 45

In order to enable the United Nations to take urgent military measures, Members shall hold immediately available national air-force contingents for combined international enforcement action. The strength and degree of readiness of these contingents and plans for their combined action shall be determined within the limits laid down in the special agreement or agreements referred to in Article 43, by the Security Council with the assistance of the Military Staff Committee.

Article 46

Plans for the application of armed force shall be made by the Security Council with the assistance of the Military Staff Committee.

Article 47

1. There shall be established a Military Staff Committee to advise and assist the Security Council on all questions relating to the Security Council's military requirements for the maintenance of international peace and security, the employment and command of forces placed at its disposal, the regulation of armaments, and possible disarmament.
2. The Military Staff Committee shall consist of the Chiefs of Staff of the permanent members of the Security Council or their representatives. Any Member of the United Nations not permanently represented on the Committee shall be invited by the Committee to be associated with it when the efficient discharge of the Committee's responsibilities requires the participation of that Member in its work.
3. The Military Staff Committee shall be responsible under the Security Council for the strategic direction of any armed forces placed at the disposal of the Security Council. Questions relating to the command of such forces shall be worked out subsequently.
4. The Military Staff Committee, with the authorization of the Security Council and after consultation with appropriate regional agencies, may establish regional sub-committees.

Article 48

1. The action required to carry out the decisions of the Security Council for the maintenance of international peace and security shall be taken by all the Members of the United Nations or by some of them, as the Security Council may determine.

2. Such decisions shall be carried out by the Members of the United Nations directly and through their action in the appropriate international agencies of which they are members.

Article 49

The Members of the United Nations shall join in affording mutual assistance in carrying out the measures decided upon by the Security Council.

Article 50

If preventive or enforcement measures against any state are taken by the Security Council, any other state, whether a Member of the United Nations or not, which finds itself confronted with special economic problems arising from the carrying out of those measures shall have the right to consult the Security Council with regard to a solution of those problems.

Article 51

Nothing in the present Charter shall impair the inherent right of individual or collective self-defence if an armed attack occurs against a Member of the United Nations, until the Security Council has taken measures necessary to maintain international peace and security. Measures taken by Members in the exercise of this right of self-defence shall be immediately reported to the Security Council and shall not in any way affect the authority and responsibility of the Security Council under the present Charter to take at any time such action as it deems necessary in order to maintain or restore international peace and security.

CHAPTER VIII

REGIONAL ARRANGEMENTS

Article 52

1. Nothing in the present Charter precludes the existence of regional arrangements or agencies for dealing with such matters relating to the maintenance of international peace and security as are appropriate for regional action provided that such arrangements or agencies and their activities are consistent with the Purposes and Principles of the United Nations.
2. The Members of the United Nations entering into such arrangements or constituting such agencies shall make every effort to achieve pacific settlement of local disputes through such regional arrangements or by such regional agencies before referring them to the Security Council.
3. The Security Council shall encourage the development of pacific settlement of local disputes through such regional arrangements or by such regional agencies either on the initiative of the states concerned or by reference from the Security Council.
4. This Article in no way impairs the application of Articles 34 and 35.

Article 53

1. The Security Council shall, where appropriate, utilize such regional arrange-ments or agencies for enforcement action under its authority. But no enforce-ment action shall be taken under regional arrangements or by regional agencies without the authorization of the Security Council, with the exception of mea-sures against any enemy state, as defined in paragraph 2 of this Article, pro-vided for pursuant to Article 107 or in regional arrangements directed against renewal of aggressive policy on the part of any such state, until such time as the Organization may, on request of the Governments concerned, be charged with the responsibility for preventing further aggression by such a state.
2. The term enemy state as used in paragraph 1 of this Article applies to any state which during the Second World War has been an enemy of any signatory of the present Charter.

Article 54

The Security Council shall at all times be kept fully informed of activities under-taken or in contemplation under regional arrangements or by regional agencies for the maintenance of international peace and security.

CHAPTER IX

INTERNATIONAL ECONOMIC AND SOCIAL CO-OPERATION

Article 55

With a view to the creation of conditions of stability and well-being which are necessary for peaceful and friendly relations among nations based on respect for the principle of equal rights and self-determination of peoples, the United Nations shall promote:
a. higher standards of living, full employment, and conditions of economic and social progress and development;
b. solutions of international economic, social, health, and related problems; and international cultural and educational cooperation; and
c. universal respect for, and observance of, human rights and fundamental free-doms for all without distinction as to race, sex, language, or religion.

Article 56

All Members pledge themselves to take joint and separate action in co-operation with the Organization for the achievement of the purposes set forth in Article 55.

Article 57

1. The various specialized agencies, established by intergovernmental agree-ment and having wide international responsibilities, as defined in their basic instruments, in economic, social, cultural, educational, health, and related fields, shall be brought into relationship with the United Nations in accor-dance with the provisions of Article 63.

2. Such agencies thus brought into relationship with the United Nations are hereinafter referred to as specialized agencies.

Article 58

The Organization shall make recommendations for the co-ordination of the policies and activities of the specialized agencies.

Article 59

The Organization shall, where appropriate, initiate negotiations among the states concerned for the creation of any new specialized agencies required for the accomplishment of the purposes set forth in Article 55.

Article 60

Responsibility for the discharge of the functions of the Organization set forth in this Chapter shall be vested in the General Assembly and, under the authority of the General Assembly, in the Economic and Social Council, which shall have for this purpose the powers set forth in Chapter X.

CHAPTER X

THE ECONOMIC AND SOCIAL COUNCIL

COMPOSITION

Article 61

1. The Economic and Social Council shall consist of fifty-four Members of the United Nations elected by the General Assembly.
2. Subject to the provisions of paragraph 3, eighteen members of the Economic and Social Council shall be elected each year for a term of three years. A retiring member shall be eligible for immediate re-election.
3. At the first election after the increase in the membership of the Economic and Social Council from twenty-seven to fifty-four members, in addition to the members elected in place of the nine members whose term of office expires at the end of that year, twenty-seven additional members shall be elected. Of these twenty-seven additional members, the term of office of nine members so elected shall expire at the end of one year, and of nine other members at the end of two years, in accordance with arrangements made by the General Assembly.
4. Each member of the Economic and Social Council shall have one representative.

FUNCTIONS and POWERS

Article 62

1. The Economic and Social Council may make or initiate studies and reports with respect to international economic, social, cultural, educational, health, and related matters and may make recommendations with respect to any

such matters to the General Assembly to the Members of the United Nations, and to the specialized agencies concerned.

2. It may make recommendations for the purpose of promoting respect for, and observance of, human rights and fundamental freedoms for all.
3. It may prepare draft conventions for submission to the General Assembly, with respect to matters falling within its competence.
4. It may call, in accordance with the rules prescribed by the United Nations, international conferences on matters falling within its competence.

Article 63

1. The Economic and Social Council may enter into agreements with any of the agencies referred to in Article 57, defining the terms on which the agency concerned shall be brought into relationship with the United Nations. Such agreements shall be subject to approval by the General Assembly.
2. It may co-ordinate the activities of the specialized agencies through consultation with and recommendations to such agencies and through recommendations to the General Assembly and to the Members of the United Nations.

Article 64

1. The Economic and Social Council may take appropriate steps to obtain regular reports from the specialized agencies. It may make arrangements with the Members of the United Nations and with the specialized agencies to obtain reports on the steps taken to give effect to its own recommendations and to recommendations on matters falling within its competence made by the General Assembly.
2. It may communicate its observations on these reports to the General Assembly.

Article 65

The Economic and Social Council may furnish information to the Security Council and shall assist the Security Council upon its request.

Article 66

1. The Economic and Social Council shall perform such functions as fall within its competence in connexion with the carrying out of the recommendations of the General Assembly.
2. It may, with the approval of the General Assembly, perform services at the request of Members of the United Nations and at the request of specialized agencies.
3. It shall perform such other functions as are specified elsewhere in the present Charter or as may be assigned to it by the General Assembly.

VOTING

Article 67

1. Each member of the Economic and Social Council shall have one vote.
2. Decisions of the Economic and Social Council shall be made by a majority of the members present and voting.

PROCEDURE

Article 68

The Economic and Social Council shall set up commissions in economic and social fields and for the promotion of human rights, and such other commissions as may be required for the performance of its functions.

Article 69

The Economic and Social Council shall invite any Member of the United Nations to participate, without vote, in its deliberations on any matter of particular concern to that Member.

Article 70

The Economic and Social Council may make arrangements for representatives of the specialized agencies to participate, without vote, in its deliberations and in those of the commissions established by it, and for its representatives to participate in the deliberations of the specialized agencies.

Article 71

The Economic and Social Council may make suitable arrangements for consultation with non-governmental organizations which are concerned with matters within its competence. Such arrangements may be made with international organizations and, where appropriate, with national organizations after consultation with the Member of the United Nations concerned.

Article 72

1. The Economic and Social Council shall adopt its own rules of procedure, including the method of selecting its President.
2. The Economic and Social Council shall meet as required in accordance with its rules, which shall include provision for the convening of meetings on the request of a majority of its members.

CHAPTER XI

DECLARATION REGARDING NON-SELF-GOVERNING TERRITORIES

Article 73

Members of the United Nations which have or assume responsibilities for the administration of territories whose peoples have not yet attained a full measure of self-government recognize the principle that the interests of the inhabitants of these territories are paramount, and accept as a sacred trust the obligation to promote to the utmost, within the system of international peace and security established by the present Charter, the well-being of the inhabitants of these territories, and, to this end:

a. to ensure, with due respect for the culture of the peoples concerned, their political, economic, social, and educational advancement, their just treatment, and their protection against abuses;

b. to develop self-government, to take due account of the political aspirations of the peoples, and to assist them in the progressive development of their free political institutions, according to the particular circumstances of each territory and its peoples and their varying stages of advancement;

c. to further international peace and security;

d. to promote constructive measures of development, to encourage research, and to co-operate with one another and, when and where appropriate, with specialized international bodies with a view to the practical achievement of the social, economic, and scientific purposes set forth in this Article; and

e. to transmit regularly to the Secretary-General for information purposes, subject to such limitation as security and constitutional considerations may require, statistical and other information of a technical nature relating to economic, social, and educational conditions in the territories for which they are respectively responsible other than those territories to which Chapters XII and XIII apply.

Article 74

Members of the United Nations also agree that their policy in respect of the territories to which this Chapter applies, no less than in respect of their metropolitan areas, must be based on the general principle of good-neighbourliness, due account being taken of the interests and well-being of the rest of the world, in social, economic, and commercial matters.

CHAPTER XII

INTERNATIONAL TRUSTEESHIP SYSTEM

Article 75

The United Nations shall establish under its authority an international trusteeship system for the administration and supervision of such territories as may be placed thereunder by subsequent individual agreements. These territories are hereinafter referred to as trust territories.

Article 76

The basic objectives of the trusteeship system, in accordance with the Purposes of the United Nations laid down in Article 1 of the present Charter, shall be:

a. to further international peace and security;

b. to promote the political, economic, social, and educational advancement of the inhabitants of the trust territories, and their progressive development towards self-government or independence as may be appropriate to the particular circumstances of each territory and its peoples and the freely expressed wishes of the peoples concerned, and as may be provided by the terms of each trusteeship agreement;

c. to encourage respect for human rights and for fundamental freedoms for all without distinction as to race, sex, language, or religion, and to encourage recognition of the interdependence of the peoples of the world; and

d. to ensure equal treatment in social, economic, and commercial matters for all Members of the United Nations and their nationals, and also equal treatment for the latter in the administration of justice, without prejudice to the attainment of the foregoing objectives and subject to the provisions of Article 80.

Article 77

1. The trusteeship system shall apply to such territories in the following categories as may be placed thereunder by means of trusteeship agreements:
   a. territories now held under mandate;
   b. territories which may be detached from enemy states as a result of the Second World War; and
   c. territories voluntarily placed under the system by states responsible for their administration.
2. It will be a matter for subsequent agreement as to which territories in the foregoing categories will be brought under the trusteeship system and upon what terms.

Article 78

The trusteeship system shall not apply to territories which have become Members of the United Nations, relationship among which shall be based on respect for the principle of sovereign equality.

Article 79

The terms of trusteeship for each territory to be placed under the trusteeship system, including any alteration or amendment, shall be agreed upon by the states directly concerned, including the mandatory power in the case of territories held under mandate by a Member of the United Nations, and shall be approved as provided for in Articles 83 and 85.

Article 80

1. Except as may be agreed upon in individual trusteeship agreements, made under Articles 77, 79, and 81, placing each territory under the trusteeship system, and until such agreements have been concluded, nothing in this Chapter shall be construed in or of itself to alter in any manner the rights whatsoever of any states or any peoples or the terms of existing international instruments to which Members of the United Nations may respectively be parties.
2. Paragraph 1 of this Article shall not be interpreted as giving grounds for delay or postponement of the negotiation and conclusion of agreements for placing mandated and other territories under the trusteeship system as provided for in Article 77.

Article 81

The trusteeship agreement shall in each case include the terms under which the trust territory will be administered and designate the authority which will exercise the administration of the trust territory. Such authority, hereinafter called the administering authority, may be one or more states or the Organization itself.

Article 82

There may be designated, in any trusteeship agreement, a strategic area or areas which may include part or all of the trust territory to which the agreement applies, without prejudice to any special agreement or agreements made under Article 43.

Article 83

1. All functions of the United Nations relating to strategic areas, including the approval of the terms of the trusteeship agreements and of their alteration or amendment shall be exercised by the Security Council.
2. The basic objectives set forth in Article 76 shall be applicable to the people of each strategic area.
3. The Security Council shall, subject to the provisions of the trusteeship agreements and without prejudice to security considerations, avail itself of the assistance of the Trusteeship Council to perform those functions of the United Nations under the trusteeship system relating to political, economic, social, and educational matters in the strategic areas.

Article 84

It shall be the duty of the administering authority to ensure that the trust territory shall play its part in the maintenance of international peace and security. To this end the administering authority may make use of volunteer forces, facilities, and assistance from the trust territory in carrying out the obligations towards the Security Council undertaken in this regard by the administering authority, as well as for local defence and the maintenance of law and order within the trust territory.

Article 85

1. The functions of the United Nations with regard to trusteeship agreements for all areas not designated as strategic, including the approval of the terms of the trusteeship agreements and of their alteration or amendment, shall be exercised by the General Assembly.
2. The Trusteeship Council, operating under the authority of the General Assembly shall assist the General Assembly in carrying out these functions.

CHAPTER XIII

THE TRUSTEESHIP COUNCIL

COMPOSITION

Article 86

1. The Trusteeship Council shall consist of the following Members of the United Nations:
   a. those Members administering trust territories;
   b. such of those Members mentioned by name in Article 23 as are not administering trust territories; and
   c. as many other Members elected for three-year terms by the General Assembly as may be necessary to ensure that the total number of members of the Trusteeship Council is equally divided between those Members of the United Nations which administer trust territories and those which do not.
2. Each member of the Trusteeship Council shall designate one specially qualified person to represent it therein.

FUNCTIONS and POWERS

Article 87

The General Assembly and, under its authority, the Trusteeship Council, in carrying out their functions, may:

a. consider reports submitted by the administering authority;

b. accept petitions and examine them in consultation with the administering authority;

c. provide for periodic visits to the respective trust territories at times agreed upon with the administering authority; and

d. take these and other actions in conformity with the terms of the trusteeship agreements.

Article 88

The Trusteeship Council shall formulate a questionnaire on the political, economic, social, and educational advancement of the inhabitants of each trust territory, and the administering authority for each trust territory within the competence of the General Assembly shall make an annual report to the General Assembly upon the basis of such questionnaire.

VOTING

Article 89

1. Each member of the Trusteeship Council shall have one vote.
2. Decisions of the Trusteeship Council shall be made by a majority of the members present and voting.

PROCEDURE

Article 90

1. The Trusteeship Council shall adopt its own rules of procedure, including the method of selecting its President.
2. The Trusteeship Council shall meet as required in accordance with its rules, which shall include provision for the convening of meetings on the request of a majority of its members.

Article 91

The Trusteeship Council shall, when appropriate, avail itself of the assistance of the Economic and Social Council and of the specialized agencies in regard to matters with which they are respectively concerned.

CHAPTER XIV

THE INTERNATIONAL COURT OF JUSTICE

Article 92

The International Court of Justice shall be the principal judicial organ of the United Nations. It shall function in accordance with the annexed Statute, which is based upon the Statute of the Permanent Court of International Justice and forms an integral part of the present Charter.

Article 93

1. All Members of the United Nations are *ipso facto* parties to the Statute of the International Court of Justice.
2. A state which is not a Member of the United Nations may become a party to the Statute of the International Court of Justice on conditions to be determined in each case by the General Assembly upon the recommendation of the Security Council.

Article 94

1. Each Member of the United Nations undertakes to comply with the decision of the International Court of Justice in any case to which it is a party.
2. If any party to a case fails to perform the obligations incumbent upon it under a judgment rendered by the Court, the other party may have recourse to the Security Council, which may, if it deems necessary, make recommendations or decide upon measures to be taken to give effect to the judgment.

Article 95

Nothing in the present Charter shall prevent Members of the United Nations from entrusting the solution of their differences to other tribunals by virtue of agreements already in existence or which may be concluded in the future.

Article 96

1. The General Assembly or the Security Council may request the International Court of Justice to give an advisory opinion on any legal question.
2. Other organs of the United Nations and specialized agencies, which may at any time be so authorized by the General Assembly, may also request advisory opinions of the Court on legal questions arising within the scope of their activities.

CHAPTER XV

THE SECRETARIAT

Article 97

The Secretariat shall comprise a Secretary-General and such staff as the Organization may require. The Secretary-General shall be appointed by the General Assembly upon the recommendation of the Security Council. He shall be the chief administrative officer of the Organization.

Article 98

The Secretary-General shall act in that capacity in all meetings of the General Assembly, of the Security Council, of the Economic and Social Council, and of the Trusteeship Council, and shall perform such other functions as are entrusted to him by these organs. The Secretary-General shall make an annual report to the General Assembly on the work of the Organization.

Article 99

The Secretary-General may bring to the attention of the Security Council any matter which in his opinion may threaten the maintenance of international peace and security.

Article 100

1. In the performance of their duties the Secretary-General and the staff shall not seek or receive instructions from any government or from any other authority external to the Organization. They shall refrain from any action which might reflect on their position as international officials responsible only to the Organization.
2. Each Member of the United Nations undertakes to respect the exclusively international character of the responsibilities of the Secretary-General and the staff and not to seek to influence them in the discharge of their responsibilities.

Article 101

1. The staff shall be appointed by the Secretary-General under regulations established by the General Assembly.
2. Appropriate staffs shall be permanently assigned to the Economic and Social Council, the Trusteeship Council, and, as required, to other organs of the United Nations. These staffs shall form a part of the Secretariat.
3. The paramount consideration in the employment of the staff and in the determination of the conditions of service shall be the necessity of securing the highest standards of efficiency, competence, and integrity. Due regard shall be paid to the importance of recruiting the staff on as wide a geographical basis as possible.

CHAPTER XVI

MISCELLANEOUS PROVISIONS

Article 102

1. Every treaty and every international agreement entered into by any Member of the United Nations after the present Charter comes into force shall as soon as possible be registered with the Secretariat and published by it.
2. No party to any such treaty or international agreement which has not been registered in accordance with the provisions of paragraph 1 of this Article may invoke that treaty or agreement before any organ of the United Nations.

Article 103

In the event of a conflict between the obligations of the Members of the United Nations under the present Charter and their obligations under any other international agreement, their obligations under the present Charter shall prevail.

Article 104

The Organization shall enjoy in the territory of each of its Members such legal capacity as may be necessary for the exercise of its functions and the fulfilment of its purposes.

Article 105

1. The Organization shall enjoy in the territory of each of its Members such privileges and immunities as are necessary for the fulfilment of its purposes.
2. Representatives of the Members of the United Nations and officials of the Organization shall similarly enjoy such privileges and immunities as are necessary for the independent exercise of their functions in connexion with the Organization.
3. The General Assembly may make recommendations with a view to determining the details of the application of paragraphs 1 and 2 of this Article or may propose conventions to the Members of the United Nations for this purpose.

CHAPTER XVII

TRANSITIONAL SECURITY ARRANGEMENTS

Article 106

Pending the coming into force of such special agreements referred to in Article 43 as in the opinion of the Security Council enable it to begin the exercise of its responsibilities under Article 42, the parties to the Four-Nation Declaration, signed at Moscow, 30 October 1943, and France, shall, in accordance with the provisions of paragraph 5 of that Declaration, consult with one another and as occasion requires with other Members of the United Nations with a view to such joint action on behalf of the Organization as may be necessary for the purpose of maintaining international peace and security.

Article 107

Nothing in the present Charter shall invalidate or preclude action, in relation to any state which during the Second World War has been an enemy of any signatory to the present Charter, taken or authorized as a result of that war by the Governments having responsibility for such action.

CHAPTER XVIII

AMENDMENTS

Article 108

Amendments to the present Charter shall come into force for all Members of the United Nations when they have been adopted by a vote of two thirds of the members of the General Assembly and ratified in accordance with their respective constitutional processes by two thirds of the Members of the United Nations, including all the permanent members of the Security Council.

Article 109

1. A General Conference of the Members of the United Nations for the purpose of reviewing the present Charter may be held at a date and place to be fixed

by a two-thirds vote of the members of the General Assembly and by a vote of any nine members of the Security Council. Each Member of the United Nations shall have one vote in the conference.

2. Any alteration of the present Charter recommended by a two-thirds vote of the conference shall take effect when ratified in accordance with their respective constitutional processes by two thirds of the Members of the United Nations including all the permanent members of the Security Council.

3. If such a conference has not been held before the tenth annual session of the General Assembly following the coming into force of the present Charter, the proposal to call such a conference shall be placed on the agenda of that session of the General Assembly, and the conference shall be held if so decided by a majority vote of the members of the General Assembly and by a vote of any seven members of the Security Council.

CHAPTER XIX

RATIFICATION AND SIGNATURE

Article 110

1. The present Charter shall be ratified by the signatory states in accordance with their respective constitutional processes.

2. The ratifications shall be deposited with the Government of the United States of America, which shall notify all the signatory states of each deposit as well as the Secretary-General of the Organization when he has been appointed.

3. The present Charter shall come into force upon the deposit of ratifications by the Republic of China, France, the Union of Soviet Socialist Republics, the United Kingdom of Great Britain and Northern Ireland, and the United States of America, and by a majority of the other signatory states. A protocol of the ratifications deposited shall thereupon be drawn up by the Government of the United States of America which shall communicate copies thereof to all the signatory states.

4. The states signatory to the present Charter which ratify it after it has come into force will become original Members of the United Nations on the date of the deposit of their respective ratifications.

Article 111

The present Charter, of which the Chinese, French, Russian, English, and Spanish texts are equally authentic, shall remain deposited in the archives of the Government of the United States of America. Duly certified copies thereof shall be transmitted by that Government to the Governments of the other signatory states.

IN FAITH WHEREOF the representatives of the Governments of the United Nations have signed the present Charter.

DONE at the city of San Francisco the twenty-sixth day of June, one thousand nine hundred and forty-five.

Selected Bibliography

A vast quantity of official documentation and secondary writing is available to anyone wanting to know more about the work of the United Nations. Electronic access to almost all of the official documents, plus press releases and many other reports, publications and links to other organizations, is available at: http://www.un.org. This site also offers material in UN working languages other than English.

Most of the work of deliberative organs is published on paper in the *Official Records* series, which is arranged under the name of the main organs, such as the Security Council or General Assembly, that is responsible for the work. Official documents are available in UN-appointed depository libraries, many of which are in universities and research institutions, as well as in official government installations in member countries. Official publications eventually appear in six official languages: Arabic, Chinese, English, French, Russian, and Spanish. In addition, the UN Secretariat publishes official reports and unofficial public information materials. These materials, available in UN Information Centers in many parts of the world, include statistical publications and guides to, and summaries of the work of the organization.

A comprehensive account of the work of the United Nations can be found in the *Yearbook of the United Nations*, published annually by the UN Department of Public Information. These yearbooks lag some years behind. The yearbooks, which are standard items in reference libraries all over the world and are available on compact disks, contain the texts of the most important resolutions adopted by the deliberative organs, as well as brief versions of debates and a summary of the earlier treatment of the topics by the several organizational agencies. A briefer source that gives structural details and is much favored by diplomats, is *United Nations Handbook* (Wellington: New Zealand Ministry of Foreign Affairs, annual). Another handy source is United Nations, *Basic Facts About the United Nations* (New York, UN Department of Public Information, 2004).

A more independent reference source on current activities is the annual volume, *A Global Agenda: Issues before the ..th General Assembly of the United Nations*, prepared by the United Nations Association of the United States of America. It appears each September at the opening of the General Assembly. A source of scholarly articles and comment UN activities is the journal, *Global Governance*, published by the Academic Council on the United Nations System, whose office is at Wilfrid Laurier University, 75 University Ave.w., Waterloo, ON, CAN N2L 3C5; Internet address: www.acuns.wlu.ca.

General and legal references

For an authoritative legal and historical commentary on the structure and intended operation of the United Nations, see Leland M. Goodrich, Edvard

Hambro, and Anne Patricia Simons, *Charter of the United Nations. Commentary and Documents*, 3rd rev. ed., New York: Columbia University Press, 1969. A more recent legal treatment of UN developments is Bruno Simma (ed.), *The Charter of the United Nations: a commentary*, Oxford & New York: Oxford University Press, 1994. See also Philippe Sands & Pierre Klein (eds), *Bowett's Law of International Institutions*, 5th ed., London: Sweet & Maxwell, 2001; Christopher C. Joyner. (ed.), *The United Nations and International Law*, Cambridge: Cambridge University Press, 1997; Henry G. Schermers, *International Institutional Law*, 3 vols., Leyden: Sijthoff, 1972; Robert C.R. Siekmann, *Basic Documents on United Nations and Related Peace-Keeping Forces*, Dordrecht: Martinus Nijhoff Publishers, second enlarged edition, 1989.

Many general accounts of the United Nations for university study and for broader audiences are available. A noteworthy forthcoming volume is Thomas G. Weiss and Sam Daws (eds), *The Oxford Handbook on the United Nations*, to be published in 2006 by Oxford University Press. Among other helpful general books are: Thomas G. Weiss, David P. Forsythe & Roger A. Coate, *The United Nations and Changing World Politics*, 4th ed., Boulder, CO.: Westview Press, 2004; Inis L. Claude Jr., *Swords into Plowshares*, 4th ed., New York: Random House, 1971; H.G. Nicholas, *The United Nations as Political Institution*, 5th ed., London: Oxford University Press, 1975; Harold K. Jacobson, 2nd ed., *Networks of Interdependence*, New York: Knopf, 1984; Adam Roberts and Benedict Kingsbury (eds), *United Nations, Divided World: The UN's Roles in International Relations*, 2nd ed., Oxford: Clarendon Press, 1993.

Chapter 1   Introduction

Hildebrand, Robert. *Dumbarton Oaks: the Origins of the United Nations and the Search for Postwar Security*. Chapel Hill, NC: University of North Carolina Press, 1990.

Luard, Evan. *A History of the United Nations: The Years of Western Domination*. London: Macmillan, 1982.

Russell, Ruth B. *A History of the United Nations Charter. The Role of the United States*. Washington D.C.: Brookings Institution, 1958.

Schild, Georg. *Bretton Woods and Dumbarton Oaks*. New York: St. Martin's Press, 1995.

Schlesinger, Stephen L. *Act of Creation: the Founding of the United Nations*. Boulder, CO: Westview Press, 2003.

Walters, Frank P. *A History of the League of Nations*, 2 vols. London: Oxford University Press, 1952.

Chapter 2   Charter and Structure of the United Nations

Bailey, Sydney D. and Sam Daws. *The Procedure of the UN Security Council*. Oxford: Oxford University Press, 1998.

Bloed, A. and van Dijk, P. *Forty Years International Court of Justice: Jurisdiction, Equity and Equality*. Utrecht: Europa Instituut, 1988.

Boutros-Ghali, Boutros. *The Unvanquished: a U.S.-U.N. Saga*. New York: Random House, 1999.

Bowett, D.W. *et al. The International Court of Justice: Practice and Procedure.* London: B.I.I.C.L., 1997.

Eyffinger, A. *The International Court of Justice, 1946–1996.* The Hague: Kluwer Law International, 1996.

Finkelstein, Lawrence S. (ed.). *Politics in the United Nations System.* Durham and London: Duke University Press, 1988.

Gordenker, Leon. *The UN Secretary-General and Secretariat.* London: Routledge, 2005.

Matanle, Emma. *The UN Security Council: Prospects for Reform.* London: Royal Institute of International Affairs, 1995.

Meron, Theodor. *The United Nations Secretariat.* Lexington, MA: D.C. Heath, 1977.

Peterson, M.J. *The General Assembly in World Politics.* Boston: Allen & Unwin, 1986.

Rivlin, Benjamin and Gordenker, Leon. (eds). *The Challenging Role of the Secretary-General.* Westport, CT: Praeger, 1993.

Urquhart, Brian. *Hammarskjöld.* New York: Knopf, 1972.

Chapter 3   Membership and Decision-making

Alger, Chadwick F., Lyons, Gene F., Trent, John E. (eds). *The United Nations System: the Policies of Member States.* Tokyo: United Nations University, 1995.

Baehr, Peter R. and Castermans, Monique C. (eds). *The Netherlands and the United Nations: Selected Issues.* The Hague: T.M. Asser Institute, 1990.

Karns, Margaret and Mingst, Karen. *The United States and Multilateral Institutions.* London: Routledge, 1992.

Kaufmann, Johan. *United Nations Decision Making.* Alphen aan den Rijn: Sijthoff & Noordhoff, 1980.

Kaufmann, Johan. *Conference Diplomacy: An Introductory Analysis,* second revised ed. Dordrecht: Martinus Nijhoff Publishers, 1988.

Righter, Rosemary. *Utopia Lost: the United Nations and World Order.* New York: Twentieth Century Fund Press, 1995.

Chapter 4   The Maintenance of Peace and Security

Abi-Saab, Georges. *The United Nations Operation in the Congo 1960–1964.* New York: Oxford University Press, 1978.

Barnett, Michael H. *Eyewitness to a Genocide: the United Nations and Rwanda.* Ithaca, NY: Cornell University Press, 2002.

Blix, Hans. *Disarming Iraq: the Search for Weapons of Mass Destruction.* London: Bloomsbury, 2004.

Boutros-Ghali, Boutros. *An Agenda for Peace: Preventive Diplomacy, Peacemaking and Peace-keeping.* New York: United Nations, 1992.

Claude, Inis L. Jr. *Power and International Relations.* New York: Random House, 1964.

Findlay, Trevor. *Cambodia: The Legacy and Lessons of UNTAC.* Oxford: Oxford University Press, 1995.

Goodrich, Leland M. *Korea: A Study of U.S. Policy.* New York: Council on Foreign Relations, 1956.

Gordenker, Leon and Weiss, Thomas G. (eds). *Soldiers, Peacekeepers and Disasters*. London: Macmillan, 1992.

Hill, S.M. and Malik, Sh. P. *Peacekeeping and the United Nations*. Aldershot: Dartmouth Publishing Co., 1996.

James, Alan. *Peacekeeping in International Politics*. Houndsmill, Basingstoke: Macmillan, 1990.

Price, Richard M. and Zacher, Mark W. (eds). *The United Nations and Global Security*. New York: Palgrave Macmillan, 2004.

Ratner, Steven R. *The New UN Peacekeeping: Building Peace in Lands of Conflict after the Cold War*. New York: St. Martin's Press, 1995.

Weiss, Thomas G. (ed.). *Beyond Subcontracting*. Houndmills, Basingstoke: Macmillan Press, Ltd., 1998.

Weiss, Thomas G. (ed.). *Collective Security in a Changing World*. London: Lynn Rienner Publishers, 1993.

Whitman, Jim. *Peacekeeping and the UN Agencies*. London: Frank Cass Publishers, 1999.

Chapter 5   Human Rights and Decolonization

Alston, Philip (ed.). *The United Nations and Human Rights: a Critical Reappraisal*, 2nd revised ed. Oxford: Clarendon Press, 2005.

Alston, Philip and James Crawford (eds). *The Future of UN Human Rights Treaty Monitoring*. Cambridge: Cambridge University Press, 2000.

Bayefsky, Anne F. *The UN Human Rights Treaty System in the 21st Century*. The Hague: Kluwer Law International, 2000.

Bayefsky, Anne F. *How to Complain to the UN Human Rights Treaty System*. The Hague: Kluwer Law International, 2003.

Boerefijn, Ineke. *The Reporting Procedure under the Covenant on Civil and Political Rights: Practice and Procedures of the Human Right Committee*. Antwerp: Intersentia/Hart, 1999.

Cassese, Antonio. *Self-Determination of Peoples: A Legal Reappraisal*. Cambridge: Cambridge University Press, 1995.

Conte, Alex, Scott Davidson, Richard Burchill. *Defining Civil and Political Rights: The Jurisprudence of the United Nations Human Rights Committee*. Aldershot: Ashgate, 2004.

Dale, Richard, 'The UN and Decolonization in Namibia', in David P. Forsythe, *The United Nations in the World Political Economy: Essays in Honour of Leon Gordenker*. Houndmills, Basingstoke: Macmillan, 1989, 165–96.

Dore, Isaak I. *The International Mandate System and Namibia*. Boulder, CO.: Westview Press, 1985.

Dugard, John (ed.). *The South-West Africa/Namibia Dispute*. Berkeley: University of California Press, 1973.

El-Ayouty, Yassin. *The United Nations and Decolonization: The Role of Afro-Asia*. The Hague: Martinus Nijhoff, 1971.

Emerson, Rupert. *From Empire to Nation: The Rise to Self-Assertion of Asian and African Peoples*. Cambridge, Mass.: Harvard University Press, 1960.

Fedorowich, K. and M. Thomas (eds). *International Diplomacy and Colonial Retreat*. London: Cass, 2001.

Forsythe, David P. *Human rights in International Relations*. Cambridge: Cambridge University Press, 2000.

Hannum, Hurst, 'Rethinking Self-Determination', *Virginia Journal of International Law*, vol. 34, no. 1 (1993).

Heyns, Christof and Viljoen, Frans. *The Impact of the United Nations Human Rights Treaties on the Domestic Level*. The Hague: Kluwer Law International, 2002.

Humphrey, John P. *Human Rights and the United Nations: A Great Adventure*. Dobbs Ferry, N.Y.: Transnational Publishers, 1983.

Jessup, Philip C. *The Birth of Nations*. New York: Columbia University Press, 1974.

Katayanagi, Mari. *Human Rights Functions of United Nations Peacekeeping Operations*. The Hague: Kluwer Law International, 2002.

Kent, Ann. *China, the United Nations and Human Rights*. Philadelphia: University of Pennsylvania Press, 1999.

McColdrick, Dominic. *The Human Rights Committee: Its Role in the Development of the International Covenant on Civil and Political Rights*. Oxford: Clarendon Press, 1991.

Moore, M. (ed.). *National Self-Determination and Secession*. Oxford: Oxford University Press, 1998.

Moris, Halim, 'Self-Determination: An Affirmate Right or Mere Rhetoric?' *ILSA Journal of International and Comparative Law*, vol. 201 (1997).

Ramcharan, B.G. *The United Nations High Commissioner for Human Rights*. The Hague: Martinus Nijhoff, 2002.

Risse, Thomas, Ropp, Stephen C. and Sikkink, Catherine (eds). *The Power of Human Rights: International Norms and Domestic Change*. Cambridge: Cambridge University Press, 1999.

Rodley, Nigel S. (ed.). *To Loose the Bands of Wickedness: International Intervention in Defence of Human Rights*. London: Brassey's, 1992.

Rotberg, Robert I. (ed.). *Namibia: Political and Economic Perspectives*. Lexington, MA.: Lexington Books, 1983.

Sears, Mason. *Years of High Purpose: from Trusteeship to Nationhood*. Washington: University Press of America, 1980.

Tolley, Howard Jr. *The U.N. Commission on Human Rights*. Boulder and London: Westview Press, 1987.

United Nations, Department of Public Information. *The United Nations and Decolonization (2000–2001)*, available at: http://www.un.org/Depts/dpi/decolonization/main.htm.

Toussaint, Charmian E. *The Trusteeship System of the United Nations*. Westport, CT: Greenwood Press, 1976.

Van Boven, Theo. *People Matter: Views on International Human Rights Policy*. Amsterdam: Meulenhoff, 1982.

Chapter 6   Cooperation for Economic and Social Progress

Belgrad, Eric A. and Nachmias, Nitza (eds). *The Politics of International Humanitarian Aid Operations*. Westport, CT: Praeger, 1997.

Berthelot, Yves. *Unity and Diversity in Development Ideas*. Bloomington, IN: Indiana University Press, 2004.

Commission on Global Governance. *Our Global Neighborhood*. Oxford, Oxford University Press, 1995.

Cox, Robert W., Harold K. Jacobson *et al.* (eds). *The Anatomy of Influence: Decision Making in International Organization*. New Haven: Yale University Press, 1973.

Emmerij, Louis, Jolly, Richard and Weiss, Thomas G. *Ahead of the Curve: UN Ideas and Global Challenges*. Bloomington, IN, Indiana University Press, 2001.

Gordenker, Leon. *International Aid and National Decisions*. Princeton, N.J.: Princeton University Press, 1976.

Jackson, Robert. *A Study of the Capacity of the UN Development System*. New York: United Nations, 1969.

Mitrany, David. *A Working Peace System*. Chicago: Quadrangle Books, 1966.

Murphy, Craig N. *International Organization and Industrial Change: Global Governance since 1850*. New York: Oxford University Press, 1994.

Rothstein, Robert L. *Global Bargaining: UNCTAD and the Quest for a New International Economic Order*. Princeton, NJ: Princeton University Press, 1979.

Sauvant, Karl P. *The Group of 77. Evolution, Structure, Organization*. New York: Oceana Publications, 1981.

Schechter, Michael C. (ed.). *United Nations-Sponsored World Conferences: Focus on Impact and Follow-up*. Tokyo: United Nations University Press, 2001.

United Nations Children's Fund. *The State of the World's Children...* New York: UNICEF, annual.

United Nations Development Program. *Human Development Report...* New York: Oxford University Press, annual.

Weiss, Thomas and Gordenker, Leon (eds). *NGOs, the UN, & Global Governance*. Boulder, CO: Lynne Rienner, 1996.

Williams, Douglas. *The Specialized Agencies and the United Nations: the System in Crisis*. London: C. Hurst & Co., 1987.

World Bank. *World Development Report...* New York: Oxford University Press, annual.

Chapter 7   The 21st Century: a Changing UN

Annan, Kofi. *We the peoples: the role of the United Nations in the 21st century*. New York: UN Department of Public Information, 2000.

Bertrand, Maurice. *The Third Generation World Organization*. Dordrecht: Martinus Nijhoff Publishers, 1989.

Dijkzeul, Dennis and Beigbeder, Yves (eds). *Rethinking International Organizations: Pathology & Promise*. New York: Berghahn Books, 2003.

Franck, Thomas M. *Nation against Nation: What Happened to the U.N. Dream and what the U.S. Can Do about It*. New York: Oxford University Press, 1985.

Fromuth, Peter. *A Successor Vision: The United Nations of Tomorrow*. Lanham, Md.: University Press of America, 1988.

Gorbachev, Mikhail. *Realities and Guaranties for a Secure World*. Moscow: Novosti Press Agency Publishing House, 1987.

High-level Panel on Threats, Challenges and Change. *A More Secure World: Our Shared Responsibility*. New York: United Nations, 2004.

International Commission on Intervention and State Sovereignty. *The Responsibility to Protect*. Ottawa: ICISS, 2001.

Knight, W. Andy. *A Changing United Nations: Multilateral Evolution and the Quest for Global Governance*. Houndmills, Basingstoke: Palgrave, 2000.

Luck, Edward C. *Mixed Messages: American Politics and International Organization, 1919–1999*. Washington: Brookings Institution, 1999.

Meisler, Stanley. *United Nations: the First 50 Years*. New York: Atlantic Monthly Press, 1995.

Moynihan, Daniel Patrick. *A Dangerous Place*. New York: Berkley Books, 1980.

Rochester, J. Martin. *Waiting for the Millennium: The United Nations and the Future of World Order*. Columbia, SC: University of South Carolina Press, 1993.

Ruggie, John Gerard. *Winning the Peace: America and World Order in the New Era*. New York: Columbia University Press, 1996.

Urquhart, Brian and Childers Erskine. *A World in Need of Leadership: Tomorrow's United Nations*. Uppsala: Dag Hammarskjöld Foundation, 1990.

Index